C000132046

**SENATE HOUSE LIBRA**
**UNIVERSITY OF LONDON W**
Tel: 020 7862 8460 http://www.senatehous
Please note that this book is due back on the late
It may be requested if required by another n
case it will not be possible to renew the loan.
**Fines are payable on books returned after the due date.**

| SHLs ITEM BARCODE 19 1862931 1 | | |
|---|---|---|
| | | |
| | | |
| | | |
| | | |
| | | |
| | | |
| | | |
| | | |
| | | |

HENRY KEAZOR, THORSTEN WÜBBENA (EDS.)
**Rewind, Play, Fast Forward.**
**The Past, Present and Future of the Music Video**

[transcript]

BIBL.
LONDIN.
UNIV.

This publication was made possible thanks to the friendly and generous support by The Richard Stury Stiftung (Munich) and the Coneda UG (Frankfurt/Main).

**Bibliographic information published by
the Deutsche Nationalbibliothek**
The Deutsche Nationalbibliothek lists this publication in the Deutsche Nationalbibliografie; detailed bibliographic data are available in the Internet at http://dnb.d-nb.de

© 2010 transcript Verlag, Bielefeld

All rights reserved. No part of this book may be reprinted or reproduced or utilized in any form or by any electronic, mechanical, or other means, now known or hereafter invented, including photocopying and recording, or in any information storage or retrieval system, without permission in writing from the publisher.

Cover layout: Christian Jegl, Munich, www.dasneueschwarz.net
Proofread by Henry Keazor & Thorsten Wübbena
Typeset by Mark-Sebastian Schneider, Bielefeld
Printed by Majuskel Medienproduktion GmbH, Wetzlar
ISBN 978-3-8376-1185-4

Global distribution outside Germany, Austria and Switzerland:

**Transaction Publishers**
**New Brunswick (U.S.A.) and London (U.K.)**

Transaction Publishers   Tel.: (732) 445-2280
Rutgers University        Fax: (732) 445-3138
35 Berrue Circle          for orders (U.S. only):
Piscataway, NJ 08854      toll free 888-999-6778

# Contents

## *FAST FORWARD*: THE FUTURE
## OF THE MUSIC VIDEO

# Rewind – Play – Fast Forward

## The Past, Present and Future of the Music Video: Introduction

HENRY KEAZOR/THORSTEN WÜBBENA

> "Art presses the "Stop"- and "Rewind"-
> buttons in the stream of life: It makes
> time stop. It offers reflection and re-
> collection, it is an antidote against lost
> certitudes."[1]

Like perhaps no other medium, the music video clip is marking and shaping our everyday culture: film, art, literature, advertisements – they all are clearly under the impact of the music video in their aesthetics, their technical procedures, visual worlds or narrative strategies. The reason for this has not only to be sought in the fact that some of the video directors are now venturing into art or advertisement, but that also people not working in the field of producing video clips are indebted to this medium.[2] Thus, more or less former video clip-directors such as Chris Cunningham or Jonas Åkerlund have established themselves successfully with their creations which very often are based on ideas and concepts, originally developed for earlier music videos: both Cunningham's works *Flex* and *Monkey Drummer*, commissioned in 2000 respectively 2001 by the Anthony d'Offay Gallery, evolved out of his earlier music videos.[3] *Flex* relies on the fantastic and weightless underwater cosmos Cunningham designed for the images that accompanied Portishead's *Only you* in 1998. *Monkey Drummer*[4] is heavily based on the soundtrack written by the Irish musician Aphex Twin (Richard David James) for whom Cunningham had previously directed famous videos such as *Come to Daddy* (1997) and *Windowlicker* (1999). Åkerlund, on the other hand, made an even more direct recourse to his earlier music video. His film, *Turn the Page*, presented in 2004 at the Schirn in Frankfurt in the context of the short-film exhibition *3-minutes*, uses exclusively footage he had shot six years earlier for the video clip, accompanying the song *Turn the Page* by the band Metallica (which also is used as a soundtrack for the film).[5]

In the field of literature not only directors such as Chris Cunningham have served as models for characters in novels like William Gibson's 2003 novel *Pattern Recognition* in which the clip of a fictitious music video-director who puts "robot girls in his video"[6] is characterized by the following words: "No sci-fi kitsch for Damien. Dreamlike things in the dawn half-light, their small breasts gleaming, white plastic shining faints as old marble"[7] (this a clear reference to Cunningham's music video for Björk's *All is Full of Love*, directed in 1999: fig. 1).[8]

*Fig. 1: Still from the music video by Chris Cunningham:*
Björk, All is Full of Love, *1999*

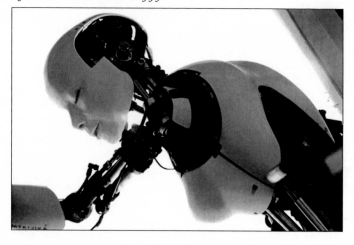

But also narrative structures and devices are taken over from the music video. For example, the writer Jasper Fforde (who had previously worked as a cameraman) was obviously inspired by a music video when he endowed its heroine Thursday Next[9] with the capacity to read and thus insert herself physically into the context and the setting of any given book and to thus allow its plot to feature abrupt changes in places, times and contexts – exactly as seen in the famous clip shot by John Landis for Michael Jackson's song *Black or White* in 1991 where the singer also abruptly changes from one cultural and narrative setting to the other.[10] And as a hint that his novel also deals with the history of pop- and rock music, Fforde equips Thursday Next with a car that is more or less identical with Janis Joplin's famous Porsche 356c Cabriolet (figs. 2 & 3).[11]

*Fig. 2: Janis Joplin's Porsche 356c Cabriolet (left)*
*Fig. 3: Mark Thomas: Cover Illustration for Jasper Fforde,* Something Rotten,
*2004 (right)*

It may sound strange to state that the music video is also influencing advertisements, given that a video clip is more or less an advertisement itself, but the influence is increasingly evident. In 2006, for example, an advertisement for the computer company Apple (fig. 4, left) stirred pop music fans and music journalists, as well as the general press because the advertisement relied on images which were nothing more than a remake of a music video produced three years earlier for the song *Such Great Heights* by the pop group The Postal Service (fig. 4, right).[12]

*Fig. 4: Comparison of stills taken from an "Apple"-advertisement by
Josh (Melnik) and Xander (Charity), 2006 (left) and from their
music video for The Postal Service,* Such Great Heights, *2003 (right)*

Likewise, a recent advertisement for the candy mint "Tic Tac"[13] is heavily indebted to Spike Jonze's groundbreaking music video for Fatboy Slim's track *Weapon of Choice* from 2001. Both the commercial and the music video feature a tired salesman (fig. 5 & 6), sitting in an armchair in a hotel lobby, next to a trolly with cleaning products and a radio (fig. 7 & 8). Whereas the salesman in Spike Jonze's video hears Fatboy Slim's music coming from the radio and is incited to dance, the salesman in the "Tic Tac" commercial requires the additional help of a slim blonde who shakes a box of "Tic Tacs".

*Fig. 5: Still from the music video by Spike Jonze: Fatboy Slim,* Weapon of Choice, *2001*

*Fig. 6: Still from the advertisement by Jacky Oudney for "Tic Tac", 2008*

*Fig. 7: Still from the music video by Spike Jonze: Fatboy Slim,* Weapon of Choice, *2001*

*Fig. 8: Still from the advertisement by Jacky Oudney for "Tic Tac", 2008*

The possibility that the means of a music video could be instead used one day as a vehicle for election campaigns was already envisioned in 1992 by director/actor Tim Robbins who in his satire *Bob Roberts* plays a homonymous singing conservative politician whose revisionist approach is – among others – underlined by his adaptation of Don Alan Pennebaker's legendary (and for the music video: highly influential) film sequence for Bob Dylan's *Subterranean Homesick Blues* from 1965. The content of Dylan's skeptical and liberal approach is not only reversed by Roberts into its exact opposite by substituting the title of Dylan's album *The Times They Are A-Changin'* (1964) against the cynical "Times are Changin' Back", or by replacing the lyrics on Dylan's famous cue cards (fig. 9) with slogans such as "By any means necessary, make millions", but also by exchanging the famous bystanders in Pennebaker's clip – among them the pop poet Allen Ginsberg (fig. 9) – with two bankers and sexy dancers (fig. 10). That this political use of music videos as a – in the end: very successful – part of an election campaign is not just an exception, but a consequently followed strategy becomes even clearer in the course of the film when Roberts again relies on this medium in order to also advertise his patriotism.

Fig. 9: *Still from the film by Don Alan Pennebaker: Bob Dylan, Subterranean Homesick Blues, 1965*

Fig. 10: *Still from the film by Tim Robbins: Bob Roberts, 1992*

Interestingly, in "real life" (as opposed to the reality depicted in a film) it was rather in the politically opposed party of the democrats that video clips were used as part of the recent election campaign in America: famous sympathizers of Barack Obama (such as, among others, the actress Scarlett Johansson, the singers Nicole Scherzinger and John Legend and the musician Herbie Hancock) had interpreted his now famous "Yes, we can"-speech in February 2008 under the direction of Will. I. Am (from the group Black Eyed Peas) and Jesse Dylan (the son of Bob Dylan) in the form of a music video in order to promote the candidate (fig. 11).

Fig. 11: *Still from the music video by Will. I. Am and Jesse Dylan, Yes We Can, 2008*

In three short days, the video garnered more than a million views on YouTube and 10 million on the host site, yeswecan.dipdive.com, and was even awarded an Emmy in June 2008 in the new category "Best New Approaches in Daytime Entertainment".[14]

To finish our short survey of forms indebted to the music video, we want to briefly mention the cinema where the style, narration and the technical means, developed in the field of the music video have had a great impact – be it that movie directors, obviously impressed by the music video, have adapted for example its imagery [15],editing or pace (as just one early example one could refer to Tony Scott's film *Top Gun* from 1986), or that directors of music videos were and are shifting to film making, thus bringing with them and importing some of the hallmarks of the music video into the cinema. One can think here about directors such as David Fincher, Mark Romanek, Michel Gondry or the already mentioned Spike Jonze. But such a shift from music advertisement to film already happened in the 60s when directors such as Claude Lelouch, Francis Ford Coppola or Robert Altman first learned the filmic ropes by shooting so-called "Scopitones", more or less direct antecedents of the music video, and then changed over to the cinema of the Nouvelle Vague without forgetting what they had learned while making the musical short films.[16]

But exactly such a change from helming a music video to directing a film now symptomizes a crisis in which the video clip finds itself after years of both financial and aesthetic prosperity (for which the notorious 7 million dollars reportedly paid for Mark Romanek's video for Michael and Janet Jackson's song *Scream* in 1995 is perhaps the most incisive example).[17] Due to economic declines over the past years the record companies have invested increasingly less money into the production of music videos while in turn their way of presentation has also drastically changed. Whereas music videos were once shown on television on music channels such as MTV [18], the Internet, cellphones and other emerging platforms with their, however, reduced quality considering vision and sound, have overtaken the market. Thus, already in June 2000 Mark Cohn and Ken Martin (under the name "The Broad Band") mocked the former hymn of the music video, the song "*Video Killed the Radio Star*" by The Buggles, chosen by MTV on the 1st August 1981 in order to inaugurate and hail its airplay, by sneering: *Internet Killed the Video Star.*[19]

Since that time, the authors of articles, blogs and books have asked time and again whether or not the music video is dead (fig. 12).

*Fig. 12: Screenshot from website forum*
*http://videos.antville.org/ (15 July 2006)*

More often than not, the answer has been: yes.

Nevertheless it has to be asked if this answer is not perhaps premature and at least moot: while one might not want to argue with the viewpoint that the music video in its up to now familiar and known form might have started to cease to exist, one might however ask if perhaps it will just continue to exist in another, new form. "Music TV was yesterday. Today, you best watch music videos together with friends late in the evening, tightly pressed together in front of the computer screen – or on the big movie screen", the journalist Sarah Stähli writes in her introduction to the section *Sound & Stories* of the 45th Solothurn Film Festival 2010 in which the best Swiss music videos were presented and awarded.[20]

Moreover, it can be read as a sign of enduring sturdiness that the music video furthermore tries to come at hands with the factors threatening it instead of blindly continuing to do its business as usual. This might be eased by the fact that it was in the genre of the music video in the first place that the idea of an online presence of a musical star was conceived and visualized: In Paul Hunter's clip for Jennifer Lopez' song *If You Had My Love*, released in May 1999, the singer was presented as a sort of a "belle captive" (as one could put it by quoting the title of a novel by Alain Robbe-Grillet), because she seems to be confined to a series of white, clinical rooms where everything is under observation. While she performs her song, cameras, controlled by online viewers, are following her movements, broadcasting them to different locations such as a garage, a call center, private homes, a dance hall etc. where J.Lo's performance is followed on TV- and computer-screens by her audience. That Lopez is indeed more or less the marionette of an interactive display, becomes evident when a user out of given menu chooses to view the lyrics sung by her or selects a certain dance style she then has to perform during her song – or when he chooses to see her taking a shower.

Of course, the reality as it was viewable on Internet TV and from February 2005 on at the YouTube-platform[21] was much less glamorous and stylish than the surroundings of J.Lo, but it went more or less into the same direction.

In any case, the genre of the video clip nowadays does not ignore the YouTube-phenomenon, but instead tries to benefit from it, as two briefly discussed examples, both produced in Spring 2008, show.

In May 2008 the band Weezer, the 1995 winners of four MTV-music video awards for the video directed by Spike Jonze for their song *Buddy Holly*, released a clip for their latest single "Pork and Beans". It is not by chance that this video did premiere not on MTV or any other TV-channel, but on YouTube. This was appropriate insofar as the video features many people made famous by YouTube and the Internet, some of them not even known by their proper names but being characterized rather by their activities on YouTube such as "catching Raybans with one's face", the "Free Hugs Campaign", the "Dancing Banana", "Diet Coke and Mentos eruptions" or "Will it blend" (the latter two featuring phony records and experiments). Partially chosen by the members of Weezer, each of whom picked their favorites, all these people were contacted by the director of the clip, Mathew Cullen, after which they were flown over to Los Angeles for the four-day shoot. Whereas an episode of the cartoon series *South Park* had previously rather mocked these celebrities[22], Cullen followed the path indicated by the music video for the Canadian rock band The Barenaked Ladies, who in the clip for their song *Sound of Your Voice* from February 2007 have also replaced their own appearance with the presentation of several YouTube-celebrities, lip-synch the song and pursue their own original and inventive activities.

While Cullen declared his clip to be a "celebration of that creativity", it is quite obvious that the video – by featuring YouTube-celebrities – was also trying hard to generate greater attention by the YouTube-audience as well as by other media which are carefully and/or distrustfully observing YouTube and its cult and culture. The strategy was successful. The video had over 1.2 million views in its first 24 hours on YouTube and after only four days 3.6 million people had watched it. The video quickly attained the status of being the most watched video on the Internet during those days[23] – a success which recalls the time when John Landis' groundbreaking video for Michael Jackson's *Thriller* was announced and broadcasted on MTV and broke records with respect to audience ratings.

The other example comes from Germany: Also in Spring, in April 2008, the German band Wir sind Helden released a video to accompany the single *Die Konkurrenz*. Instead of hiring a director, the band had posted a notice on their website the February before, which encouraged their audience to shoot their own video to suit the song and to hand it in. Arguing that self made things are somehow nicer, the band invited their fans under the title "Mehr Wettbewerb mit der Konkurrenz" to let their creativity flow (the title, in English meaning "More competition with the concurrence", already indicates the conceptual nature of the approach: videos were invited to compete with one another in order to accompany a song on "concurrence").[24] Whether reference was made to the lyrics of the song or not was irrelevant – on their website the band just stated that everything, except naked women and helicopters, was welcome.[25] Out of the many submissions received, rather than choose the best video, the band took just the best scenes from the various entries and then edited them into a music video for their song.[26]

The final result is not only interesting insofar as it combines heterogeneous material, reminiscent of Weezer's *Pork and Beans*, but also because of the way this material was framed and presented. On the one hand the small screen space, featuring the clickable "Play"-icon, with below the control device (fig. 13) clearly makes reference to the typical YouTube-appearance (fig. 14): thus, despite the fact that the shown snippets were not taken from YouTube, the video ironically present itself as a typical YouTube-video.

*Fig. 13: Still from the music video by and for Wir sind Helden, Die Konkurrenz, 2008*

*Fig. 14: Screenshot from YouTube, displaying the music video by Mathew Cullen: Weezer, Pork and Beans, 2008*

But the self-made character of the whole screen does not look like something from the Internet, but rather like something tinkered out of roughly cut and painted cardboard in order to just artlessly simulate a typical YouTube-screen. It is interesting to state that this look was not conceived originally by Wir sind Helden themselves but that this, too, is – so to speak – second hand, which means: borrowed from somewhere else. The correct term in order to describe the appearance of the child-like, rough style would be certainly "sweded", because this is the word coined by Jerry, the protagonist of Michel Gondry's feature film *Be Kind – Rewind* (2008). Faced with the dilemma of having accidentally erased the entire collection of his friend Mike's video-rental-store, Jerry decides to re-make the lost films with the simplest means and with him and his friends as the actors, taking on roles such as characters from *Rambo, The Lion King, Rush Hour, Ghostbusters, When We Were Kings, Driving Miss Daisy* and *Robocop* – with charmingly amateur results which, surprisingly, meet the taste of the customers of the store who request more and more movie remakes of that kind. Since Jerry, in order to explain his source for these films, claims that they are coming from Sweden (thus also justifying the long waiting times and especially the high prices he asks for these European "imports"), the redone films are quickly branded as "sweded". It is exactly this "sweded" look of the rough and handcrafted tinkering that has successfully proven itself, appearing not only as part of such a re-modeled YouTube-screen (fig. 15), but, apart from the Wir sind Helden-clip, even in advertisements for TV Soap Operas.[27]

*Fig. 15: Screenshot from the former website for the film*
Be Kind – Rewind, 2008

However, it is important to remember that the director of *Be Kind* was and still is a music video director and that he had designed and developed the "sweded" aesthetics already in the context of his earlier music videos (such as the video for *Walkie Talkie Man* by the band Steriogram, shot in Spring 2004).[28] While the rough reproduction of things in the video such as helicopters, a recording studio, musical instruments and cars (fig. 16) gives the clip a wild and funny appearance, Gondry sanctioned this look in the context of his feature film as due to the modest means Jerry and his friends have at their disposition when trying to re-make a Hollywood blockbuster.

*Fig. 16: Still from the music video by Michel Gondry:*
Steriogram, Walkie Talkie Man, 2004

At the same time, this is in a certain way a comment Gondry also makes on the genre of the music video itself which was often considered as the cheap little sister of the big, expensive Hollywood blockbuster.[29] It is perhaps also due to this parallel that Jerry's "sweded" films in *Be Kind* have more or less the same duration like a music video, that is of around 3 minutes in which the content of a whole film – as sometimes also in the case of a music video – is condensed, and that this short, cheap, "sweded" versions, however, are then more appreciated by the customers than the long, expensive Hollywood-originals (author Matt Hanson's words "Music video has become meta-cinema" come to the mind).[30]

One could continue this thread even by putting Jerry's cheaply looking "sweded" films into relation to the current video clips which have also lost their once sometimes blockbuster-like budgets and have now to try to also charm the audience with most modest means – this not only by making recourse to the humble YouTube-style[31], but also by coming up with clever ideas. One can here directly refer to the example of the most recent endeavour of the Los Angeles band OK Go: In a music video (directed by James Frost, the band itself in cooperation with Syyn Labs[32] and released in March 2010) for their song *This Too Shall Pass*[33], they tried to set something against Hollywood and its costly digital effects by putting their credo "Back to the mechanical"[34] into visual action. With the intention "to create cool stuff which you can see is also really real"[35], they designed together with their collaborators a machine, displayed over the two storeys of a warehouse and involving "more than 700 household objects, from flying rat traps to a plummeting piano" into a frenetic chain reaction, triggered by a toy lorry, then going on continuously for four minutes (the song's length) and finding its climax in a series of paint-loaded canons, being fired off against the four band members. The result, as journalist John Harlow concludes: "Even by the overheated standards of the internet, the success of the (...) video (...) has been extraordinary. In its first few days of release on the web, it has attracted more than 8.7m viewers."[36]

Interestingly, with this approach OK Go in a certain way did nothing else than to repeat the earlier success of a very similar video which, although conceived as an advertisement for a car, was nevertheless directed in 2003 by the renowned music video director Antoine Bardou-Jacquet.[37] In this advertisement, Bardou-Jacquet staged a kind of "Ballet Mécanique" by combining components of the then new Honda Accord to a very similar, complicated 1:45 minute chain reaction which in the end did lead to nothing else than the closing of the car's trunk which, eventually, did made the car roll from a tilting platform – an action accompanied by an off-voice asking "Isn't it nice when things just work?"[38] Given the meticulous interaction of the isolated car parts, starting with a small, single, rolling cog, and ending with the entire rolling car, the choreography of the components suggests an assembly belt which in the end launches the sum of all these interacting pieces, the finished car.

The short film has become a huge success on YouTube where it is often presented under the catch-name "Honda – The Cog". So it seems as if – again – a YouTube-success would have triggered the inspiration for another, latest YouTube-success. However, as Thomas Elsaesser has recently emphasized, the Honda-advertisement itself is heavily indebted to a forerunner:[39] In 1987 the artist duo (Peter) Fischli & (David) Weiss presented a 30 minute video at the Kassel *documenta 8* under the title *Der Lauf der*

*Dinge* ("The Way Things Go") which did mark their international break-through. As in the case of the Honda-advertisement, it shows a chain reaction of different items, put together in a 70-100 feet long structure inside a warehouse, but while the Honda-advertisement relies mainly on mechanical interaction, Fischli & Weiss also included chemical procedures which often enhance the suspense because the viewer has to wait for them to take place and to have their effect, so that there is always the uncertainty if the process is successfully continuing or if it will get interrupted. According to some sources the artist duo tried to sue the Honda-company because they considered the advertisement as a plagiarism[40], but it certainly would have been very difficult to prove this, given that *Der Lauf der Dinge* itself could be put into a long line of similar, earlier conceptions: Not only did director Richard Donner (who has a weak spot for such chain-reacting ballets – see for example also the beginning of his 1983 movie *Superman III*) already in 1985 include a scene into his movie *The Goonies* where a simple door-opener is conceived as a chain-reacting contraption, but the entire concept can be traced back to the idea of Reuben Lucius Goldberg (mainly known today as Rube Goldberg: 1883-1970), a Jewish American sculptor, author, engineer, inventor, and cartoonist, who is today famous for exactly the invention of complex, chain-reaction driven devices that perform astonishingly simple tasks in most complicated and convoluted ways (in his comics Goldberg from 1934 on made his character "Professor Lucifer Gorgonzola Butts" invent and build such machines) – thus his name became the epitome for these "Rube Goldberg machines".[41]

To return to the OK Go-video and his ancestors: They are not only linked by the basic concept of such a "Rube Goldberg machine", being each time at the center of the films, but, especially in the case of the Fischli & Weiss-project and the OK Go-video, also by the underlying bias of the works. Adapting Elsaesser's word, originally addressed to a comparison of the Fischli & Weiss-video with the Honda-advertisement, but actually even fitting better concerning the OK Go-clip, one can state: "(...) in both works, one notes a studied anachronism, a retrospective temporal deferral at work. (...) Fischli & Weiss produced their tape around the time when artists were seriously considering their respone to the new media technologies of video compositing and digital editing. Their work is clearly a manifesto in favor of materiality and indexicality, an ironic middle finger stuck in the face of the digital to come, and taking their stand in the heated debate about the loss of indexicality in the post-photographic age."[42] Exactly such an emphasis and celebration of the "visble, tangible world" and the insistence "on a linear causality vanishing in the media" (as opposed for example to Lady Gaga-clips), can be also observed in the OK Go-video.

All this shows that the music video continues to do what it used to do for decades: to look for all kinds of possible inspiration, to try to do something new with it and to thus inspire itself as well as other media forms.

However, the signs of its crisis can't be denied either – it is perhaps not wonder that discussions about the music video very often feature the words "rethinking" and "reinventing". As two examples among many others we'd like to refer first to the book published by Matt Hanson in 2006, titled *Reinventing Music Video – Next Generation Directors*. Second we want to mention the Swedish designer Jakob Trollbäck who, in March 2007, delivered a talk with the title "Rethinking the music video" in the context of the TED-conferences (the letters standing for "Technology, Entertainment, Design", a series of talks started in 1984 where people from these three areas come together).[43]

It is, however, interesting to see that both the book published by Hanson as well as the talk given by Trollbäck repeat rather than advance history: "Re-thinking" resp. "re-inventing" in their case thus takes on more the colors of an approach where already existing things of the past are taken up and thought through or invented again.[44] Trollbäck's claim for example to have created a music video for Brian Eno's and David Byrne's 1981 song *Moonlight in Glory*[45] that is more directed by the music than driven by a filmmaker's concept and which thus achieves "to show purely the expression of a great song"[46] (fig. 17), in our view ultimately leads to nothing more than a rather tame and even not as original renewal of older videos which already showed the lyrics of a song while trying to translate its music into abstract patterns of light and colors (the most advanced masterpiece here is perhaps Bill Konersman's clip for *Sign 'O' the Times* by Prince, produced in 1987: fig. 18).[47]

*Fig. 17: Still from the music video by Jakob Trollbäck: Brian Eno and David Byrne,* Moonlight in Glory, *2007*

*Fig. 18: Still from the music video by Bill Konersman:* Prince, Sign 'O' the Times, *1987*

Especially in Trollbäck's case the well-known phrase "If you don't know history, you are doomed to repeat it" springs to mind. The unconscious orientation on the past (since it seems that Trollbäck's claim to have created such a pioneering video is only possible because he apparently doesn't know about the Prince-clip) touches upon another important aspect of the crisis of the music video: it's historic dimension.

Apart from the fact that books such as the one by Hanson or endeavours such as the one by Trollbäck are simply repeating history, the current crises shows clear parallels to a crisis which had previously beset the music video in the early 90's. Just like today it was of a financial as well as consecutively aesthetical nature, and already then some heralded this as the end of the music video while others saw it as a healthy process which would further allow only "good" musicians to have likewise "good" music videos (as opposed to the prior situation where, as the music video director Rudi Dolezal did put it, "there was a video clip for every idiotic band").[48]

This shows, however, that the music video has not one, but several histories[49], which are separated by ruptures, breaks, endings and starting points. Therefore, what we are witnessing now may not be the symptoms of an irretrievable end, but rather a point where the clip – once again – begins to change, differentiate, evolve into something new.

This view is confirmed if we take a look at other histories of the music video in which the antecedents of the form did not tie into each other, but followed each other paratactically. For example, the early "Phonoscènes", which after 1907 were produced with a certain routine and exhibited a refined correlation between the music, the lyrics and the images (see the article by Thomas Schmitt in this volume) did not directly lead into the "Soundies" of the 40s and 50s. Jazz musicians often did star in these short films which also and again presented a quite elaborated narrative in order to interpret the music, its sections and structures. Their sometimes very artful visual style actually did anticipate already some of the stylistic features which were used later in the 70s during the rise of the music video (Gjon Mili's and Norman Granz's film for *Jammin' the Blues* from 1944 for example anticipates with its optical multiplication of a single musician some moments of Bruce Gowers' famous music video for Queen's *Bohemian Rhapsody*, made in 1975: figs. 19 & 20).[50]

*Fig. 19: Still from the film by Gjon Mili and Norman Granz:* Jammin' the Blues, *1944*

*Fig. 20: Still from the music video by Bruce Gowers: Queen,* Bohemian Rhapsody, *1975*

The same happened concerning the "Panoram Jukebox" and the subsequent "Scopitones" whose directors didn't rely on the aesthetic achievements of the Soundies, but started afresh instead. This was also perhaps due to the fact that the "Scopitone", which started to spread in the early 60s, was considered a technical improvement over the "Panoram" when the latter fell out of fashion due to the Second World War. The user of the "Panoram" didn't have any choice to view a particular film, but had to watch a sequence of black and white films as they were edited together (much in the same way the audience of MTV later had to watch the sequence of clips chosen by the producers of the show or dictated by the charts). Instead, the user of a "Scopitone" could directly pick a particular film (much in the same way the Internet currently allows)[51] which was, moreover, in color. Such features made the "Scopitone" a rival of black and white television, which was dominant at the time.[52] Following the decline of the Scopitones, the first directors of music videos didn't use and view the "Scopitones" in order to learn from what had already been achieved there in terms of visual styles and the possible linking of music, words and images, but rather started afresh (the "Scopitones" were actually only re-discovered much later and then first rather as collector's items).

Given that the histories and pre-histories of the music videos stretch far further back than 1981 when MTV appeared (see already the fact that MTV had to rely upon earlier shot clips in order to fill its program), the consensus is that the beginning of the genre must be sought much earlier. The debate remains open regarding how far one should go back when seeking the earliest ancestor, however. As we suggested earlier, short films made for and with music had been already produced around 1900, and it seems that one origin can be seen in the way Thomas Alva Edison had devised his "Kinteophone" in 1891 (fig. 21) – we say deliberately "devised" because actually the technical realization wasn't up to Edison, who only dreamed about the possibility of sitting comfortably in an armchair at home while following a performance at an opera house in sight and sound.[53]

*Fig. 21: Thomas Alva Edison's "Kineto-phone", 1895*

In fact, this vision really describes what the television set would make possible later. But Edison's dream was more about making a performance accessible to the home viewer (much in the way, DVDs with a "Live on stage"-film do this), while a music video doesn't limit itself to this, even though it was and is clearly and mainly designed to work as a substitute for such a live performance (already the pop group ABBA in the middle of the 70s deliberately used their music videos in such a way because one band-member loathed big international tours – so the group came up with so called "promo films" and later music videos; thanks to them the fans were recompensed for this lack of live presence by, for example, granting them visual access into the studio while the band records a song, or by even giving them glimpses inside the everyday life and the emotional re-lationships of the group members).[54] But already this example shows that a music video didn't and doesn't limit itself to just record a live perform-ance, but that it emancipates itself from this very tight context and instead comes up with a style which – in its best moments – aims at interpreting the music on a visual level. Thus, a second element has to be considered when dealing with music videos: the fact that music here receives a visual and reproducible interpretation. It is exactly this point of the possibility to exactly reproduce the always same performance that distinguishes the music video from the opera[55] while the fact that the interpretation of mu-sic in a music video can be freed from any narrative also discerns the video clip from forms such as the musical. A possible candidate as one of the first antecedents for such a reproducible performance can be seen in Philippe Jacques de Loutherbourg 's "Eidophusikon" (fig. 22), a small pic-ture theatre, introduced in 1781, where mainly non-narrative phenomena of nature such as storms and waterfalls were mounted on a small stage.

*Fig. 22: Edward Francis Burney, Watercolor-Drawing of Philippe Jacques de Loutherbourg's "Eidophusikon" (London, British Museum, ca. 1782)*

Given that the theatre was exclusively mechanical, the phenomena could be reproduced the same way continuously. Since music and sounds were an essential part of the whole show (and film director Werner Nekes even claims that no other than famous composer Johann Sebastian Bach's youngest son, Johann Christian, composed the music for these performances)[56], one can agree with those authors who call the "Eidophusikon" the most significant multi media picture theatre of the 18th century.[57]

With this research for one of the earliest antecedents and forerunners of the music video we have, at the same time, already deeply stepped into the question what actually characterizes and defines a music video, and this leads further to the question about the methods we have at our hands in order to analyze the music videos.[58] Because only an approach which has previously reflected upon the characteristics, elements, ingredients and components of a music video will also be able to accordingly analyze it and to appreciate all its single levels and parameters as well as their mutual relationship and interaction.

Whereas earlier research has focused entirely on the images (given that music videos were considered to be nothing else than a derivate of the cinema) and neglected the music and especially the lyrics[59], more recent attempts have attempted to encompass all the different factors composing and concerning a music video. Apart from the images themselves, these include the music, the lyrics, the whole context of the particular song and video such as the album, and the image of the musician or band, as it has been shaped also by former videos etc. By comparing the results of such a fully formed research with the analysis of other, especially earlier videos and their predecessors, we can better understand not only the past of the music video as a genre as well as its changes and developments, but also its present and – perhaps even –its future. This all the more since one might ask not only questions about which specific histories to deal with, but also with which versions of the present, given that the genre of the music video finds itself at different points of development in each country.[60]

This volume thus tries to tackle all the three time parameters – the past, the present and the future of the music video (which, as we have tried to show, are deeply interwoven), as well as the geographical aspect.

Thus, Part one ("Rewind") deals with the past by first looking back to the Golden Era of the American music video (Saul Austerlitz), the history of the antecedents of the music video in France (Thomas Schmitt), the close relationship between visual arts and short music films between the 60s and the 80s (Barbara London) and the history of the Italian music video and the awareness and use of this history among contemporary Italian directors (Bruno di Marino).

This awareness brings us into the present ("Play") where we will have a closer look at the contemporary reception of the music video (Klaus Neumann-Braun and Axel Schmidt), before raising questions concerning the methods in the analysis and interpretation of the music video (Giulia

Gabrielli, Matthias Weiß). This leads to issues concerning the actual state of the music video as an aesthetic medium (Paolo Peverini, Laura Frahm) and to the problem how to address and tackle this medium properly in the future (Christoph Jacke).

The opening of the music video towards other media-forms (Holger and Cornelia Lund) and protagonists (such as artists making video clips: Antje Krause-Wahl) brings us to the question about the future ("Fast Forward") of the music video: Will YouTube resurrect the music video (Gianni Sibilla, Carol Vernallis) or will it experience completely different transformations (Christian Jegl and Kathrin Wetzel)?[61]

The articles published in this volume, with the exception of Antje Krause-Wahl's essay, are based on papers given during an international and inter-disciplinary symposium, which was organized by the editors and held in October 2008 at the Goethe-University Frankfurt/Main.[62] The conference was financially supported by the Volkswagen-Stiftung, the Vereinigung von Freunden und Förderern der Goethe-Universität, the Stiftung zur Förderung der internationalen wissenschaftlichen Beziehungen der Goethe-Universität, the Fazit-Stiftung and the Mainova. Without their support, this publication would have been impossible, so we would like to thank these institutions once again.

The Richard Stury Stiftung in Munich most generously supported this publication, and we would like to thank its chairman, Dr. Helmut Heß, as well as Dr. Friederike Wille (Frankfurt/Main); our thanks also go to the Coneda UG (Frankfurt/Main) for its friendly support.

Finally, we would like to thank our translators, Eva Ehninger (Frankfurt/Main) and Steven Lindberg (Berlin), but especially Anthony Metivier (Berlin) who not only corrected and revised the texts linguistically[63], but who also, with his stimulating questions and suggestions, helped to improve them concerning their content.

*Henry Keazor/Thorsten Wübbena,*
*Saarbrücken and Frankfurt/Main, August 2010*

**Note**
The text by Klaus Neumann-Braun and Axel Schmidt has been translated by Henry Keazor, the text by Matthias Weiß has been translated by Eva Ehninger, the texts by Laura Frahm and Christoph Jacke have been translated by Steven Lindberg.

# REFERENCES

**1** | Liebs 2009: "Die Kunst drückt Stopp- und Rücklauftasten im Lebensfluss: Sie hält die Zeit an. Sie bietet Reflexion und Rückbesinnung; ein Antidot gegen verlorengegangene Gewissheiten."

**2** | See for this also Thompson 2009.

**3** | See for this Keazor/Wübbena 2007: p. 319-322.

**4** | The title is not only referring to a children's toy, but at the same time to the highly influential track *Funky Drummer* by James Brown and his band, recorded in 1969, whose drum solo (performed by Clyde Stubblefield) is hailed as one of the most frequently sampled rhythmic breaks in hip hop and popular music, if not even the most sampled recording ever - see for this http://www.webwire.com/ ViewPressRel.asp?aId=16717 (last access 16.3.2010).

**5** | See for this Keazor/Wübbena 2007: p. 323-325 and Keazor/Wübbena 2006: p. 46.

**6** | Gibson 2003, p. 5.

**7** | Ibid., p. 7.

**8** | See Keazor/Wübbena 2007: p. 25, note 50.

**9** | See his tetralogy *The Jane Eyre Affair* (2001), *Lost in a Good Book* (2002), *The Well of Lost Plots* (2003) and *Something Rotten* (2004) as well as the sequel *First Among Sequels* (2007).

**10** | Keazor/Wübbena 2006: p. 46f.

**11** | The car in the novel is not only described as a (Fforde 2001: p. 59) "brightly painted sports car", but even its model – (ibid.: p. 88) a "356 Speedster" – is specified.

**12** | In this case this was due to the fact that the directors of the music video and of the advertisement, the duo Josh (Melnik) and Xander (Charity) were identical: see for this Keazor/Wübbena 2006, p. 46-47.

**13** | See the TV-spot, designed by the agency Heimat (Berlin), directed by Jacky Oudney (for the production company Telemaz Commercials, Berlin) and released in summer 2008 also on http://www.tictac.de ("aktuell", "spot 3").

**14** | See for this http://en.wikipedia.org/wiki/Yes_We_Can#cite_ref-2 (last access 16.3.2010). The video inspired spoofs and parodies such as for example the anti-McCain-song *john.he.is* (see for this the article by Carol Vernallis in this volume, p. 248).

**15** | The most recent example here seems to be Roland Emmerich's disaster movie *2012* (2009): several scenes (such as the car chase through a cityscape, disintegrated by an earthquake) seem to be inspired by the car race and the earthquake-sections in the music video, directed in 2002 by Jonathan Dayton and Valerie Faris for *Californication* by the Red Hot Chili Peppers.

**16** | See for this Keazor/Wübbena 2007: p. 59, Bovi (2007), p. 110/115 and Scagnetti 2010: p. 70/114-116.

**17** | Keazor/Wübbena 2007: p. 302, note 53.

**18** | See for this also the telling title of the article by Phull 2010: "I want my MTV back" which is provoked by the journalist's observation that MTV by now has even dropped the "Music Television" strapline underneath its logo, thus indicating that it doesn't consider itself anymore as a TV station devoted to broadcasting music. Phull's reaction: "I was genuinely choked." In his article he reflects upon the possible impact MTV could still have today, even in the guise of a TV station not devoted to music anymore and concludes: "(...) we can only imagine what MTV could still do for someone with discernable talent – if it only chose to."

**19** | The clip was produced by eStudio.com (a Silicon Valley-based interactive branding and animation company, founded in 1998, among others, by Mark Cohn and Ken Martin. The company did run one of the then first flashsites; in this context eStudio did present (as part of the so-called "regurge"-series) cartoon parodies of music videos such as The Buggles (episode 1), The Back Street Boys (episode 2), Limp Bizkit (episode 3) and Cyndi Lauper (final episode 4). In 2002, the founders of eStudio, Cohn, Martin and Ivan Todorov opened Blitz Digital Studios, an animation studio and integrated marketing firm, which did supersede eStudio.

**20** | Stähli 2010: "Musikfernsehen war gestern. Musikvideos sieht man sich am besten spätabends mit Freunden an, dicht zusammen gedrängt vor dem Computerbildschirm – oder auf der großen Kinoleinwand."

**21** | For YouTube in general and its different aspects see Burgess/Green 2009 as well as Snickars/Vonderau (2009).

**22** | See the fourth episode of the twelfth season of *South Park*, "Canada on Strike!", first aired on the 2nd of April 2008. Later, somewhat consequently, *South Park* fans would then also produce a parody of the Weezer-clip with *South Park* characters singing a new text. See for this the article by Carol Vernallis in this volume, p. 256, note 11.

**23** | According to http://en.wikipedia.org/wiki/Pork_and_Beans_(song) (last access 16.3.2010) "it reached more than four million viewers in its first week and was that week's most-watched video. It was the most popular video of the month in June, reaching 7.3 million views by June 16, 2008."

**24** | http://www.wirsindhelden.de/news/archive (last access 16.3.2010), under the 25.02.2008: "(...) mehr Wettbewerb mit der Konkurrenz."

**25** | http://www.wirsindhelden.de/news/archive (last access 16.3.2010), under the 25.02.2008: "Keine nackten Weiber, keine Hubschrauber [...]."

**26** | For a similar concept see the project for the music video for C-Mon & Kypski's song *More is Less*, where the visitors of the website http://oneframeoffame. com are invited to photograph themselves with a webcam while copying the pose from a given frame of already existing footage from the music video. The picture is then uploaded and added to a suited moment of the music video which is thus populated and made with/by the fans and "friends" of the band. Similar (so-called "audience-based") projects have been started in the meantime for example also in the fashion world: fashion photographer Nick Knight recently did upload raw footage for a promotional film on a website and asked the users to edit a short film out of it by using at least 25 % from the original material while also adding own footage. Out of the submitted films he then did choose usable ideas and incorporated them into his final advertisement – see for this Piepgras 2010, p. 33.

**27** | In 2008, the German soap-opera "Marienhof" for example featured in their adverts also a YouTube-player which mimicked a "sweded" style.

**28** | http://www.director-file.com/gondry/steriogram.html.

**29** | See for this and its discussion Keazor/Wübbena 2007: p. 248.

**30** | Hanson 2006: p. 11.

**31** | See for this also the contributions by Paolo Peverini and Gianni Sibilla in this volume.

**32** | Syyn Lab is a Los Angeles group of creative engineers who joined in 2008 with the objective to "twist together art and technology": see http://syynlabs. com/about (last access 21.3.2010).

**33** | The band actually launched two music videos to accompany the song: The first one, directed by Brian L. Perkins and released in January 2010, features a live performance of the song in collaboration with the University of Notre Dame Marching Band, filmed in October 2009. See for this http://en.wikipedia.org/ wiki/This_Too_Shall_Pass_(song) (last access 21.3.2010).

**34** | Harlow 2010.

**35** | Ibid.

**36** | Ibid. Interestingly, the same issue of *The Sunday Times* in which Harlow's article is published, features also (p. 14: "News Review") a report on the world-wide success of the music video, shot in March 2010 by Jonas Åkerlund for Lady Gaga's *Telephone*: "(...) it's on its way to become one of the most watched videos of all time." This shows clearly that still different concepts in music videos can be successful: While Åkerlund's video relies on the by now almost hackneyed scandal-strategy by stirring media-attention thanks to a recourse to a "all-singing, all-dancing, lesbian-prison-sex and mass-murder"-scenario (so the above mentioned report), while being moreover heavily indebted to Quentin Tarantino's *Pulp Fiction* (1994), the music video for OK Go instead opts for a more modest and at the same time non-narrative approach. The above stated phrase "If you don't know history, you are doomed to repeat it" applies especially to the case of the music videos for Lada Gaga since almost all of them are more or less spiced-up and stylish rehashes of earlier video clips, especially those made for Madonna and Britney Spears (whose directors Lady Gaga tellingly also took over by hiring for example Francis Lawrence or Jonas Åkerlund). Given her succesful drawing-by-numbers-approach, one would almost wish for the sake of originality that Stefani Joanne Angelina Germanotta alias "Lady Gaga" – reportedly being a studied media scientist with a NYU-degree in music – will one day expose her career as the mere practical part of a research project on the ways and mechanisms the pop business functions todays.

**37** | Already in 2005 director Mike Palmieri did conceive his music video for the song *An Honest Mistake* by the American rock band The Bravery by putting a similar chain reaction (consisting of dominoes and other mundane household objects) into the center of the band's performance.

**38** | This – seemingly natural – "working" was, however, in some moments helped by digital post production.

**39** | See Elsaesser 2009.

**40** | http://de.wikipedia.org/wiki/Der_Lauf_der_Dinge_(Film)    (last    access 13.5.2010).

**41** | See for example http://en.wikipedia.org/wiki/Rube_Goldberg (last access 13.5.2010).

**42** | Elsaesser 2009, p. 176.

**43** | http://www.ted.com/talks/lang/eng/jakob_trollback_rethinks_the_ music_video.html (last access 16.3.2010).

**44** | Thus, Hanson's book mainly deals with directors who – as interesting as their works might be – are rather developing before invented concepts further instead of actually inventing new techniques, designs and aesthetic strategies. Tellingly for the historical amnesia reigning in Hanson's book is the fact that the reader never encounters any production or release dates for the presented videos – thus, the (also historical) difference between the (as Hanson p. 14 calls them) "Icons of the Genre" (that is, groundbreaking directors such as Chris Cunningham, Jonathan Glazer, Michel Gondry, Hammer & Tongs and Spike Jonze) and the "Next-generation directors" is more or less blurred. Since Hanson also never displays his criteria for assigning certain directors to this "next generation", it almost seems as if only the technology, used by the directors, would be decisive for him: he presents them (p. 24) under the heading "digital-age music video".

**45** | From the album "My Life in the Bush of Ghosts" which was re-released in expanded and remastered form in 2006.

**46** | So Trollbäck in his introduction.

**47** | For the music video see Vogt 2008 and Keazor/Wübbena 2010: 229.

**48** | Dolezal 1994: 169: "Es wird nicht mehr (...) für jede Idiotenkapelle automatisch ein dazu passendes Video produziert."

**49** | See for this for example already the title of the book by the Italian historian Paolo Mieli, "La storia – le storie" (Milan: Rizzoli 2000), where the difference between one singular historical narrative ("The history") and its manifold counterpart ("The histories") is stressed. Carrier (2000), p. 118 reports a suggestion of Paul Barolsky according to whom also "The story of art is really lots and lots of very particular stories."

**50** | Keazor/Wübbena 2010: p. 225.

**51** | See for example the conclusion by Phull (2010): "(...) for the technically savvy, finding or hearing the music they like is no longer a matter of watching television for hours (...) in the hope of hearing a song that appeals to you."

**52** | For the Panoram and the Scopitones see Keazor/Wübbena 2007: p. 57-59, Herzog 2007 and Scagnetti (2010).

**53** | See for this Keazor/Wübbena 2007: p. 57 and Keazor/Wübbena 2010: p. 223-224.

**54** | See for this Keazor/Wübbena 2007: p. 64-65.

**55** | Nevertheless, Liggeri 2007: p. 53 sees Richard Wagner's concept of a "synthesis of the arts" at the origin of the "synaesthesia" of the music video.

**56** | See http://wernernekes.de/00_cms/cms/front_content.php?idart=101# Eidophusikon (last access 15.3.2010).

**57** | See Mungen 2006, vol. 1: p. 168-175 and Keazor/Wübbena 2010: p. 223.

**58** | Middleton/Beebe 2007: p. 6 are still diagnosing an "apparent standstill in the theorization of music video", apparently due to a lack of "new and innovative models for analysis."

**59** | Middleton/Beebe 2007: p. 5: "One difficulty in music video studies (...) is the fact that theorists of the visuals are often not trained in musical analysis and perhaps are not even particularly familiar with or interested in popular music itself." See for this also the article by Jacke in this volume.

**60** | See here also the admonition by Phull 2010 who reminds us of the still prominent role of music TV in other parts of the world: "It should not be forgotten, however, that in the wider world, where people don't have the time to spend hours trawling through trend-setting blogs, or to sit at their laptops downloading MP3s, TV is still a dominant medium." See also the essay by Hayward 2007.

**61** | Other possible forms, not discussed here, into which the music video could and certainly will diffuse are the fashion film (see for this Piepgras 2010, p. 33) and modern museum displays: The Bach-Museum in Eisenach for example grants their visitors the possibility to "enter" a composition by Johann Sebastian Bach by stepping into a multimedia room where the music is "translated" into immersive visuals. The installation, designed by the director and media-artist Marc Tamschick did win the award of the "Finalist Diploma" during the 2008 World Media Festival in Hamburg. See for this http://www.tamschick.com ("projects", "Begehbares Musikstück").

**62** | See http://www.muvikon08.net.

**63** | Nevertheless, possible mistakes are not his responsibility.

## Bibliography

Bovi, Michele (2007): *Da Carosone a cosa nostra – gli antenati del videoclip*, Coniglio Editore.

Burgess, Jean/Green, Joshua: *YouTube. Online Video and Participatory Culture*, Cambridge/Malden: Polity Press 2009.

Carrier, David (2000): *The Aesthetics of Comics*, Pennsylvania State University Press.

Dolezal, Rudi (1994): "Musikvideos – Die Avantgarde der 90er Jahre", in: Cecilia Hausheer/Annette Schönholzer (eds.): *Visueller Sound – Musikvideos zwischen Avantgarde und Populärkultur*, Lucerne: Zyklop, p. 168-169.

Elsaesser, Thomas (2009): "Tales of Epiphany and Entropy: Around the Worlds in Eightly Clicks", in: Pelle Snickars/Patrick Vonderau (eds.): *The YouTube Reader*, Stockholm: National Library of Sweden, p. 166-186.

Fforde, Jasper (2001): *The Eyre Affair*, London: Hodder and Stoughton.

Gibson, William: *Pattern Recognition*, Berkley Books 2003.

Hanson, Matt (2006): Reinventing Music Video. Next-Generation Directors, Their Inspiration and Work, Mies: Rotovision.

Harlow, John (2010): "How a group of geeky scientists created the world's coolest pop video", in: *The Sunday Times*, 21.3.2010, p. 16 ("Focus").

Hayward, Philip (2007): "Dancing to a pacific beat: music video in Papua New Guinea", in: Jason Middleton/Roger Beebe (2007): *Medium Cool.*

*Music Videos from Soundies to Cellphones*, Durham & London: Duke University Press, p. 152-173.

Herzog, Amy (2007): "Illustrating music: The impossible embodiments of the Jukebox film", in: Jason Middleton/Roger Beebe (2007): *Medium Cool. Music Videos from Soundies to Cellphones*, Durham & London: Duke University Press, p. 30-58.

Keazor, Henry/Wübbena, Thorsten (2006): "Kulturelle Kannibalen? Videoclips prägen Erscheinungsbild und Ästhetik unserer Kunst- und Alltagskultur", in: *Forschung Frankfurt*, April 2006), p. 44-47.

Keazor, Henry/Wübbena, Thorsten (2007²): *Video thrills the Radio Star. Musikvideos: Geschichte, Themen, Analysen*, Bielefeld: transcript.

Keazor, Henry/Wübbena, Thorsten (2010): Chapter and Entries for the lemma "Music Video", in: Dieter Daniels/Sandra Naumann/Jan Thoben (Eds.): *See this Sound. An Interdisciplinary Survey of Audiovisual Culture*, Cologne: Walther König 2010, p. 223-233.

Liebs, Holger (2009): "Das Ende des Kanons. Die Hysterie des Kunstbooms ist vorbei", in: *Süddeutsche Zeitung*, 30.12.2009, No. 300, p. 11.

Liggeri, Domenico (2007): *Musica per i nostri occhi. Storie e segreti dei videoclip*, Milan: Bompiani.

Middleton, Jason/Beebe, Roger (2007): Medium Cool. Music Videos from Soundies to Cellphones, Durham & London: Duke University Press.

Mungen, Anno (2006): *"BilderMusik", Panoramen, Tableau vivants und Lichtbilder als multimediale Darstellungsformen in Theater- und Musikaufführungen vom 19. bis zum frühen 20. Jahrhundert*, Remscheid: gardez! Verlag, 2 Vols.

Phull, Hardeep (2010): "I want my MTV back", in: *The Sunday Times - Culture*, 21.2.2010, p. 26.

Piepgras, Ilka (2010): "Der grosse Nick. Das Internet revolutioniert die Modewelt - und der Fotograf Nick Night ist ihr Prophet", in: *Zeit-Magazin*, 18.2.2010, No. 8, p. 30-34.

Scagnetti, Jean Charles (2010): *L'aventure scopitone 1957 – 1983. Histoire des précurseurs du vidéoclip*, Paris: Éditions Autrement.

Snickars, Pelle/Vonderau, Patrick (eds.) (2009): *The YouTube Reader*, Stockholm: National Library of Sweden.

Stähli, Sarah (2010): "MTV, selbst gebastelt", in: *Program and Catalogue of the 45th Solothurn Film Festival*, Solotuurn, p. 334

Thompson, Krista (2009): "The Sound of Light: Reflections on Art History in the Visual Culture of HipHop", in: *Art Bulletin*, Volume XCI, No. 4, p. 481-505.

Vogt, Tobias (2008): "Ein Buchstabenballett als Zeitzeichen. Selbstreflexion im Musikvideo Sign 'O' The Times", in: Klaus Krüger/Matthias Weiß (eds.): *Tanzende Bilder. Interaktionen von Musik und Film*, München: Wilhelm Fink, p. 173-187.

# *Rewind*:
# The History, Collecting, and Reception
# of the Music Video

# "Don't You Cry Tonight"

## Guns N' Roses and the Music Video Folly

Saul Austerlitz

Film critic Stuart Klawans has coined the term "film folly" to refer to outlandishly ambitious films like D.W. Griffith's *Intolerance* or Mikhail Kalatozov's *I Am Cuba* (Klawans 2000) – epic productions stemming from vast budgets and gargantuan egos. Film follies, by their very nature, are always doomed to fail at some level, but their ambitiousness also renders them uniquely fascinating, and anomalous – the white elephants of film history. The Guns N' Roses' videos *Don't Cry*, *November Rain*, and *Estranged*, directed, respectively, in 1991, 1992, and 1993 by Andy Morahan, meet the definition of film folly beyond a shadow of a doubt. Where the average video confined itself to a narrow set of locations, and a modest budget, the Guns N' Roses trilogy ballooned to epic size, with all the trappings of a Hollywood blockbuster. Their enormousness made them ripe for parody (in fact, a 1994 *Spin* article poked fun at their tangled symbolism: Loffreda 1994), but they remain marvels of the video's ambitions to cultural significance, and emotional heft. And with the ever-shrinking promotional budgets for videos in the new century, clips like these are a vanishing breed. If the early era of the music video was a gathering of strength, moving toward ever bigger, ever grander productions, these Guns N' Roses videos were the form's apex, the high point in a curve that swung downward in their aftermath toward the smaller, more economical, less heroically ambitious videos of today.

Snickers often break out during Guns N' Roses videos – the vision of Slash's seething (possibly homoerotic) jealousy toward his romantically fulfilled bandmate, as expressed in his keening guitar solo in *November Rain*, is a particular favorite – but the videos do not mind. They are too much in love with their own swooning grandiosity, their opulence rendering all questions of taste entirely moot. To criticize them overly much is to demand of the music video that it be something other than what it is – grandiose, opulent, fantastic, and absurd. Guns N' Roses' extravagant ambitions, which led them to release two overstuffed albums on the same day, and lead singer Axl Rose's tendency toward outsized displays of emotion, culminated in this trio of clips, the biggest and brightest follies in music video history. Easy to disdain, but hard to hate, *Don't Cry*, *November Rain*, and *Estranged* are the epitome of the music video's crass magnificence.

Even the video for Michael Jackson's *Thriller* (directed in 1983 by John Landis) paled in comparison with Axl Rose and Co.'s megalomaniacal, magnificently melodramatic trio of clips, which tell a discombobulated, symbolically fraught tale of lost love and shattered dreams. Having risen to take hold of the mythical "Biggest Band in the World" title after the enormous success of their 1987 debut album *Appetite for Destruction*, Guns N' Roses attempted to make a series of videos that would match the band's outsized ambitions in their gigantitude. Assisting the band in bringing their vision onto the screen was director Morahan, formerly best known for helming those celebrations of artful stubble, George Michael's *Father Figure* and *Faith* (both produced in 1987). And what genre befits gigantitude more than the melodrama? Griffith and Kalatozov and the other exemplars of the film folly had leaned heavily on melodrama – outsize emotions conjoined with outsized budgets and city-sized sets. For Guns N'Roses and Morahan, the melodrama they sought was that familiar one of tormented, impossible love, tinged with the ever-present specter of death.

Since when did music videos concern themselves with such downbeat themes? Music videos have always been – as both fans and detractors would tell us – celebrants of the gloriously ephemeral. Music videos were fantasies of a perfect world just beyond our reach. It was the realm of "money for nothing and chicks for free" (to quote the lyrics of the homonymic 1985 song by the Dire Straits). The last thing a music video would want to do would be to depress its audience. And yet, the progress of the music video toward ever-grander spectacles demanded a shift in themes – Oscar-worthy videos must have Oscar-worthy themes. And so, we have the Guns N' Roses trilogy, simultaneously marvelous and ludicrous, moving and absurd, charming and dispiriting. In short, these videos are the music video in a nutshell – they are the largest-scale version of an artform whose every pore demanded bigger, grander, more spectacular.

We begin with *Don't Cry*, which stars Rose and then-girlfriend Stephanie Seymour as a couple on the rocks. This is music video with pretensions to the epic; witness the first few seconds of the video, in which Axl, shrouded in snow and lugging a pistol, looks more like an Eisenstein hero than a rock star. The genre is melodrama, and the inspiration is Douglas Sirk; here, the stormy weather of the unhappy couple is reflected in the landscape. *Don't Cry* would have been a field day for Freud; symbols of entrapment are everywhere. Axl is drowning; he is buried alive; he is a bird, unable to take flight. Axl confronts his other selves; he walks into a mirror and vanishes. Axl and Stephanie take comfort in their memories, but even those are unpleasant: bickering and arguing. In the next scene, a somber

Rose drives by the cemetery in his limousine, touring the far reaches of his own memory. Rose finds himself thrashing in the water, tugged down into the depths, toward death, by Seymour.

In the meantime, guitarist Slash has his own female problems. Driving along the coastline with his lady friend, she yells and curses at him, and he calmly veers his car over the cliff. Death is always followed by rebirth in *Don't Cry*; after presumptively dying in a fiery car crash, Slash magically reappears at the top of the mountain to play his solo, in perhaps the second-most snicker-inducing moment in the trilogy, and Axl returns to the cemetery later in the video to visit his own grave. Tainted love is a form of death here, wrecking egos and poisoning even the charmed existences of big-time rock stars. At the end, Axl is at Stephanie's grave, enduring a living death of his own. Half short film, half performance clip, *Don't Cry* must find a way to match the heightened emotion of the tempestuous couple, and so the band play atop a skyscraper, searchlights seeking them out, helicopters hovering around them. Like the bird that is his companion underground, this Axl is desperate to get out, and unable to find a way. *Don't Cry* provides a solitary ray of hope at its conclusion, the rebirth implied in the bookending shots of a baby undergoing baptism promising escape from the seemingly eternal cycle of psychic pain and degradation.

*November Rain* is like *The Godfather Part II* of the GNR trilogy, extending backward and reaching forward from its predecessor. The band are playing a packed concert hall, complete with orchestra and backup singers, and Axl and Stephanie are getting married at a perfect little church somewhere in the middle of nowhere. The lushness of the music – its swooping strings, swooning guitar, and carefully plucked piano – is matched by the lushness of the surroundings. The happy couple are beaming – Stephanie looking gorgeous, Axl looking like he borrowed Jerry Seinfeld's puffy shirt for the day. The bride and groom French kiss – surely an eye-opener for many 12-year-olds when this video was first released – and Slash stomps out, stalking the Midwestern pampas, his guitar solo kicking up a dust storm as a helicopter shot swoops in, around, and over him.

Why is Slash angry? Is he jealous? We don't know, and truthfully we don't particularly care. The music creates a mood – sensual, multi-faceted, elegiac – and the images do their best to keep up, but there is simply no time to explain. And frankly, explanations would only be a drag. We are in the land of illogic, where a cut or a chord is enough explanation as long as the mood holds. And so, the happy wedding reception is permanently spoiled by a rainstorm – note the return of water as a harbinger of doom. Guests dash for cover, floral arrangements fall into a puddle, and a guy dives right into the wedding cake. Red wine spills on the virginal white tablecloth, and the bloody stain is a cue for the video's coda. Matching the musical shift in tone in the song itself, the last two minutes of the nine-plus-minute *November Rain* are tragic. Stephanie is dead, a day of happiness having become one of mourning. Axl mourns at her grave as another rainstorm falls. Axl shakes uncontrollably in bed, picturing Stephanie throwing her wedding bouquet. It flies through the air, only to land on her own coffin, its pinkish-red color soaking into the black coffin. What had first appeared to be a respite from *Don't Cry's* relentless gloom reveals itself to be both an extension and an explanation. Love and death are so closely related that the one can become the other, almost without our realizing.

By the time we get to *Estranged*, the final, and longest, entry in the trilogy, Axl's demons have stripped him of all illusion – all "naïve faith and trust", as the dictionary definition offered here has it. A SWAT team rushes his hilltop estate, bursting in on Axl recumbent on the floor. Axl's family is gone, his love is gone, and he is left alone amidst the soulless trappings of fame. A series of flash-motion shots usher in a wave of GN'R fans into a stadium, where the band begins to play. Fame, at this rarefied level, is both the cause of, and the balm for, his pain. The outsized performances in these three videos – skyscraper, theater, stadium – are in some obscure way a justification for the outsized melodrama of the videos' storylines. Music this big, they posit, must have a video every bit as outrageously oversized. The videos celebrate size for its own sake – exhibit A in its definition as a video folly. Axl airplanes across the stage, his Charles Manson T-shirt some obscure statement of rebellion, as the dream-Axl rises from his slumber, and showers fully clothed, his face devoid of all feeling. Needless to say, sadness does not distract Mr. Rose from the need to keep his facial hair perfectly sculpted. The song's piano bridge ushers in a transition. We are back at home, only now it is day, and Axl is packing up and leaving. Axl gets into the back seat of a limousine, and as the trunk closes, we spot a small dolphin figurine. As Slash's dolphin-call-esque guitar solo rings out, dolphins are everywhere: on television, heading westbound on Sunset Boulevard, on a billboard above the Rainbow club, bursting out of the cargo hold of an airplane.

Dolphins? Perhaps there was a secret message to be found here, about the music video. Even sinking in the ocean of mediocrity, there was the possibility of grace – of being lifted, on the backs of dolphins, to wonder.

Suddenly, Axl is stalking the length of an enormous tanker ship. He leaps into the water, refusing offers of help from an onlooker tossing a life preserver, or an outstretched hand from a nearby rowboat, like the man waiting in vain for heavenly assistance in the famous religious parable. Sinking below the surface, Axl finds himself surrounded by a team of dolphins. Water is no longer the preserve of death, but rather of renewed life. Not one to be left out of the good times, Slash emerges from the storm-tossed waters for a guitar solo, water cascading off his axe, because – why not? Eventually, a search and rescue team salvages Axl from the water, pulling him into the sky as one boot drops into the water.

Axl emerges from the trilogy of videos older, sadder – and wiser. Having had and lost his love, he saves himself, and although no longer in possession of his illusions, he lives to see another day. For all their bombast, *Don't Cry*, *November Rain*, and *Estranged* are deeply adult in their evocation of wounded spirits, their summoning of the bittersweet and the tragic a far cry from the fantasy wish-fulfillment of the average music video. These videos' desire to be the biggest, most video videos ever made also leads them to be something other than their predecessors: sadder, more emotional, and more bittersweet. They are what happens when music videos are pushed to their breaking point, and become a little real.

To simply dismiss these videos as trash, or as the misguided monomania of a multi-platinum superstar, is to misunderstand the essence of the music video. To put it bluntly, the music video is trash. Glorious trash, trash that occasionally strives for the condition of art, but trash nonetheless. Videos are advertisements for music, their stated intent to move widgets with maximum efficiency. This is the music video's limitation, and its source of strength. Music videos are rarely subtle. To create a history of the music video that is all *Sledgehammer* and Michel Gondry is well and good, but it does not properly honor the actual history of the form, and the follies that form its extremes, be they these videos, *California Love*, or any of a dozen Michael Jackson epics. *Don't Cry*, *November Rain*, and *Estranged* are the music video's *Gone With the Wind*. They may be outlandishly oversized, they may be crass, they may even occasionally be foolish. They also are, at some elemental level, the music video when it is most itself. We are unlikely to see their equals again.

## BIBLIOGRAPHY

Austerlitz, Saul (2007): *Money for Nothing: A History of the Music Video from the Beatles to the White Stripes*, New York, Continuum.

Klawans, Stuart (2000): *Film Follies: The Cinema Out of Order*, New York, Continuum.

Loffreda, Beth (1994): "Guns N'Roses 101: Music Video As Texts", in: *Spin*, August 1994, p. 24.

# The Genealogy of the Clip Culture

Thomas Schmitt

Following Immanuel Wallerstein's "Modern World-System" and reading universal history since the Renaissance as the development of a world economy (Wallerstein 2006: p. 43), recent trends toward globalization seem to represent a new episode of the progressive crystallization of mass culture as world culture. Inside this movement, the Culture Industry has presented its own history as a positive, affirmative and linear progression since World War II.

But what about Culture Industry before 1944? Before 1927? Or Before 1918?

The more we study the forerunners and the antecedents of the music video (like the six "Cinéphonies" produced by Emille Vuillermoz between 1935 and 1939), the better we understand how our view on the subject has been influenced by it. Video music came and presented itself as a bold new object. It has to be true because television told us so. But once we rewind and watch again all these TV-70's shows where music video first appeared, a new view begins to arise.

This article will (1) rewind the construction of the object of the music video as a discourse in France since the late 70's. (2) It presents facts about the "Phonoscène" phenomenon (1902-1917). (3) It discusses what we can learn from the comparison. (4) It proposes to extend the history of the video music in order to describe it with a different perspective.

## 1. THE CONSTRUCTION OF A DISCOURSE

### 1.1 The Anecdote

On Sunday, October the 28th, 1979, Michel Drucker, the most famous French Sunday TV show host ever (still on air as of 2010) was embarrassed. On the one hand he was glad to have received this tape. On the other hand he did not know how to deal with it. Sure, the song was a hit in the UK. Yet, its broadcasting was not that simple. Because The Buggles was a completely unknown band at the time, the situation was awkward. As long as Michel Drucker could present a clip from a movie such as Roman Polanski's film *Tess*, everything was fine, since the viewer knew that this was just a brief glimpse, a promotional side-moment in another medium. But a promo was not that simple to introduce. Michel Drucker could not pretend that the band was performing in some other place in the studio. The discontinuity in the televised discourse was too obvious. He could not hide the gap between the big show he was hosting and the tiny one, the performance, he was about to present. So he decided to present the alien recording as what it was: a video tape, and thus Drucker became one of the first French VJs: "We are now about to meet again... Nino Ferer was just talking about the problems of creation ...well, in the realm of film and variety film... the English never stop mesmerizing us...Look what they have done with Buggles... Buggles is an English band, two Englishmen... They sing 'Video Killed the Radio Star'...And you will see that with a film you can do...you can really innovate things in the realm of variety...."[1]

Two weeks later, the French version of *Video Killed the Radio Star*, performed by a French singer (and at the same time: 'air guitarist') named Ringo, was broadcasted on French television. Here are the lyrics, translated from French to make them rhyme in English:

> "My space rocket's a wreck, it has been a long journey
> I look my way to reach to you my dear honey
> But my devices have all just broke away
> oh – ah – oh – ah
>
> I'm connected to a wide symphony net
> The music people ear on this planet
> I can not say I have been distracted yet
> oh – ah – oh – ah
>
> Change the channel
> oh – ah – oh – ah
> So I understand
>
> Tell me who is this huge big black crow x 2
>
> I am so lost in the night
> oh – ah – ah – oh
>
> I can see fine upstanding people through my window
> Sitting in their armchairs, they all own their stereo
> Their own personal problems and their video

oh – ah – oh – ah
Change the channel
oh – ah – oh – ah
So I understand

Tell me who is this huge big black crow x 2

In my heart like on your screen
The color of my blood is green

If you really want to see me tonight
I can land in your courtyard
(...)."[2]

A few weeks later, The Buggles finally crossed the Channel in order to perform on French television. When Trevor Horn was asked about the "huge black crow" supposedly mentioned in the lyrics of his song, his jaw dropped since it doesn't feature in the original lyrics at all.

## 1.2 A Growing Feeling of Hysteria

It is very difficult to narrate the early days of the music video in France without evoking the contemporary political context which presented itself as a major change ("le changement"). Did the election of François Mitterrand in May 1981, leading to the presence of four communist ministers in the government, really represent a turning point? Just as only Richard Nixon could go to China, only a socialist leader could liberalize the French mass media. As in the United Kingdom under Margaret Thatcher (1979), in the United States under Ronald Reagan (1980) and would soon occur in Germany under Helmut Kohl (1982), the feeling of experiencing a new wave may have been also caused by the politic turnover. Was music video, as a sign of a cultural free trade among the west, a fad, a subject of infatuation, some kind of self-fulfilling prophecy?

## 1.3 The Shows that Made Video Music History

In the late 70's, the three (and then only) French government-owned channels (TF1, Antenne 2, and FR3) were infrequently interrupted by commercials, which meant that music videos represented a visible intrusion into the accustomed discourse of French television.

The first show to present promos on a weekly basis was *Studio 3*, which aired from July 1979 to February 1982. With a bizarre set that evoked the interior of a spacecraft from the British sci-fi series *Doctor Who*, *Studio 3* was entirely different from Michel Drucker's On-the-couch-Variety show. This time, the host was clearly dealing more with audio-visual recordings than with physically present artists. But, since a precise vocabulary did not yet exist, it was still difficult to describe the situation. This lack of specific vocabulary appeared, for example, when *Studio 3* presented the clip for the song *Another Brick In the Wall* by Pink Floyd, made in 1979 by Gerald Scarfe, calling it "a melting of comic strip and film tapes".

This period of early enthusiasm (1978-1985) can be studied in France as the constitution of a "field" of interaction between political power, economic interests, and the critics. In February 1983 the French minister of communication (Mr. Georges Fillioud) declared that the official name for our object should be from then on "Bande vidéo promotionnelle" ("promotional video tape"). The daily paper *Libération* should promote instead, against Fillioud's recommendation, the notion "clip". At that time "vidéo" was mainly used in order to describe video art, video games, and the VHS phenomenon. "Vidéomusique", the contemporaneous official appellation, was coined by the Ministry of Culture in the early 90's. Ever since, the word "clip" has entered French film criticism as the equivalent of the term "montage" in English. The term carries, however, a pejorative meaning.

Before MTV Europe started its broadcasting in 1987, some kind of "gentleman agreement" had been televised on June the 20th, 1985. Just like the BBC, French television wanted to establish a connection between music video and "the past". So they showed a "Scopitone" and invited Jean-Christophe Averty. But Mr. Averty (who invented a new form of variety show with *Les Raisins Verts* in 1963 and directed a few "Scopitones") strongly rejected any kind of responsibility for helping create the new genre and declared, after having followed the video for the song *You might think* by The Cars, directed in 1984 by Jeff Stein & Alex Weil: "One must know nothing about the aesthetics and the history of the cinema, the history of editing ("montage"), the history of collage, to find anything new in this."

## 1.4 Serge Daney's Intuition

In October 1985, a special issue of the newspaper *Libération* was published. "Paysage du clip" ("Landscape of the clip") was the title of a supplement of 16 pages, linked to a forty day exhibition at the Centre Georges Pompidou. Italian and German "clip situations" are also mentioned.

The last page presents a "Genealogy of the video clip from the caves until today" (the term undoubtedly alludes to the concept of genealogy as introduced by Michel Foucault who had died the year before: Foucault 1977). According to this document, the clip supposedly would have been ten years old at the time. Bruce Gowers' video for *Bohemian Rapsody*, shot in 1975, is therefore considered as a "first step" and the music video for *Video killed the Radio Star*, made by Russel Mulcahy in 1979 as a "starting point". Thus, 'Mama' "Soundie" (supposedly only used in jazz clubs) and 'Daddy' "Scopitone" (associated exclusively to the "Yéyé", the phenomenon of the French rock variety) are pushed back into prehistoric times (1930-

1960). In his article "Critic Question", Serge Daney writes: "We should try to understand how clip culture, because it is essentially musical, brings us way back into the past to a time we do not know, when films – even if they were qualified mute – were shot and seen with a musical background."

Following Serge Daney's suggestion, we'll take a look at these forgotten times.

## 2. THE PHONOSCÈNE PHENOMENON

The "Phonoscène" phenomenon has been regarded as the prototype of the first sound films, a sort of "rehearsal" of their later beginning (Abel 1994; Burch 1991; Chion 2003: p. 40). Here are arguments in order to discuss such a judgment.

### 2.1 The Hardware

The "Chronophone" (see Barnier 2002) combined a gramophone and a "cinematographe" (a "chronographe", to be precise), linked by a synchronizing mechanism patented by Gaumont in 1902.

The different models of the "Chronophone", such as the "Chronomegalophone", presented so called "Phonoscènes". Thus, a "Phonoscène" is not one, but two objects: it is a disc which can be heard and a film which can be seen at the same time. The disc was recorded first. It was then played during the shooting of the film. "Phonoscènes" were already recorded by using the lip sync method.

At the times when the "Phonoscène" is present (1902-1917), the market, within which these cultural merchandises are exchanged, is not stable. Until the turn around 1908, only films and records were sold. As a result of the Pathé-initiative in 1908, films were rented rather than sold. This represented the end of cinema as a mere funfair attraction, particularly because of the concurrent appearance of the first "movie theatres". Meanwhile, discs took over from cylinders as a standard recording medium.

### 2.2 The Chronology

The very first "Phonoscènes" were presented by Léon Gaumont at the Société Française de Photographie on the 7th of November 1902. Other demonstrations took place at the Musée Grevin (Schwartz 1999: p. 193) at the end of the same year and at the Moulin-Rouge on summer 1906. The invention was then brought to London and presented to the Queen Consort Alexandra on April 4th 1907. This entertainment lasted about an hour. The program consisted of a selection from song pictures which had been staged at the Hippodrome. They included *The Miserere - Scene from Giuseppe Verdi's Opera "Il Trovatore"*, *The Captain Song* from the Gilbert and Sullivan operetta *H.M.S. Pinafore*, *Tit-Willow* from Gilbert and Sullivan's comic opera *Mikado, This Little Girl and That* from the musical play *The Little Michus* by Albert Vanloo, Georges Duval and André Messager, and *The Serenade* from Charles Gounod's opera *Faust*.

When Gaumont opened his own cinema theatres in Paris (the "Cinéma-Théatre Gaumont" in June 1908 and the famous "Gaumont-Palace", "the greatest cinema of the world" in September 1911), "Phonoscènes" were exhibited every week until 1917. Léon Gaumont himself, in his letters, claims that the industrial exploitation of the "Chronophone" actually started in January 1910 at the Olympia, the first Music Hall in Paris. According to the same sources, a presentation had been also shown in New York, at the 39th Street Theatre on the 5th, 6th and 7th of June 1913.

The "Chronophone" was not the first sound-on-disc system, but it was the better one, at least until the arrival of Warner's "Vitaphone". The last known projection of a "Phonoscène" took place on September 1917 in Paris.

## 2.3 The Archive Material

A collection of programs, sold in Gaumont cinemas, tells us which "Phonoscènes" were likely shown in Paris from 1908 to 1917. Catalogues have been published in July 1906, January 1908, March 1911, and July 1912.

Printed in January 1908, the Gaumont "Projections Parlantes"-catalogue (the catalogue of the "Talking Projections") is a 160-pages brochure, divided into three main sections. First, we find corporate material that presents the sales conditions ("the merchandise travels at the client's risk..."), a presentation of the company itself and a description of the factories and of the studio, which was called "theatre" at the time. This section is eight pages long and is followed by a "hardware section" of 40 pages and a "software section" of 110 pages.

The hardware section presents the cameras, projectors, lightning devices, and paraphernalia. A section of 20 pages, for example, is dedicated to editing tools. Then comes the "Talking Projection"-section that presents Gaumont main product: the "Chronophone": "To show our clients our deep interest in the industry of chronophonie, we give, as a simple piece of information, an overview of the patents we own. This will prove that our house is the first in dealing especially with Talking Projections."[3]

This is followed by a brief history of the techniques of synchronising the "Cinematographe" (with a capital C) and the "Phonographe" (with a capital P). The presentation of the "Chronophone Gaumont" itself appears on page 36. According to this commercial literature, the "Chronophone" entirely resolves the problem of synchronizing the two technical devices, something that had presented a challenge since the invention of the "cinematographe" and the "phonographe" (written this time without capital letters): "A lot of inventors – and not the least – have tried to solve this problem. None of them gave such a complete resolution of it, as we did."[4] "Life itself reconstituted! What a joy! What a wealth to be able to keep and store for the ones who will come after us the portrait, the gesture and the voice of all our great orators, of all our great artists."[5] "Some sad and timid minds did go that far to claim that the Chronophone would be the death of the artists. We thank them for this mark of success which would outweigh any possible advert. But we nevertheless would like to put also these artists at ease. Did the phonograph kill the singers? Wasn't its appearance also sided by similar silly predictions? What is the result? The singers did never earn so much money; we know some of them – and not a few – who tripled their annual income (...). We could also prove that watching and listening to our Phonoscènes will make them very popular in the whole wide world (...)."[6] "If you would have listened to a good record ["record" in English in the text] and you would have the chance to see the artist in a theatre, wouldn't you try to be among the audience? You will agree that the same argument is valuable for the projections and that showing a scene is the best publicity for this scene."[7] "It's the progress. You can't go against it! If we wouldn't have reached the solution of the synchronism, some other would have. But let's go briefly back to business. (...) Success goes to the new inventions, and it is as much bigger as these inventions are sensational. Where at the moment is an invention which can gain the interest of the audience in the same way as our talking projections?"[8] "If your budget is limited, just address yourself to our made-to-measure model: We have foreseen every case."[9] "Are you afraid to be one day without food for your device? We'll answer you that we already spent over two millions on our film studios and laboratories (...). Our cinematographic theatre is the biggest in the world. (...) We are not shying away from any sacrifice in order to give our Phonoscènes the maximum amount of artistic effect possible, be it the choice of sets, the position of the camera or the interpretation of the idea of the author of the script."[10] "If you look at our catalogue of phono-scènes, you'll see we've already edited more than hundreds of them (...)."[11]

Pages 71 to 190 are dedicated to "films cinématographiques". These are short silent movies. Pages 51 to 72 are dedicated to "Phonoscènes". Every even page features a list of 28 "phonoscènes". Every uneven page presents 28 illustrations, one for each "Phonoscène". The last pages presents only eight "Phonoscenes" out of a total of 288. Each "Phonoscène" has a number, a telegraphic code, a title, and a "genre" assignment (Italian opera, French song, Spanish song, English song etc.). Also indicated are the approximative length of the scene (around 60 meters), its price (without coloration, around 150 Francs) and the price of a disk, around 10 Francs.

## 2.4 The Corpus

According to Jean-Jacques Meusy (Meusy 1995: p. 518), 774 "Phonoscènes" were produced. The first, directed in France by Alice Guy (Guy 1976), were followed by examples from Louis Feuillade. In London Arthur Gilbert directed 33 "Phonoscènes" for the Gaumont-British Picture Corporation Limited in 1906, 54 in 1907 and 15 in 1908. The majority of the "Phonoscènes" have been shot in French, but many also in English, Spanish, Italian and German. Édouard Arnoldy (Arnoldy 2004: p. 42) describes the German "Phonoscène" for the song *Die Macht des Walzers* (*The Power of the Waltz*) with Lucie Bernhardo and Martin Martens in which two drunk dancers destroy a bourgeois interior.

The corpus of the "Phonoscènes" can be divided in two main categories: operetta or opera (such as *Carmen, Pagliacci, Otello, Tosca, Faust*, etc.) and songs. A minority of the "Phonoscènes" show dances, instrumental solos (cornet, ocarina), fencing bouts, and comedy sketches which were called "talkingfilms" (filmparlants). The opera/operetta "Phonoscènes" are reproducing the operatic *mise en scène* from the perspective of a front row spectator. The song-"Phonoscènes" instead are not that homogenous. Some of them focus on the performance of the singer, others on the narrative described by the song.

## 2.5 The *Belle Époque* Celebrities

Félix Mayol, Armand Dranem and Pierre-Paul Marsalés (called "Polin") are three very well known (if not the three best known) French singers of the era between 1895 and 1918 (Caradec/Weill 2007; Condemi 1992; Jacques-Charles 1966). Each of them recorded a dozen of "Phonoscènes". Their success was so huge that a lot of copycats made their living by imitating them in other towns. The three singers performed in places called "Café-Concert", where the audience could drink and smoke (both activities usually forbidden in theatres) while listening (and/or booing the artists). One of the key characteristics of such entertainments was that, since 1864, the artists were authorized to dress up as their characters. Thus, a huge variety of different "genres" in singers and songs appeared. Éloi Ouvrard for example is considered to be the inventor of the "comique troupier" genre, the funny soldier genre. Polin was his successor, dressed up as simple cavalry soldier. Dranem was an "eccentric", "absurdist" singer, performing in the costume of a clown, while Mayol donned the uniform of a crooner. These French *Belle Époque* celebrities had to build a complex cluster of recognizable signs by melting their personalities and their characters' features in order to create their own genre. Thus, Mayol kept the same hairdo for twenty years, Polin always used the same red and white checked handkerchief and Dranem notably performed with closed eyes.

Dranem's, Mayol's and Polin's "Phonoscènes" can be described as "tableaux". They present fixed long shots of the artist lip-synching in front of a decorated curtain. Mayol, who always presented himself wearing a Lily of the Valley in his buttonhole, sings in front of a curtain, decorated with Lilies of the Valley. In a certain way, the personality of the artist thus contaminates the set. A few years later (in 1910), Mayol would buy his own entertainment place, the "Concert Mayol", thus reaffirming his leadership among the French Belle Époque celebrities. Dranem can be seen standing in his "Phonoscènes" in front of a painted canvas representing an avalanche of bouquets. This metaphor of success may have been borrowed from a poster by the French artist Adrien Barrère, promoting Dranem on the walls of Paris. Similarly, Polin's "Phonoscène" shows him in front of a canvas depiction of a garden, and this may be related to a poster by the artist Georges Goursat (also called Sem).

## 2.6 The Narrations

The "Phonoscène #4", sang by M. Ribière is entitled *Le Couteau* (*The Knife*). This 1898 song, written and composed by Théodore Botrel, is a dialogue between a tramp and a peasant. When the tramp asks if he could sleep in the barn, the peasant offers him a place to sleep in his house. When the tramp replies that he is dirty, the peasant gives him clothes and shoes. And when the tramp asks for water, the peasant gives him wine. At the end, when the peasant is asleep, the tramp takes his knife... and cuts a slice of bread. The "Phonoscène"-catalogue of July 1906 specifies: "Just as in Montmartre cabarets the singer of the mimed scene is on one side." Further research has to be done about this "mimed songs"-tradition which was already fading at the time when the "Phonoscènes" appeared. At the same time, the action was sometimes also represented by silent actors and narrated by the singer. *The Knife* seems to be the only example of its kind in the corpus.

In the "Phonoscène" *Anna, qu'est ce que t'attends?* (*Anna, what are you waiting for?*) the narrator prompts his wife in the first verse to hurry up. The train is about to leave and they may miss it. What we see is what we hear: In front of their house, the husband takes a basket and fills it with food and a bottle of wine. While his spouse puts her hat and gloves on, the husband mimes with his hands, singing that she spends too much time. While singing the chorus, the man takes the basket and a kid on his shoulder. Two other children are coming out the house and the whole family walks off. Cut. As the second verse starts, the family in now sitting on the grass by the side of a river. The man ties a napkin around his neck and asks "What are you waiting for?", declaring that he is hungry, while pouring wine into the glasses: "This food is delicious. Next time we'll invite the president." As the song lyrics clearly presents two separated moments

BIBL.
LONDIN.
UNIV.

of the narration (before and during the picnic), the montage follows this structure by accordingly showing two different "tableaux".

The same division can be observed in *Chemineau chemine* (*Wandering Wanderer*), a "Phonoscène" from 1914. The first shot/verse takes place in a wheat field, the second one in a farm courtyard. The first "tableau" is a presentation of the singer/character as a free wanderer. In the second shot, the verse evokes what we first see: the vagabond gives bread to two poor children.

In *Fumeur d'Opium* (*Opium Smoker*), the singer (maybe Adolphe Bérard) is seen lying on a sofa in an Asian opium den. The lyrics do not evoke such a place, but explain what lead the character to use drugs: "Since Ninon left me, my head is a mess. So to forget her, I smoke opium."[12] As the character/narrator describes his hallucinations in which he sees his love again, the Asian waitress seated next to him prepares his next pipe, giving him quick glances from time to time. In the second verse, the singer gets up. Gazing at the audience, he mimes the chorus, waving his hands: "Little smoke, take my illusions away in a too short blue dream." Then, pointing his finger to the camera, with budging eyes, he roars: "You are not Ninon. I can't love you!"[13] Putting his hands before him as if to protect himself from a ghost, he falls on the sofa. The Asian waitress immediately gives him a new opium pipe. *Fumeur d'Opium* was shown in May 1913 at the Gaumont Palace.

*J'ai du cinéma* (*I've got cinema*) is a song in two verses, originally sung by Edmond Bouchaud a.k.a. Dufleuve. In the "Phonoscène", we see the singer Laurent Nalet in front of a café. He tells the first verse of his story to a waiter:

> I was wandering the other week
> when a cinematographer
> asked me to pose for the ciné.
> I said ok.

> He then made me pull faces, make gestures and contortions.
> And since then I've got the cinéma - a - a - a - a.
> In the heart, in the liver, in the lungs, everywhere,
> I've got cinematography.

While repeating the chorus, the singer starts to jump and to pull faces just like in a silent movie. The cinema seems to be contagious: the waiter also starts to jump. Then the music stops and Laurent Nalet asks a female customer:

> Dear madam, am I bothering you when moving like this? Don't look at me
> madam or you will get cinema too!

All the customers look a bit afraid. The café manager arrives. Laurent Nalet laughs at him and tells him the second verse:

> Since I've been cinematographied,
> I cannot longer stay still.[14]

And, gazing at the camera, he starts jumping like a madman. A cop arrives
to arrest him.... *J'ai du cinéma* is one of the last "Phonoscènes" showed at
the Gaumont Palace in June 1917.

## 2.7 The Diffusion

From 1908 to 1917, at least one "Phonsoscène" was shown each week in
one of the two Parisian Gaumont cinema theatres.

This the transcription of a "Gaumont Palace" program, dating from the
last week of June 1917.

First part :
1 Orchestra, The Ace March Chapelier
2 Kineto-Scientific Series, In the Insects World, Our Countryside Inhabitants
3 Phonoscène Gaumont, I've Got Cinéma
4 The Gorges Of Rumel, Panorama
5 The Bluff, comedy
6 Cinema at the Army, War annals
7 It's Springtime, Ciné-Vaudeville Gaumont interpreted by M. Marcel Levesque

Ten minutes break ("entr'acte")

Second part :
1 Orchestra, Russian Danse (G. Fosse)
2 Attraction : Horly's Trio (acrobats)
3 The Duty, a dramatic comedy in three parts, interpreted by [...]
4 Gaumont-Palace Actualities, day to day events from all over the world.

An orchestra of 50 musicians, directed by Mr. Paul Fosse and Mr. Eugène
Poncin.

## 3. DISCUSSING THE COMPARISON

### 3.1 Parallel Histories

A new network (cinema theatres, cable tv, the Internet), a new hardware (discs and films, VHS and CDs, digital files) and a major player (Gaumont, Warner, YouTube): comparing today (2010) and yesterday (1980) with the "Phonoscène"-phenomenon period (1908-1917) makes one aware of significant echoes.

These parallel histories make evident the difficulty to fully embrace the subject since all these forms are not only recorded moving images, consisting of music, lyrics and sounds, but they are also complex cultural artifacts that interact with the *Zeitgeist*. Because they represent history, they interact with it. And they are also self-referential: the "Phonoscène" *I've got cinema* makes jokes about its medium, numerous examples of self-representation exist among the "Scopitone"-films, and *Video killed the Radio Star* already did put the blame on itself etc. These forms are time capsules, remembrance of things present.

### 3.2 Material History

The industrialization of culture, described by Adorno and Horkheimer in 1944, was already producing artifacts at the end of the 19th century (Adorno/Horkheimer 1944). By the time songs were sold as folded color illustrated "sheet-music", the industry was producing illustrated song slides projected on screen (Altman 2004: p. 183). You could buy a music sheet, a record, but the song slides were not for sale.

These objects, as clues of a rising economy of the spectacle, led us to Vaudeville, Music-hall, Cabaret, Café-Concert and maybe juke joints (an informal establishment featuring music, dancing, gambling, and drinking, primarily operated by African American people in the southeastern United States). These cultures, in a dialectic relation with the opera, have produced significant codes of representation. For example the "Corbeille", painted by Edgar Degas in his works *Les Café-Concert des Ambassadeurs* (1876-1877, Lyon, Musée des Beaux-Arts) and *Cabaret* (Washington, Corcoran Gallery of Art), was a Café-Concert tradition until circa 1885 (see Coquiot 1896). Without any other reason save for the satisfaction of the male gaze, women were on stage while an artist was singing.

# 4. SINCE WHEN?

## 4.1 Forgetting Post-Modernism?

Instead of considering "Phonoscènes" as yesterday promos, we invite the reader to imagine video music as today "Phonoscènes".

By doing so, we will reevaluate our knowledge about a popular mass culture before it was identified by the cultural studies in the 50's, by Adorno and Horkheimer in the 40's, and by Siegfried Kracauer in the mid 20's. Making the genealogy of culture?

This grey patient (Foucault used this definition of "Genealogy" as given by Nietzsche) work would not aim at discovering a mythical beginning. Yet, this crisis of historiography (see Altman 2004: p. 15) could be useful to build a new method of analysis.

## 4.2 Beyond Modernity

A brooch, a badge, a campaign button, a pre-historical fibula. All these object have a double nature: they are decorative and functional. The same applies to the music video clip.

"Phonoscènes", "Cinéphonies", "Scopitones", "Promos": the techniques have changed, but the function has remained the same. Following the thesis developed by Nicolas Deville about music video and tarot (Deville 1990), we wish to confront the aesthetics of the music video with inherited medieval iconography, namely heraldry because a coat of arms and its description ("blazon") can be compared to the relationship between the audio-visual and the textual elements of a music video. Since this rather complex dialectic relationship makes it so difficult to study the phenomenon of the music video, it may be useful to get back to medieval imagery in order to deduce from there and establish a coherent stable uniformed clip theory.

Instead of using the word "genre", we propose to identify the general impression achieved by an audio-visual-textual fragment as *tincture* (a term which in heraldry designates the colors used to emblazon a coat of arms).[15] Since some genres such as "blues" (in music), "giallo" (Italian for "yellow", referring to crime stories in literature) or "film noir" in cinema are already referring to colors, the paradigm shift is possible. Just as a coat of arms is usually composed by combining two or more other coat of arms, two or more master clips are often combined in a music video. Heraldry gives us a vast vocabulary to describe the variety of these combinations such as for example a *mise en abyme*. Clip theory could use this aesthetic algebra in order to identify and name the structures, figures and beauties of the music video.

## References

1 | "Nous allons maintenant retrouver...Nino Ferrer parlait justement du problème de la création...et bien dans le domaine du film et du film de variété... les anglais n'ont pas fini de nous épater! Regardez ce qu'ils ont fait avec Buggles... Buggles est un groupe anglais, deux anglais...Ils chantent 'Vidéo kills the radio star'...Et vous allez voir qu'avec le film on peut...on peut vraiment innover en matière de variété...".

2 | "J'arrive de loin et ma fusée fuit de partout
　　Je cherche mon chemin pour aller à ton rendez-vous
　　Mais mon radar et mon moteur ont tourné fous...
　　oh – ah – oh – ah
　　Je suis branché sur un réseau de symphonies
　　Sur la musique que les gens écoutent par ici
　　Je peux pas dire que ça m'éloigne de mes soucis
　　oh – ah – oh – ah

　　Changez la chaîne
　　oh – ah – oh – ah
　　Que je comprenne

　　Dites-moi qui est ce grand corbeau noir x 2

　　Je suis perdu dans le soir
　　oh – ah – oh – ah

　　De mon hublot je vois des gens très comme il faut
　　Dans leur fauteuil ils ont chacun leur stéréo
　　Et leur radio, leurs ennuis et leur vidéo

　　oh – ah – oh – ah
　　Changez la chaîne
　　oh – ah – oh – ah
　　Que je comprenne

　　Dites-moi qui est ce grand corbeau noir x 2

　　Sur vos écrans et dans mon cœur
　　Mon sang est de la même couleur

　　oh – ah – oh – ah x 2

　　Dites-moi qui est ce grand corbeau noir x 2

　　Sur ton écran et dans mon cœur
　　Mon sang est de la même couleur

Si tu veux vraiment me voir
Je me pose dans ton jardin ce soir
(...)."

**3** | Translated from the French – the original reads: "Afin de bien montrer à no-
tre clientèle toute l'importance que nous attachons à la nouvelle industrie de la
Chronophonie, nous donnons ci-dessous, à titre de simple renseignement, un
aperçu des brevets que nous avons pris ou que nous exploitons. Ceci constitue,
en outre, la preuve évidente que notre Maison est la première s'occupant spécial-
ement des Projections Parlantes."

**4** | "Bien des inventeurs, et non des moins illustres, ce sont occupés de ce prob-
lème. Aucun n'a donne cette solution complète, telle qu'elle fut présentée par
nous (...)."

**5** | "La vie reconstituée! Quelle joie! Quelle richesse que de pouvoir conserver
pour ceux qui viendront après nous le portrait, le geste et la voix de tous nos
grands orateurs, de tous nos grands artistes (...)."

**6** | "Quelques esprits chagrins ou timorés ont été jusqu'à prétendre que notre
Chronophone était la mort des artistes. Nous le remercions de cette marque de
succès. Elle vaudrait à elle seule mieux que toutes les publicités; mais cepend-
ant nous voulons rassurer ces mêmes artistes. Est-ce que le phonographe a tué
les chanteurs? N'a-t-on pas prédit la même ineptie à son apparition ! Quel est le
résultat ? Jamais ils n'ont gagné autant d'argent; nous en connaissons, et non
des moindres, qui triplent annuellement le revenue (...). Nous pourrions prouver
de même que la vue et l'audition des nos phonoscènes leur vaudront une popu-
larité considérable dans le monde entier (...)."

**7** | "Si vous aviez entendu un bon record phonographique et qu'il vos eût pos-
sible, quelques jours après, de voir l'artiste dans un théâtre, n'eussiez-vous cher-
ché à être au nombre des spectateurs ? Vous admettrez que le même argument
est valable pour les projections et que le fait de montrer une série de vues prises
d'une scène est la meilleure publicité pour cette scène."

**8** | "C'est le progrès. Il n'y a pas à aller contre. Si nous n'avions pas trouvé la
solution du synchronisme, c'eût été un autre qui y aurait atteint. Revenons un peu
maintenant à la partie commerciale (...). Le succès va aux nouveautés, et il est
d'autant plus grand qu'elles sont sensationnelles. Où existe-t-il actuellement une
invention propre à intéresser le public autant que nos projections parlantes?"

**9** | " Votre budget est-il limité, reportez-vous à notre modèle à main. Nous avons
prévu tous les cas."

**10** | "Craignez-vous un jour ou l'autre d'être sans aliment pour votre appareil,
nous vous répondrons que nous avons dépensé plus de 2 millions pour avoir un
établissement de prises e vues et des laboratoires d'édition hors de pair. Notre
théâtre cinématographique est le plus grand du monde. (...) Nous ne reculons
devant aucun sacrifice pour donner à nos phono-scènes le maximum d'effet ar-
tistique qu'il soit possible d'obtenir tant par le choix des décors, l'emplacement
de la prise de la vue et l'interprétation de l'idée de l'auteur du scénario."

**11** | "Si vous consultez nos listes de phono-scènes, vous pourriez remarquer que
nous en avons déjà édité plusieurs centaines (...)."

**12** | "Depuis que ma Ninon est partie

Ma tête est un capharnaüm
Et pour oublier mon amie
Je fume le troublant opium."

**13** | "Petite fumée emporte mon rêve
Dans un songe bleu qui trop tôt s'achève. (...)
Tu n'es pas Ninon, tu n'es pas Ninon
Je ne peux pas t'aimer."

**14** | "Je me baladais la semaine dernière lorsqu'un cinématographeur
M'Dis 'voulez-vous pour vous distraire poser devant un ciné un quart d'heure?'
Je consent, il met l'appareil en place et me fait faire un tas de contorsion
Des gestes et des grimaces
J'ai fait des trucs et des machins
Et depuis ce temps-là crénom d'un chien
Y a pas à dire j'ai du cinéma – ha – ha – ha – ha
Ainsi qu'un peu de cinémato – ho – ho – ho –ho
Dans le cœur, dans le foie, dans le mou, dans la tête, dans les bras, dans les jambes, dans le cou,
Cina cinéma c'est au cinématographe, de la cinématographie partout.
Petite madame, je vous énerve à remuer comme ça ?
Ne me regardez pas madame!
Sinon ça vous prendra comme moi!
Vous aurez du cinéma, et demain, vous y reviendrez au cinéma
Vous avouerez que c'est cocasse,
Depuis que j'ai posé devant ce fourbi,
Je ne tiens plus une minute en place,
Je gigote le jour et la nuit,
Sitôt que je sors dans la rue
Les badauds, les gosses, les passants,
Les trottins et les petites grues,
Disent en riant:
Regardez donc ce ouistiti
Qui nous fait la danse de Saint-Guy."
(Au refrain)

**15** | To give a short example: in the music video, directed by Sophie Muller in 1996 for the song *Don't Speak* by the band No Doubt, we can discern (at least) two "tinctures", a "live" one (referring to documentaries and filmed concerts) and a "narrational" one (relying on features such as fiction, composed scenes, lip sync etc.).

## BIBLIOGRAPHY

Abel, Richard (1994): *The Ciné Goes to Town: French Cinema, 1896-1914*, Berkeley: University of California Press.

Abel, Richard/Altman, Rick (2001): *The Sounds of Early Cinema*, Bloomington: Indiana University Press.

Adorno, Theodor W./Horkheimer, Max (1944): *Dialectic of Enlightenment*, New York: Social Studies Association.

Altman, Rick (2004): *Silent Film Sound*, New York: Columbia University Press.

Arnoldy, Edouard (2004): *Pour une histoire culturelle du cinéma*, Liège: Editions du Céfal.

Burch, Noël (1991): *La Lucarne de l'infini, naissance du langage cinématographique*, Paris: Nathan Université.

Caradec, François/Weill, Alain (2007): *Le Café Concert 1848-1914*, Paris: Fayard.

Chion, Michel (2003): *Un art sonore, le cinéma*. Paris: Cahiers du Cinéma.

Condemi, Concetta (1992): *Les cafés-concerts, histoire d'un divertissement (1849-1914)*, Paris: Editions Quai Voltaire Histoire.

Coquiot, Gustave (1896): *Les Cafés-concerts*, Paris: Librairie de l'art.

Deville, Nicolas (1990): *Essai sur les figures de Dionysos dans le videoclip et leur incidence sur l'émergence de quatre images macluhaniennes*, Ph.D. dissertation (Sociologie, Paris V, num. national de thèse: 1990PA05H067)

Foucault, Michel (1977): "Nietzsche, Genealogy, History". In: Donald F. Bouchard (ed.): *Language, Counter-Memory, Practise. Selected Essays and Interviews*, Ithaca: Cornell University Press, p. 139-164

Guy, Alice (1976): *Autobiographie d'une pionnière du cinéma, 1873-1968*. Paris: Denoël-Gonthier.

Jacques-Charles (1966): *Le Caf Conc'*, Paris: Flammarion.

Meusy, Jean-Jacques (1995): *Paris-Palaces ou le temps des cinémas (1894-1918)*, Paris: CNRS Editions.

Schwartz, Vanessa R. (1999): *Spectacular Realities: Early Mass Culture in Fin-de-Siècle Paris*, Berkeley: University of California Press.

Wallerstein, Immanuel (2006): *Comprendre le monde. Introduction à l'analyse des système-monde*, Paris: Editions La Découverte.

# Looking at Music

Barbara London

Minimal music gave us maximal video. The frenetic pace of early MTV might seem removed from the extended duration of phasing or ambient drones, but sensory assault and perceptual slowness are far more closely intertwined than we might think. Indeed, the short form of the music video seems to contain within it both pop decadence and avant-garde asceticism. Now that the music video has in many ways become the signature form of all media – migrating away from MTV toward YouTube and scaled down to iPhones – it is worth considering the genre's relationship to experimental, interdisciplinary activities of the 60's and 70's.

A dense yet twisted braid of connections ties video to music during this period. Such a composite history is all too often treated as a series of separate strands: video, for example, has been considered largely in the province of the visual – whether as a continuation of documentary photographic practices, of textual communication, or of pictorial abstraction. But the aural and temporal aspects of video are, of course, no less important; despite a spate of exhibitions focusing on the tradition of "visual music" in recent years, divisions between media and the senses seem as rigid as ever. To understand these continually latent links and interactions, we must turn to the plane of technology: not as a deterministic engine of innovation, but as a common platform where music and video were treated as translatable signals or codes.

In the 60's, advanced, room-size computers were the focus of collaborations among engineers, musicians, and artists. Under the auspices of technical research or groundbreaking residency programs, artists were invited to such high-tech corporate enterprises as Bell Laboratories in New Jersey and Siemens Studio for Electronic Music in Munich. Much of the experimentation in electronic and computer music was directly related to the rise of minimalism and automated compositional structures: artists illustrated common sounds, repetitive words, and unhurried actions, often for long intervals. These inter-media endeavors owed as much to John Cage's embrace of ambient noise and chance operations and David Tudor's use of signal processing and feedback as to the work of film-sound pioneers such as Mary Ellen Bute, who based many of her intricate film animations on oscilloscope patterns or on mathematical formulas for transposing music into graphics. Bute's works had actually screened as shorts preceding feature films in regular movie theaters (such as the Radio City Music Hall) in the 40's and 50's – deploying sophisticated technology and arcane notational systems simultaneously to induce a timely pause or break in mainstream entertainment.

Others in the decades following Bute would continue to explore the tempo, distribution, and production of mass media, taking up electronic instruments that came on the consumer market at the same time as the first portable video cameras. Many of these artists, such as Tony Conrad and Steina in the U.S., were engaged in developing distinct personae through recorded actions. They might extend time, repeating an action for the length of an open-reel videotape, either thirty or sixty minutes. Or they might opt for succinctness and make work that adhered to the length of a pop song or a one-minute television commercial. Rooted in the historical exploration of slowness, the intersections of music and video began to traverse technology's exponentially increasing upgrades, from high-end equipment and broadcast television to lo-fi improvisations.

While Nam June Paik (1932-2006) later became known for his rapid-fire editing style, he started out slowly. At the University of Munich, he studied with composer, musicologist, pianist and building engineer Thrasybulos Georgiades and then with Wolfgang Fortner at the Conservatory of Music in Freiburg (Paik/Hanhardt 2003: p. 20). Paik's compositions in Freiburg already included experimentation with pre-recorded sounds. In 1958, at the lively gathering known as the International Summer Course for New Music in Darmstadt, Paik first met John Cage. The avant-garde composer, who felt electronic music was dead as a doornail, was notorious for treating all manner of noise – and silence – as music. Paik recalled: "Germany, in 1958, was a superficially serious culture of postwar, middle-class art and music. It was quite stifling. Suddenly, here were John Cage and David Tudor's lightweight lyricism, which was really fresh." (Stoss/Kellein 1993: p. 62)

Paik moved on to Cologne that fall, invited by the composer Karlheinz Stockhausen to be a fellow at Westdeutsche Rundfunk's (WDR) Center for Electronic Music. Stockhausen had just completed *Gesang der Jünglinge* (*Song of the Youths*) for electronic sounds and the recorded voice of a boy soprano. The work, generally considered the first musical piece for multi-track tape, used a four-track machine plus a second mono machine for a fifth track of playback.

Paik's interest in things technical was growing, but he relied on found sound (musique concrète) rather than the electronically generated sounds then in vogue at WDR. Paik's irreverence led him to include bits of Beethoven and Stravinsky alongside shrieks, test tones, and other, unidentifiable sounds. Despite the seemingly random juxtapositions and reliance on surprise, Paik's collaged music reflects the discipline of his WDR training. The pieces never resort to chaos (Zvonar 2000).

In the early 60's, Paik drew on his background in classical music and Buddhism to enact "action music" works. In these performances, after a whimsical foreplay of slowly moving about the stage, he would typically conclude with one mesmerizing note, usually played on a piano.

Moving to New York, Paik famously obtained one of the first portable video cameras to reach in New York and began making short minimal pieces. But these spare events and compositions soon appeared in other contexts, marked by sensory profligacy rather than reduction. In October 1965, Paik screened his first videotapes as part of a series of "happening nights" at the Greenwich Village nightclub *Café au Go Go* – a venue that included Lenny Bruce and the Grateful Dead among its roster of performers. The young Japanese composer Takehisa Kosugi, who had recently immigrated to the city, provided live accompaniment. *Beatles Electroniques*, 1966-69, made with the experimental filmmaker Jud Yalkut, is nothing less than an early black-and-white music video. Paik grabbed bits from the mock documentary *A Hard Day's Night* (directed by Richard Lester in 1964), refilming and further distorting the footage through his video synthesizer (developed with engineer Shuya Abe). Snippets of the Beatles' faces are caught in a loop of warped abstraction. To accompany the endlessly folding imagery, Paik created a sound track with Kenneth Lerner, which featured fragmented Beatles songs recited again and again. Whereas the original film is an upbeat paean to Beatlemania, Paik's strategies of appropriation and repetition are conceptually closer to Andy Warhol's silk-screened paintings of celebrities such as Marilyn Monroe, 1962, and Steve Reich's phasing of spoken words from a publicized racial incident in his sound composition *Come Out* (1966). Like these works, *Beatles Electroniques* brought seriality into the realm of sensory overload.[1]

The arrival of portable video gear meant that artists as well as garage bands with homegrown agendas were equipped to play with image and sound – and the dream of democratic and total media distribution as well. Yet this anarchic enterprise simultaneously paralleled the rise of the short-format music video as a promotional tool for musicians and record labels. In 1970, Captain Beefheart (aka Don Van Vliet) garnered free time on public-access cable television in Los Angeles and aired the promo he had made for his new album, *Lick My Decals Off, Baby*. In a scant ninety seconds, a TV announcer refers to band members by their oddball names as he performs Clarabell-the-Clown-like madcap actions. A hand tosses cigarette butts through the air, and then, sporting a fez, Beefheart's bandmate Rockette Morton paces, winding an eggbeater. Echoing William Wegman's concurrent short vignettes made in his studio with his dog, Beefheart's prototypical music video draws on the contingent rhythm of slapstick. Just as his musical sound was an eclectic sampling of shifting time signatures (influenced by free jazz) and Frank Zappa (Beefheart's close friend and collaborator), this initial video exploration resonated with the surrealistic character of psychedelic environments, such as Joshua White's well-known light shows at the Fillmore East in New York, which accompanied the pitch distortion and feedback of Jimi Hendrix and others (Brougher/Mattis/Strick/Wiseman 2005: p. 161-162). Akin to Bute's insertion into the Hollywood film screening, Beefheart's videos introduced a bizarre instance of both interruption and continuity into broadcast-television programming.

Beefheart got in early, and musicians paid attention. As the nascent music video slowly emerged as an effective marketing vehicle for the recording industry, its forms and outlets were left wide open. Following Beefheart, the Residents (based in San Francisco), for example, were anticipating a broad audience for music videos and believed that they could shape the format – less to sell records, though, than to infiltrate systems of television and radio promotion. Their famous 1976 album *The Third Reich 'n' Roll* features Dick Clark in an SS uniform holding a carrot on the record cover. De-skilled tracks started out with pilfered clips of classic rock and funk songs that were spliced, overdubbed, and layered with new instrumentation. To accompany the songs, the group immediately produced brief music videos (after having attempted, from 1972 to 1976, to film the first long-format music video; this was never released in its entirety). These shorts were shot on film and initially screened in art-house theaters and in film festivals. Once the Residents began to perform live in 1982, however, the videos also began airing on the newly launched channel MTV and the influential late-night television program *Night Flight*. Like the group's aural pastiche, their "expressionistic" videos drew on the dark montage of John Heartfield as well as that of fellow Bay Area artists Bruce Conner and Wallace Berman. But the Residents' samples and cut-ups managed to enter wider and more diversified streams of circulation, flouting institutional boundaries that the art world was just beginning to breach. The interlude became the centerpiece.

 Music video arose as an interstitial arena in which to toy with popular modes of distribution – and it was also the perfect field for testing new kinds of televisual celebrity. Paik had already presaged this with his audio-visual deformations of the Beatles, yet perhaps it was David Bowie who most forcefully exploited the music video to make the subcultural into the iconic. As Thurston Moore has observed, Bowie "burst into the psychosis of the young and restless intellectuals around the world" with his outré art school look and mannered androgyny (Moore 2008). And music video was the catalyst: Bowie's canonical single *Space Oddity*, recorded and released to coincide with the first moon landing in 1969, uses this persona to tell the story of Major Tom, an astronaut who becomes lost in space. The five-minute video, made in 1972 (and originally shot on 16-mm film) for the track's US release, opens and closes with what appear to be abstract waveform signals and extraterrestrial sounds of static; in between, a very young and colorfully lit Bowie is seen in close-up. Directed by Mick Rock (the photographer-filmmaker best known for his legendary shots of '70's glam rockers), the clip would have been shown in theaters or possibly on "Scopitone" apparatuses – primitive 16-mm film jukeboxes-housed in bars and clubs.[2] This precursor to the latter-day music video was, then, a kind of privatized conduit for rock-star fame, superseding rock magazines as the place where fans could connect with their idols. It should come as no surprise that at precisely the same time as the *Space Oddity* video, Bowie would assume the larger-than-life character of Ziggy Stardust, complete with what Moore has called his "alien rooster cut and spaceman glam gear." (Moore 2008)

The duo known as Suicide – vocalist Alan Vega and Martin Rev on synthesizers and drum machines – emerged in 1970 around Soho's Mercer Art Center, an early venue of the Velvet Underground and the New York Dolls. Suicide devised an unholy soup of exhaustingly long and loudly abrasive electronic textures. Terrifying and riveting, the sound came out of a structuralist milieu (of aggressive Richard Serra sculpture and Lamonte Young seriality). Suicide's song, *Frankie Teardrop*, about a poverty-stricken Vietnam vet pushed to the edge, was incisively interpreted as a 1978 music video, a collaboration between videomaker Paul Dougherty, and Walter Robinson and Edit DeAk, editors of the zine, *Art-Rite*. The scratchy film-video hybrid combines superimposed projector manipulations and high-end video post-production.

*Frankie Teardrop* evolved at a time when a bankrupt New York City was a haven for young renegade artists, who often doubled as musicians and poets. Art and music cross-fertilized with a vengeance. Artists commandeered abandoned buildings, turning vacant garages into makeshift theaters for Super 8 film screenings and raucous performances. They plastered city walls with self-designed posters announcing upcoming events or containing their aphorisms. Many found the experimental music scene more vital and relevant for their contrarian ideas than the handful of contemporary art galleries. They formed bands, performing in clubs and subsequently in non-profit art galleries. They designed and self-published their own records and zines, and used the recently formed public-access cable channels as a venue for media experiments and funky talk-show-like cultural debates.

Glenn O'Brien's weekly cable series, *TV Party*, featured young graffiti artists Fred Brathwaite (a.k.a. Fab 5 Freddy) and Jean-Michel Basquiat, who were using subway cars and city walls as blank canvases for their paintings. They tracked rap music emerging uptown and the hip downtown clubs (where they were often the only blacks in a room), regularly hanging out with Debbie Harry and the up-and-coming Madonna. Never one to be outdone, Basquiat self-produced his record *Beat Bop* with Rammellzee and K. Rob in 1983.

Debbie Harry's easy-going band Blondie came up with the song *Rapture*, inspired by an off-the-cuff rap of Brathwaite. The band's *Rapture* (1981) music video, made by "Keef" (this the working name for director Keith MacMillan and producer John Weaver) was the first rap video to be broadcast on MTV. It opens with choreographer William Barnes dancing in white suit and top hat on the Upper East Side, watching Harry and the Blondie musicians at a (as it seems) dance party. In the final sequence – one single-take – they dance down a street, passing graffiti artists Brathwaite and Lee Quinones in action, and Basquiat poised at DJ turntables. The work marks the transition into the next, more commercial decade.

Art video and music video arrived at the type of conjunction we know best: MTV. The advent of MTV was a no less heterogeneous affair, its beginnings stirring in both the celebrity-driven commodification of music and the aesthetic testing of perception. The station actually presented brief "Art Breaks" that it commissioned from artists such as Dara Birnbaum and Jenny Holzer (see Klanten/Meyer/Jofré 2005). But other videos not labeled as such were equally vanguard: Think of the wittily mordent Devo, or of Laurie Anderson, who made her renowned music video *O Superman* for Warner Bros. Records in 1981 – just in time for the start of MTV. Multimedia artist Perry Hoberman (who had been turning obsolete technologies such as 3-D slide systems into droll animated narratives) joined Anderson as artistic director. Accommodating the consumer TV set's small scale, they concentrated on close-up shots of Anderson, exaggerated silhouettes of her shadow-puppet hands, and her glowing face, illuminated by a small light placed inside her mouth. She lip-synched, moving her lips and thus the blinking light in unison with her prerecorded words. Anderson's video aired in rotation in between both "Art Breaks" and "mainstream" videos – the long duration and sustained sensations of past sonic and visual experiments now a series of fast gaps and fills.

If artists have historically been attracted to music for its dream of a universal language, a latter-day harmony of the spheres, then music video is perhaps the inverse incarnation: a particulate and fragmented form that mapped the individualized and diversified paths of media today.[3] What is most dated to us now – the fleeting, analog sounds and images of the small screen – is also becoming more familiar again.

## REFERENCES

**1** | Unpublished program notes from *Café au Go Go*. In: Artist Files, MoMA, NY Library.

**2** | See for this the introduction, p. 7, and the article by Thomas Schmitt in this volume.

**3** | See for this also the article by Antje Krause-Wahl in this volume.

## BIBLIOGRAPHY

Brougher, Kerry/Mattis, Olivia/Strick, Jeremy/Wiseman Ari (eds.) (2005): *Visual Music: Synaesthesia in Art and Music since 1900*. Los Angeles: Museum of Contemporary Art; London: Thames & Hudson.

Klanten, Robert/Meyer, Birga/Jofré, Cristián (eds.) (2005): *On Air – The Visual Language and Global Language of MTV*, Berlin: Die Gestalten.

Moore, Thurston (2008): Unpublished introduction at MoMA screening of David Bowie music videos December 1, 2008.

Paik, Nam June/Hanhardt, John (2003): *The Worlds of Nam June Paik*, New York: Guggenheim Museum.

Stoss, Tony/Kellein, Thomas (editors) (1993): *Nam June Paik: Video time-Video Space*, New York: Harry N. Abrams.

Zvonar, Richard (2000): *An Extremely Brief History of Spatial Music in the 20th Century*, http://cec.concordia.ca/econtact/Multichannel/spatial_music_short.html (last access 8.3.2010).

# "Pride and Prejudice"

## A Brief History of the Italian Music Video

Bruno Di Marino

1. In order to prevent my paper from being too historic, I suggest that I begin at the end by talking about a videoclip created by the brother-director team of Marco and Antonio Manetti. Together, they have made dozens of music videos with a rather recognizable style, which often combines its narration character with a funny and comic-book-like style. *Che Idea*, which was created in 2005 for a Hip Hop group called Flaminio Maphia, is nothing other than a small catalogue of 'tributes' to and parodies of other Italian video clips of the last 10 years, made with the Flaminio Maphia who, every time, take the roles of their colleagues: from *Serenata Rap* by Jovanotti (directed in 1994 by Ambrogio Lo Giudice) to *Una Vita da Mediano* by Luciano Ligabue (shot in 1999 by Luca Lucini), from *Quelli Che Benpensano* by Frankie Hi-NRG (made by the group itself in 1997) to *Salirò* by Daniele Silvestri (2002, Andrea Linke), up to the Hip Hop artist CapaRezza, who in his clip for *Fuori dal Tunnel*, made in 2004 by Riccardo Struchil, is chased by an enormous white ball (thus becoming, in the context of the Flaminio Maphia-video, a quote within a quote: the motive is taken from the English tv "cult" series *The Prisoner* where these white balls were chasing fugitives), including naturally some clips made by the Manetti brothers themselves such as the one made in 2006 for *Supercafone* by another Roman rapper called Er Piotta.

Towards the end of the video the camera pulls back to reveal the directors as they simulate the set of yet another video clip. One thus gets the idea that, if the Italian music video reaches the stage of self-quotation and of a mostly shameless self-referentiality, this means that it has somehow become a classic.

Another similar case of plagiarism/parody, even more spectacular and perhaps unique, did first appear in 2003: the music video for *Dedicato a Te* which Domenico Liggeri had made for the pop band Le Vibrazioni. The video consists of a girl, who in a single sequence wakes up in the morning and walks through the streets of Milan (close to the Navigli) until she arrives on a boat where the group is performing. This video became the target of first an instant remake by the farcical rock band Elio e le storie tese (they adapted Liggeri's clip in 2003 for their own music video, directed by Paolo Soravia, for the song *Shpalman*) and then immediately of another parody, this time by Frankie Hi-NRG (again in 2003 for their title *Chiedi Chiedi*): Each time we have same the location, the same actress and almost the same camera movements. The result: the two 'parasitic' works have given a somewhat enhanced impact to Liggeri's video by making it more famous.

The clip for *Chiedi Chiedi* differs more from the original video for *Dedicato a Te* than the one for *Shpalman*. Indeed, it includes another, very obvious quote from one of the masterworks of the avant-garde cinema, Luis Buñuel's and Salvador Dalí's 1929 *Un Chien Andalou*. In *Chiedi Chiedi*, the rapper Frankie appears in the disguise of the bizarre cyclist from the film and carries a mysterious, black and white-striped box around his neck from where – at the end of the video – he takes a cut-off hand (another key-element from the first part of *Un Chien Andalou*). He obviously thinks that he is the winner of a strange bicycle race which takes place on the same boat where all of the above-mentioned music videos take place; but he realizes immediately that there are already three winners on the podium, dressed just like him, and standing in front of a person which wears a moustache similar to the one by Dalí.[1]

The other curious element is that in the two video-plagiarisms of *Dedicato a Te* the four members of the Le Vibrazioni appear always, thus participating in the game with great self-irony while thus also emphasizing the fact that the parodies are somewhat 'authorized'.

2. It is exactly this type of *mise en abyme* at which the Italian video clip has arrived that is so striking. This kind of music video can be read as an expression of the need for self-consecration, but not out of exhibitionism or immodesty, but rather out of the need to finally recognize itself as an individual world of images. And all this after years of ghettoisation when the Italian video clip was pushed to the boarders of a history where the English or the Americans were always the protagonists.

If a change has happened in the history of the music video, it has been a change of style that first took place around the early 90's and then again around 2000. There seems to be a logical progression here, for with the passing of each decade, such changes occurred with a certain regularity.

The reasons for this are less to be sought on the production level (the average budget at the disposal of the directors has here remained unchanged for 20 years), but – if ever – on the level of post-production in which the reduction of editing and software costs, now increasingly available for everyone, does matter. And last but not least, a difference is made by the arrival of a new mentality and a new creativity which perhaps stems from the juvenescence of a domain, from a new desire for experimentation (not only with animation and the computer), which led to the production of videos which are not too spectacular, but instead firmly grounded on a strong concept.

As a result of these changes, some directors have quite quickly developed a recognizable style. Here we can refer, for example, to Gaetano Morbioli, who works with blurred, fuzzy images and plays with the relations between close ups and background in a way that includes the right dose computer-generated, graphic effects, but we could here also refer to the above mentioned Manetti-brothers.

For many others instead who are equally productive, from Alex Infascelli to Cosimo Alemà, eclecticism seems to be a good descriptive, particularly given their style, which changes continuously according to the musical contexts.

3. But what came first? With the short space we have at our disposal, we need to begin our history in chronological order with the year 1981 when the music video in Italy began to get distributed thanks to a TV-show called 'Mister Fantasy' (see for this also Massarini 2009). Before, there was yet another age: the one of the short films for the *Cinebox* (the equivalent of the French "Scopitone"), rediscovered some years ago, the era of the short films or TV-trailers and of films called "musicarelli" (a kind of Italian musical where the main characters were played by singers, who were then stars, sided by some comical actors).

However, we can't go too far backwards in our excursion for the danger of getting lost. Where to begin if not with what we can call the first 'conscious' Italian video clip in history, *Rock'n'rolling* by Scialpi, directed by Piccio Raffanini who then, together with Giandomenico Curi, Gianfranco Giagni, Marcello Avallone, Nicola De Maria and others formed the team of directors responsible for the successful show which was created by Paolo Giaccio and presented by Carlo Massarini (the 'Mister Fantasy'). This music video was produced by Franco Migliacci, the author of the famous *Volare (Nel Blu Dipinto di Blu)* by Domenico Modugno, published in 1958. But in reality already some months before, in 1980, the singer Loredana Bertè got her video for *Movie* directed by Andy Warhol: a 'classical' video in a very 80's-style, showing her interposed with neon signs of New York.

Some years later, in 1984, another event on TV changed the destiny of visible music: the birth of specialized TV channels like Videomusic, which delayed the arrival of the multinational MTV in Italy for a decade.[2] These were the years when the video clip became fashionable, even though it was seen as a commercial audio-visual form without any aesthetic value – this a judgement which has been revised in the meantime, to the point of forcing cinema-academics to deal with it and to make it the topics of Ph.D. dissertations of their students.

In 1984, Michelangelo Antonioni was convinced by Gianna Nannini to shoot the video for her song *Fotoromanza*. As so often, when a film director approaches the genre of the music video, the result was a disaster.[3] The images visualized the lyrics in the most servile and slavish way possible.

Was this a desired effect in order to emphasize the fanciful postmodern tautology of the music video? This is at least the opinion of those who defend Antonioni. Beyond its intentions, *Fotoromanza* remains an amusing pastime for the director.

Nevertheless there are examples of young singer-songwriters who in Italy, thanks to a video clip, have sold 100.000 copies of their singles. This is the case of Luca Carboni with his video *Ci Stiamo Sbagliando*, directed by Ambrogio Lo Giudice, perhaps the only valuable director who still today, after 25 years, continues to make clips.

But if we turn back into history there are not many works of the time to remember. There are typically 80's-works such as *Il Video Sono Io* by Matia Bazar, explicitly postmodern (like the clip itself) in its attitude towards design, its use of colours, the reflexion on the possibilities and the nature of television, or there are videos 'of atmosphere' such as *Il Mare d'Inverno* by Gianfranco Giagni for the before mentioned Loredana Bertè. But one of the best works of the 80's remains without a doubt *Una Notte in Italia* (1986) by the musician Ivano Fossati, directed by the Florentines Alessandro Salaorni and Fabio Bianchini. This very fine video also contains a quote from *Un Chien Andalou* and uses a very vanguard technique. The video is shot in black and white (showing mainly almost expressionistic silhouettes and shadows) followed by coloured sequences created using optical effects frame by frame.

The novelty of the music video, however, quickly faded away. Increasingly, record companies had less desire to invest money into music videos. An exception – and we are already in the 90's – are the clips for Vasco Rossi, often and preferably made in the USA with a huge budget: for example *Gli Spari Sopra*, directed by Stefano Salvati, a mediocre director, but very attached to the rock star. This clip is based on lots of action, special effects, and scenes shot from a helicopter. The location is a former prison where the rock star is presented as a mix between Steve McQueen and Sylvester Stallone. A lot of smoke and mirrors and only a little originality, because it follows the model of many American music videos. But the Italian pop song – and thus also the relative video clip – struggles to transgress the national boarder. *Penso Positivo* for Jovanotti, directed by Ambrogio Lo Giudice, has the privilege to be, in 1993, the first Italian video to be broadcasted by MTV (see for this also Di Marino 2001: p. 170f.). The location is typical for many video clips of the 90's: the supermarket, or the temple of consumption, where – in this case – apart from the goods and objects, concepts and thoughts are also on sale.

4. Compared to the advertisement, whose centre of production has always been in Milan, the video clip has its Roman school and this is not a small peculiarity. Set aside that the directors of 'Mister Fantasy' were also Romans, the renaissance also takes place in the middle of the 90's. Among the best pupils of this school there is indeed a young and extravagant man: Alex Infascelli. The rule remains always the same: to make a video with a

low budget. Indeed, Infascelli spends with *Faccio la Mia Cosa* for Frankie Hi-NRG only a little, but while using a certain scenography, he also invents a style.

Certainly, compared to other countries where directors now begin to claim fame after years of staying anonymous, in our country the makers of a clip still remain unknown until they leave the dark shadow of the video music and make their beginnings in the area of long and narrative films. Sooner or later, they all make this step. Some remain in the area of the musical film, others – such as Infascelli (who in 2000 made his film debut with the movie *Almost Blue*) or the Manetti-brothers (the directors of *Zora la vampira*, issued also in 2000) who approach the *film noir* or the comic-fantastic.

In the 90's the most important production company is perhaps Marco Balich's "Filmmasterclip" which, between 1992 and 2000, produced around 60 videos. Also foreign directors are now arriving in Italy: in 1993 Spike Lee for Eros Ramazzotti, Roman Polanski in 1996 directs *Gli Angeli* for Vasco Rossi together with Salvati (see for this also Di Marino 2001: p. 176f.), who, several years later, sues the production company of Madonna for plagiarism because *Ray of Light*, directed by Jonas Åkerlund in 1998, would have copied his video, shot in 1994 for Biagio Antonacci's song *Non è Mai Stato Subito*. Of course, the accusation can't be sustained, especially given that this type of music video tends to plunder the history of experimental cinema in general (and in this particular case, the time lapse sequences from Godfrey Reggio's 1982 movie *Koyaanisqatsi*). And we know that in this area nobody has invented anything and that everybody has invented everything.

Towards the end of the 90's, animation conquers its territory, riding on the wave of the enormous distribution of the English, American and French music videos made with the help of the computer. In the middle of the decade, in 1994, Vincenzo Gioanola had still painted frame by frame *Fight da Faida* for Frankie Hi-NRG (see for this Di Marino 2001: p. 171f.), but now it is the season of Stranemani, a group of Tuscan animators who are creating some very diverse works. The result of a sophisticated 3-D animation are clips for Tiromancino, a band which is very attentive towards this form of communication. Examples include the videos for the songs *Per Me è Importante* (2002) and *Imparare dal Vento* (2004), both conceived by the band leader Federico Zampaglione and made by Direct-2Brain, a group of animators (this time from Latium), working in the field of the production of advertisement. In a more experimental style we find instead other videos that use dadaistic photographic collage. Examples include videos for Vinicio Capossela's song *Marajà* by Ago Panini (2001)[4] or the most recent video for Daniele Luttazzi's song *Money for Dope* by the young Giovanni Scarfini (2005). This video falls somewhere between the disconcerting atmosphere of David Lynch and the strange creatures of the Quay brothers.

The formation of the Italian video clip-directors is very different. Some, for example, come from photography (such as Lo Giudice and Scarfò). But for the most part, video clip directors come from advertising or at least divide themselves between the advertising industry and the music video such as Fei, Sigon, Alemà, Paoletti, Capotondi or Alessandra Pescetta. Pescetta, however, began as a video artist. Her abstract film *InNaturale* (1994) had a strong impact on the rock star Ligabue, who, in 1995, asked her to direct a video clip for his song *Leggero*. Another director who comes from the area of the experimental video is Luca Pastore from Turin, who in 1999 made an especially original video for the band Subsonica, *Disco Labirinto*, a first attempt to visualise music for deaf-mutes with the help of lights and gestures, trying to communicate the pleasure of music and to facilitate an understanding of the text by translating it into the sign-language and having it appear in Karaoke-like subtitles at the same time.

5. I would like to conclude my brief excursion by emphasizing that – beyond the particular styles by individual directors applied to different musicians and bands – there is, on the contrary, a visual style which characterises a musician and his band, independent from the director who makes their videos. This is again the case with Elio e le storie tese, the rock band from Milan which can't be exported to foreign countries because of their frenzied lyrics which – beyond the town of Chiasso – can't be understood and whose videos are, in my opinion, among the best ever made in Italy.

They are highly experimental and from time to time disrespectful, provoking, anarchic. They baffle, bluff and entertain the viewer, particularly because the verbal content entwines and doubles with the visual contents, creating an incredible audio-visual chaos. It is again in the field of the quote, the parody, the twisting of every code that the Italian music video is a winner, even though – paradoxically – it can be only fully enjoyed in Italy. And this is really a shame.

## REFERENCES

**1** | This film by Dalì and Buñuel is very often quoted in the history of the music video, see for example the clip for Iggy Pop's and for Debbie Harry's song *Well Did You Evah*, directed in 1992 by Alex Cox.

**2** | For more information on the channel Videomusic and the relation with MTV see Baldini 2000.

**3** | See for this also the contribution by Giulia Gabrielli in this volume.

**4** | Vinicio Capossela is a musician who is very attentive towards musical as well as visual experimentation. Another interesting, animated clip done for him is the one made in 2009 for his song *Una Giornata Perfetta*: here, without making recourse to digital effects, the filmmaker Virgilio Villoresi has combined the technique of the stop-motion with animated photography of the singer who appears in a three-dimensional set, which was – especially at the beginning and at the end – inspired by the model of the pages from a pop-up book.

## Bibliography

Baldini, Mimmo (2000): *MTV. Il nuovo mondo della televisione*, Rome: Castelvecchi.

Di Marino, Bruno (2001): *Clip - 20 anni di musica in video (1981 – 2001)*, Rome: Castelvecchi.

Massarini, Carlo (2009): *Dear Mr. Fantasy*, Milan: Rizzoli.

# *Play:*
# The Methodology of Analysis
# and Interpretation

# Concerning the Transition of the Reception of the Music Video due to a Change in the Politics of Distribution of the Music Video- and the Music(-TV-)Market[1]

Axel Schmidt/Klaus Neumann-Braun

## 0. Introduction

The reception of the music video (abbreviated as 'ROTMV' throughout this chapter) was attached in the past mainly to the medium of television, hence for a research upon the audience the private resp. the public TV-setting served as the point of reference. Recently, technical and developments related to politics of the market have made that the audience dispersed on another, higher level of complexity. Taking this into account, the following paper deals with the changed conditions of the ROTMV.

However, such a reception can be researched in many different ways. Thus, we first want to make clear in which respect we are approaching the topic of the ROTMV.

First, reception can be understood as referring to the cognitive processing of the specific media genre, in this case the music video, which provokes questions about how music video is constructed in the first place. Furthermore, the question could be pursued in a quantitative respect, i.e. in the form of data concerning its use. However, in order to pursue yet another consideration of how ROTMV has changed, neither cognitive processing nor quantitative analysis pursued here, except with respect to secondary data.

This consideration takes as a starting point the question of where and how the phenomenon of the ROTMV can be (still) encountered today, particularly by embedding the question of reception within the research of media culture in social-economical and socio-cultural contexts. One then has to ask questions concerning the associated, flanking conditions of processes of reception. In other words, before it can be explained how reception happens cognitively resp. quantitatively, it has to be cleared, under which conditions resp. in which structures ROTMV is happening today.

Connected herewith are the following questions:

- Does the classic music video still exist, and if so, in which respect?
- Are there flexible boundaries between the music video and other AV-formats?
- How and by which means are clips distributed today?
- In which media environments are clips encountered?
- Which entities produce and distribute clips to which means?
- What is the role of music TV stations in this context?
- In which way have the offered choices and the programs of the classic music TV stations changed?

The main focus of the following consideration falls upon dealing with these questions by giving a sketch of the structural conditions of the ROT-MV, i.e.: to sketch the structures of the "context of reception" in a perspective which combines the historical with the systematic.

For this purpose, we are relying on web-based researches, current literature, and interviews with experts which were the base for a finished book project with the title "Viva MTV – reloaded".

The following overview should make clear the greater context of argument as well as its direction alongside the ROTMV-topic, as chosen for the paper:

A. Music video and music television yesterday: interlinking

- The *genesis* of music television: innovation ("cult") and development towards a "Monopoly Television"
- *Routine*: the ideal-typical way of functioning

B. Music video and music television today: a double-sided decoupling

- *Crisis*: collapse of the ideal-typical way of functioning and becoming every day-like

| Reasons/Causes | Reactions of the music channels | Way of change |
|---|---|---|
| - Crisis in the music industry/structural change of the classical record industry<br>- Change of the TV-/media-landscape (keyword: digitalisation)<br>- **Dissolution of the boundaries of the music video**<br>• **on the level of the genre (from the video clip to the net clip)**<br>• **on the level of distribution (music videos on the internet)** | Dissolution of the boundaries of the music television:<br>• **From being a division channel to the full program**<br>• **New ways of distribution**<br>• Extension of partnerships in advertising | Discontinuity:<br>**M**ore **T**han **V**ideos |
| | Extension of the monopoly<br><br>(in Germany: "MTVIVA") | Continuity:<br>Monopoly Television |

C. Conclusion: Changed (conditions of) reception

The central aspects appear in bold. Aspects which are only sketched appear as regular text, and those only hinted upon here appear as grey. The purpose of this synopsis is to make clear the greater context of the argument without having to repeat it throughout this paper.

Point A deploys the thesis of the interlinking of the music video and music television ("yesterday"), i.e. music video and music television forged an alliance which in the phase of the genesis did stand for innovation. MTV then becomes "cult" (as can be seen, for instance, by the success of the "I want my MTV" campaign [1982]). Subsequently, MTV developes into a global player, into a "Monopoly TV" which dominates the market. Thus, a routine is established, a lucrative ideal-typical way of functioning, which then – as argued under point B – gets into a crisis.

This happens – as will be shown – via a double-sided dissociation, which means that music television as well as the music video succumbs to a dissolution of boundaries which then condition the dissociation in their turn.

The dissolution of the boundaries of music television can be finally understood concerning the way of change as a discontinuity ("More than Videos") on the level of the media products (program, music videos), while the remaining components – the crisis of the music industry and the extension of a monopoly (in the German-speaking market: "MTVIVA") – could be taken as aspects of the production under the aspect of continuity and have here been mentioned just for the sake of completeness.

## A. MUSIC VIDEO AND MUSIC TELEVISION YESTERDAY: INTERLINKING[2]

The fact that MTV today can still operate as a global player in almost mo-nopoly-like structures stems directly from the "cult"-status the channel established from the very beginning. Indeed the value of the brand 'MTV' still benefits from its original cult standing, particulary in combination with the establishment of a new business model. By furnishing the music channel with music videos from music industry, advertisement and programming became the same thing. Contrary to the radio media with their concurrence, MTV in its beginnings could rely on an almost cost-neutral program which in an increasingly fragmented TV-market became more and more important. If the chain of the creation of value did work, a produced music video supported the selling of records while favoring the use and connection to a TV-channel. Thus, concerning the possibility of presenting the products of the major labels to the related target group, the music channels were the most important marketing instrument for a long time. During its peak period, 80 percent of the video clips shown by VIVA and MTV came from the four biggest record companies Universal, Sony BMG, Warner and EMI. In other words, the marketing model of music television was essentially based on having "found" a media form at the right time which in the crossing fields of the 'economy 1' (viewer/ TV ratings) and the 'economy 2' (gains and effects of the advert) functioned as advertising and programming at the same time.

## B. MUSIC VIDEO AND MUSIC TELEVISION TODAY: DOUBLE-SIDED DECOUPELING

Seen from a contemporary viewpoint, one can state that this relatively har-monious model fell under pressure, if not even into a crisis. The main rea-sons for this downfall were and still are the crisis of the music industry and the resulting structural change of the classic record industry on the one hand and the changed media and TV-landscape, as well as the connected needs of the receiving audience on the other hand. Neither point can be developed here, but it is enough to note at this point: When considered as an aspect of the music business, music videos have lost their importance as a means of marketing and partly can't be financed anymore; when be-ing considered under the aspect of the TV market and the changed media landscape (keyword: digitalization, mobile media) they undergo decisive changes which concern less the classic music video as such (it still exists), but more the social and media-economic context in which music videos have to compete now.

Importantly, this means a slow marginalization of the classic com-mercial music video as the linchpin of the own business and programming politics and has thus modified the music video and its reception decisively.

We have tried to sum up these developments with the notion of the "double sided decoupling on the level of the product", which means that the once very close linking of music videos and music television on the side of the music video as well as on the side of the music television has been loosened. We have used the notion of the "dissolution of the boundaries" for this process whereby the dissolutions of the boundaries of the music video are resulting in the dissolution of the boundaries of music television.

*A dissolution of the boundaries of the music video* has to be stated *on the level of the genre*. Here the range has been – roughly put – widened by now to include so-called "net clips" which means that they are recycled (i.e. usually taken from mass media) or self generated AV-excerpts which are accessible on the Internet via related video-portals such as YouTube, clipfish or MyVideo. The following types can be roughly discerned which have participated in the dissolution of the boundaries of the classic music video:

- Fragments /alienations of music videos (remixes, generated by users)
- Re-elaborations by the channels (for example the show "MTV Mash" [2003]; other remixes of music videos)
- Imitations of the genre
- Adaptation of an aesthetic of the classic clip-genre
- Filmed live-concerts as music clips
- Any other connection of sound and vision which belongs to a floating continuum of the music video (domination of the music; singing/performance) and film/TV (domination of the images; spoken words; soundtrack-function of music).
- Video clips used as ringtones on mobile phones (so-called "videotones")

Moreover there is a dissolution of the boundaries *on the level of distribution*, since music videos are lo longer coupled with the mass medium 'TV'. One therefore has to deal with "old" contents (music videos) in a frame of new, i.e. net- or mobile-based choices. Here, the following types can be roughly discerned concerning their "distribution channel":

- music videos on Web 2.0-platforms
- music videos on net supplies associated to music channels (for example MTV Overdrive)
- music videos on net supplies in cooperation with music channels (for example Joost)
- music videos on net suppliers which are not associated to music channels (for example www.popzoot.tv; tunespoon.tv)
- music videos on the homepage of individual artists
- music videos on the mobile phone

Additionally on could discern which institution is distributing, i.e.

- the artist him or herself
- the users (Web 2.0)
- possibly "net channels" (commercial/professional; similar to mass media)
- classic music television

The music channels are reacting upon these dynamics, with *a movement of the dissolution of the boundaries on the product and distribution level,* i.e. by broadening their program and by diversifying their ways of distribution.

The development of the *contents of the program* of MTV can be understood as the way from a pure channel for music towards the classic full program, where the sole focus on popular music has increasingly been abandoned in favor of a broader orientation towards pop- and lifestyle-topics of various kinds. Here, a central reason lies in the social-cultural changes which have made popular music lose its profile: Since music is no longer considered to be mainly formative, it cannot provide means for any kind of distinction anymore. Identifiable and distinct youth sub cultures for example have been increasingly substituted by a general youth-cultural orientation respectively they have stepped into higher age groups. Thus, the more pop music and life-style have merged, the more MTV has started increasingly aiming for other potentials of distinction than just (pop)music (consumed today also by people older than 40 years) in order to (further) reach their youthful audience. Hence, the distinction towards the generation of the parents functions – at least in its form of (music) television – today much less via musical predilections than according to visual boarders of taste and aesthetics and via questions about public (non-)showing. This is especially true concerning so-called "reality shows" and "docu-soaps" which in the meantime have been furnishing a third of the MTV-program (see the following survey in fig. 1).

*Fig. 1: Distribution of Programmes scheduled by MTV (2000-2007; workdays)*

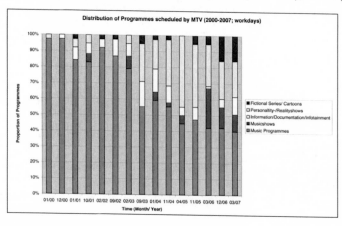

It is clear to see that there are still formats which are further orientated on popular music, but they are just making up only half of the program. This impression is enhanced by the fact that music video formats have been shifting towards the off-peak times (morning, afternoon). Other formats are now dominating their former program spaces, mainly personality- and reality-shows (around 20 %), cartoon series, and Animés for adults (more than 15 %) and docu- and infotainment-formats (around 10 %).

Dissolutions of boundaries concern not only programming, but *distribution* as well. Despite the dynamics in this field, a sketch-like overview of the different efforts music channels have made in the areas of digital TV, Internet, and mobile phone industry will be delivered in the following.[3]

## MTV digital

A look at the efforts of MTV in the realm of digital TV reveals two distinct strategies. First, the main programs of the channel are, as before, receivable in an analogue way (via satellite or cable), while the additional digital content can be ordered by paying a monthly fee (starting from 2,99 Euro) (under the label 'MTV Tune-Inn' there are seven additional digital channels in supply). This trend will continue since digital TV should be introduced to Germany nationwide up to 2010. At the moment, music(-video) shows are mainly shifted into the package of additional, payable TV-offers which finds itself moreover in concurrence with the free online supplies.

## MTV mobil

Of interest in the area of the mobile phones is the effort to make a pre-produced MTV-program receivable on a mobile device. This format is being referred to as "MTV mobil". Predestined formats of the so-called "Handy-TV" ("mobile phone-TV") are tele-shopping, music videos, and so-called Mobisoaps (soap operas for the mobile phone) – perfectly modeled for music channels in the style of MTV, as also Dieter Gorny emphasizes with the slogan "We're the kings of the short attention span". Thus, the music channel – acting as a forecaster in this area – has been available from reception via mobile phone since summer 2006. The broadcasting works via UMTS-technique in collaboration with the mobile phone companies T-Mobile, O2, and Vodafone. The channel MTV Music (an affiliation of Tune-Inn) can be received as along with a supply which shows daily updated programs of 60 minutes in an endless loop and which goes (depending from the cooperating partner) under the names MTV Shorts, MTV Snax or MTV mobile.

## MTV in the Net

Contrary to the traditional business area of music channels, the TV market, PC, and Internet represent not only an additional possibility for program distribution, but they should be considered as media genres in their own right, replete with their own rules, rules which threaten to substitute music television in its function as a medium for offering music videos and as a forum for pop culture. The engagement of the music channels in this area is thus the biggest and most complex. One can discern the following areas:

- First the usual web presences have to be mentioned; we refer here to the websites of the two big music channels in the German-speaking countries (MTV und Viva), which – with their rate of more than 10 million page impressions – were well frequented in 2006.
- The main focus, however, should be on the Streams and Video-on-demand-supplies. Considering the Streams MTV got a double concurrence from ca. 2005 on: First, a series of so-called "Videoportals" (such as YouTube or MyVideo) began where also – among others – music videos were (illegally) supplied. Moreover, alternative supplies concerning the music television (such as tunespoon.tv) and sites offering live-concert-footage (see www.fabchannel.com) established themselves. The reactions of the music channels were ambivalent (comparable to those of the record company towards music stock exchanges à la Napster): On the one hand the Viacom-trust defended itself against the usage of illegal (meaning: copyrighted) contents (see the claim for damages against Google/YouTube). On the other hand communities of interest are sought and forged: Thus, the Viacom-corporation signed a cooperation-contract with the YouTube-concurrent Joost in order to do something against such competitors. Another project in the area of the Video-Stream and – so to say – belated response to clip portals à la YouTube is the online-video-network iFilm, acquired in October 2005, which since then has been a member of the MTV Networks-family. A year later, in August 2006, Viacom bought the video- and entertainment-portal A-tom Entertainment Inc. for a sum of 200 million US-Dollars. Moreover, MTV in July 2006 started the German version of its Video-on-Demand online-service MTV Overdrive with great success, a service that allows the viewer to assemble his own program. The focus of the supply is on music videos, and the numbers of the Self-Made-MTV show how high the interest in the clips seem to be: In the first two weeks after the start of Overdrive the traffic on the homepage of the channel had doubled to 11,1 million page-impressions.
- Another area, prone to expand, is the one of the Online-Communities and of the interactive "Net-TVs". Among info- and media-supplies in the context of traditional homepages, it is here especially a range of Web 2.0-supplies which seem to be made as platforms for advertising. The so-called "Social Network Sites" (such as for example MySpace) enable users to build a virtual network of virtual interactivity and relationships. Even more drastic than in the case of the video portals it becomes clear which significance of the strategies of advertising the new sup-

plies have for the music channels: MySpace not only has the potential to make stars and to set new trends (MySpace-founder Tom Anderson is quoted in the weekly magazine *Der Spiegel* [15.01.2007] with the words "We have replaced MTV"). Moreover, Online-Communities and their offerings seem to be the forecasters of a new, changed behavior of media consumption apart from any given TV program in favor of self-created content and the ability to share this content interpersonally via the Internet. MTV has made an effort to participate in this potential: The platform MTV Flux is supposed to be run in the style of an Online-Community. It has to be seen how far this will be successful. Up to now MTV Flux is only available in Great Britain and in Ireland.

## C. CONCLUSION: CHANGED (CONDITIONS OF) RECEPTION

It should now be clear that music videos and music television have been and still are exposed to processes of the dissolution of the boundaries on many different levels (genre, context of presentation/concurrence, TV-program, distribution, areas of commerce, advert-alliances), and that this has had *serious consequences for the framing conditions of the reception of the music video*.

This shall be put into the following theses:

### 1. Emancipation

The dissociation of the phenomena 'music video' and MTV from each other due to processes of the dissolution of the boundaries on both sides not only indicates a separation, but – in a certain way, also – an emancipation: in the case of music television, it has been emancipated from its former trademark and flagship, the music video. In the case of the music video, it has been released from the framing broadcasting station, the music television. These emancipations create new latitudes for each.

### 2. De-Framing

The dissolution of the boundaries of music television comes with the consequence that the music video lacks its traditional context. It appears there as "among others" and is, moreover, outside the music television enclosed by a more diffuse program scheme which is missing the usual context. The "dissolution of the boundaries" of the music video on the level of genre also means that the product itself becomes more diffuse and that the frontier between the music video and the AV-clips area becomes more liquid. The once clearly situated phenomenon 'music video' has therefore lost its clear frame.

## 3. Shift of Meaning

Processes of emancipation and of de-framing together with the processes of music television becoming increasingly ubiquitous (MTV looses its "cult" status) are having an opposed double movement: First, the music video generally looses signification and experiences a relativization on the "highways" of mass communication (here: especially analogue television), in order to, secondly, have a renaissance on the Internet, aside from the classical mass communication. This renaissance means an increase in significance and – regarding the reception of the music video – an intensification, since chosen video clips (can) get received on the Internet. The significance of the music video therefore appears to have been shifted: instead of being cost-neutral contents of commercial TV-stations and tied to a program, they appear today as free floating entertainment- and information-segments of the popular culture.

## 4. Diversified Contexts of Reception

The reception of the music videos thus falls apart under these conditions.

- This – with respect to the *product* –
a. in an area of classic music video which has gone into niches and gets enjoyed only by minorities (such as boarder zones in the music television, special supplies on the net, digital Pay-TV, DVD-Sampler);
b. as well in an area of the "clips" in the broadest sense, where more and more also music videos are received (for example on YouTube), while they appear, however, to more and more dissolve into the more general category of the audio-visual.
- And the reception of the music video furthermore falls apart with respect to the *production/distribution*
c. in a classic (mass media/program structured) TV-area
d. as well as into a net-area where mass-media and interpersonal communication are interfering.

## 5. "Short Form"

Despite the dissolution of the social-economic structures in which the music video "grew up", it not only persists as a medial genre, but seems to have permeated the whole of popular culture in the form of aesthetic traditions of creating and shaping and ways of reception.

a. This concerns on the one hand ways of creating and fashioning television in general as well as the shaping of the full program of the music channels in particular (predominating is a style, oriented upon the "clips-aesthetics": fast editing, emphasized combination with music, unconventional perspectives and movements of the camera; shows such as "Viva la Bam" appear as "clip-like").

b.  Regarding classical forms of TV programming, this concerns, moreover, the form of the so-called "*en passant* viewing", provoked by the music videos and music television. This means, first of all, that full attention is dedicated not to the medium, but that the reception of media is embedded into other complexes of activities respectively happens parallel to them. Moreover, smaller and associatively connected units (keyword: "snippet-culture") allow a floating stepping in and out of the running program, thus favoring what has been called "Channel-Hopping".

c.  This principle of the "short form", already laid out by music television has been completed by related supplies on the net: The program as a structuring principle has disappeared in favor of individual, user-directed AV-collages. "Channel-Hopping" is unnecessary, since there are no fixed programs and the phenomenon of the "*en passant* viewing" seems to become its opposite while at the same time becoming all-embracing: "To view clips in video portals" breaks down into the organizing activity (waiting until a clip has been uploaded, new orientation and choice etc.) which invites the viewer to engage in side-activities and pauses on the one hand as well as to islands of attention (targeted viewing of the clips) on the other hand.

Summing up, one can state that the "classical" reception of music videos has been enormously fragmented and differentiated (distraction), while the formal traditions of designing a clip (as a short form, an "annex", as simply made, as trenchant, as associative etc.) as well as ways of linked reception seems to have got extended and to have been popularized (pooling).

## REFERENCES

**1** |  This paper summarizes the core results of our latest study *Viva MTV reloaded* (Schmidt, Neumann-Braun, Autenrieth 2009).

**2** |  See Banks 1996 and Schmidt 1999.

**3** |  This represents the state of research in Autumn 2007.

## BIBLIOGRAPHY

Banks, Jack (1996): *Monopoly Television. MTV's quest to control the music*, Boulder: Westview Press.

Schmidt, Axel (1999): "Sound and Vision go MTV. Die Geschichte des Musiksenders bis heute". In: Klaus Neumann-Braun (ed.), *Viva MTV. Popmusik im deutschen Fernsehen*, Frankfurt/M: Suhrkamp, p. 93-131.

Schmidt, Axel/Neumann-Braun, Klaus/Autenrieth, Ulla (2009): *Viva MTV reloaded*. Baden-Baden: Nomos.

α Grzenorein + Minkuye

# An Analysis of the Relation between Music and Image

## The Contribution of Michel Gondry

Giulia Gabrielli

## INTRODUCTION

In order to analyze any kind of audio-visual text, we need a starting hypothesis, a point of view from which we can study and examine the text. These factors vary depending on who is dealing with the text, and on the interests a person has developed throughout his studies: therefore, the same object can trigger different ideas and analysis factors. Nonetheless, any kind of analysis will be based on an attempt of accurate and in-depth comprehension of the message the author wants to convey to the recipient, and mainly of the ways through which this is achieved.

When analyzing a music video text, we cannot forgo making recourse to theories which have been developed in the context of the film, be it of a semiological, narrative or aesthetic nature. By applying the methods of Film Studies we can reach solid theoretical grounds, and we can discover connecting – or contrasting – points between these the two types of audio-video languages, i.e. the film and the music video. It is also interesting to point out the fact that concepts and theories of almost 100 years ago are today extremely resonant with contemporary issues and trends: let us think about the crucial theoretical framework by Sergei M. Eisenstein (see for this for example Keazor/Wübbena 2007: p. 95-96), and how studies about the relationship between music and image, which were developed when the talking film was introduced (for instance those by Adorno and Eisler)[1], are still useful.

Thanks to these contributions we can devote ourselves to study how different elements such as music and image manage to meet, to melt, and how they create unique and – sometimes – remarkable phenomena.

Unfortunately we have to point out that these remarkable phenomena are not so frequent and that they are rather exceptions whereas they should be the rule. We are witnessing an evolution of music videos which are more and more oriented towards the commercial and promotional aspects, to the detriment of the experimental and artistic research. A video is created and comes to life in order to promote something (a performer or a song, or both), and it would be utopist to expect these aspects to be disregarded. But it is still to be hoped that aesthetic and linguistic efforts are not totally neglected because otherwise this would lead to a situation where *only* the commercial/promotional aspects of a music video, as it is often the case at the moment, are taken into consideration when creating such a music clip.

Luckily, exceptions can always be found. Among the many good directors who have been making themselves noticeable in the past years (such as Chris Cunningham, who – though he is not very prolific – gives us real works of art, or Floria Sigismondi, Jonathan Glazer, Spike Jonze, to mention only a few), the most noteworthy and interesting to analyze is Michel Gondry. The prolific French director committed himself more than anyone else to researching and developing the potentials of synchronic bonds between music and image; this is why this essay will focus in particular on some of his works.

We will start with a general analysis of what happens when we combine images and music by trying to explore the many connections between the two. We will then try to demonstrate, through specific examples, that extraordinary and surprising results can be achieved when, as in the case of Michel Gondry, the potentials of this union are fully exploited.

## AUDIO-VISUAL TEXTS

A music video is a text typology formed by the union of two elements: a song taken in its whole and a series of images linked to it. The word "text" in the given definition is not chosen by chance, since it implies the presence of the addressee who has to receive the two elements: the spectator (Casetti 1986: p. 16). Being an *audio-visual* text then, a music video is formed by music and image: while in a film text the images – with a few exceptions – come first, in music videos the images are created later in order to be added to the song. This does not imply that we should give the visual part of the text less importance in our analysis: as we will see, it is crucial.

Besides which, it is important to underline the fact that music and images will ultimately be perceived simultaneously and as a whole. Whereas a song exists and has a more or less autonomous life, when images are linked to a song, it becomes something else, something completely different (its links with the album context, its media presence and other possible "paratexts" is much more indirect than this close combination with images). We only have a music video, when the spectator enjoys the two elements simultaneously. According to this definition, if the video is seen without the sound, what is perceived are only the *images* of a music video,

and *not the music video* itself. We only have
tor perceives this text as a whole, as a sum of
integrated into each other. Going back to the c
tian Metz, a music video is made to exist only it
(Metz 1980: p. 85).

It is now important to stress the concept of synaes.
ent phenomena such as sound and image are experienc
parts of an entity. This aspect of the audio-visual text – a pai
– is often left aside by those who create music videos, and th.        .ve
the impression to those who are analyzing them, that the link    .ween
the images and the song is purely accidental, and that the choice of different images would lead to the same result. In this regard, we need to
identify the different directions the analysis of the same text can take: a
music video can be totally dull and featureless for those who focus on the
relationship between visual and sound elements and, at the same time,
the same music video can appeal to those who analyze it from the point of
view of content, narration and aesthetics. With regard to the synaesthetic
relationships, as already indicated, those who are analyzing the music
video can get the impression that, with a choice of different images, the
same result would have been achieved. The underlying aim of the director is clearly to promote the image of the performer, a goal which is fully
understandable from a commercial point of view. By doing so, however,
the relationship between the two elements (image and music) is neglected
in favor of the image. This is why those who want to undertake an analysis
of the relationship between musical and visual elements in a music video
will face difficulties in finding suitable material. In most music videos the
two elements are used without any mutual regard, which is to say they are
used horizontally, as opposed to attempting to establish a kind of vertical
relationship between the two (with the exception of very basic relations
such as lip-synching and the synchronization of showing the image of an
instrument which is heard in that very moment). Michel Chion enlightens
this subject when he says that the clip has the only duty to disseminate
synchronization points here and there (Chion 1997: p. 74).

We can now consider the functions the two components of the audio-
visual text hold for one another.

## THE FIVE FUNCTIONS OF THE IMAGE *ɑ ( use in cluge reading )*.

First of all we can analyze the different functions of the *images* in respect
of the music: we will call them here *communicative-aesthetic functions*.

The first function of the images is to *paraphrase the verbal text of the song*.
In this case, the song text has to be taken into account: images can refer
to the content of the text they accompany, and they might draw directly
their own character from here. In this case, it may be preferable to at-

to the song's *text*, since the content of lyrics can appear as conclusive and clear than the *music* of a song where the sphere of emotions and subjectivity comes into play. On the other hand, the central visual idea of a music video can be based on the song title. For example, the music video for the song *Nightswimming* by R.E.M. (shot in 1995 by Jem Cohen) shows how the song title can function as the point of departure for the visual side of the whole clip. The same holds true concerning the music video for the song *Umbrella* by Rihanna (directed in 2007 by Chris Applebaum). There is, despite their same point of departure, a clear aesthetic difference between these two videos: while the former shows an interesting aesthetic development by presenting grainy images of bodies dipped into the water, the latter uses the song-title only as an opportunity to merely exhibit and celebrate the singer's sensuality. This last example shows us that, when paraphrasing, an author risks being didascalic, that is: preceptive – in Italy, Michelangelo Antonioni's incursion into the world of the music video with his clip for Gianna Nannini's song *Fotoromanza*, shot in 1984, is worth mentioning. In this case, the great film director, by visually repeating the song text word for word, created what is still considered an example of how to wreck a good music video.

The second function of the images with respect to the soundtrack is *facilitating the comprehension of the lyrics*, and here the most used means are subtitles and lettering. Here, for example, we can refer to *Sign 'O' the Times* (produced in 1987 by Bill Konersman for Prince), a video in which the text is almost the only visual object in the video. We also have a small masterpiece in the music video for Alex Gopher's piece *The Child* (made in 2000 by Antoine Bardou-Jacquet, Ludovic Houplain and Hervé de Crécy), where lettering is used in an innovative and smart way. As far as subtitles are concerned, *Everybody Hurts* (directed in 1992 by Jake Scott) for R.E.M. and *No Surprises* (made in 1997 by Grant Gee) for Radiohead also present good examples.

The third function of images is *creating a further reading perspective of the song*. In this case, images may develop independently from the content of the text. As a general rule, the field where this function can find the richest soil is the one of dance/electro/techno music where the verbal text – if there is any in the first place – is repeated many times and thus remains extremely simple. And – even more important – this music genre does not necessarily have the main aim to present the performing artists to the audience. In this case the director is not influenced either by the musical instruments, by the voices of musicians or by the lyrics: on the content level, images are free to follow their own path, on the narration level they can develop an autonomous story without being forced to match any elements, given by the lyrics or the appearance of the musicians. The absence or limitation of lyrics can thus open a space for the creative, narrative and experimental freedom of the visuals elements.

Obviously, this is also possible in a song with a verbal text: again, in this case a solution which can be used is subtitling. An excellent example of this is the video for the Radiohead-song *Just* (directed in 1995 by Jamie Thraves). Here, two visual levels are linked to the music which can be classified as alternative rock. One level shows the band during its perform-ance, the other shows what they apparently can see from the window of the building where they are playing: a man is lying on the ground in the middle of the street and a group of people gathers around him, as curious as the spectator to know why he is not standing up. While the music plays on, only subtitles translate what the different characters are saying. In the end, the man starts to explain his reasons, but in that crucial moment of the explanation, the subtitles suddenly stop and hence it is impossible to know what the man says. This is all the more tantalizing since all the peo-ple around him, after having listened to his words, obviously feel provoked to lie down on the ground too.

The example of the Radiohead-video shows that it is also possible to dev-elop an independent visual level for songs with a verbal text in order to cre-ate a different interpretation of the song. However, such an approach risks confusing the spectator's understanding of the intended message because the visual material might interfere with the meaning of the lyrics. We shall keep in mind that such a perceptive confusion can be seen as negative from the point of view of a merely efficiency-orientated audio-visual com-munication, but from the promotional/commercial point of view it might be seen as a positive element for the song. If the spectator does not clearly understand the meaning of the message the first time, this might actu-ally work in the music video's favor. The 'target' (this a word, not used by chance here: in this case the viewer is not just seen as a spectator, but rather as a 'target' aimed upon) will be tempted to see the video again and again, and by re-viewing it, he will listen to the song time and again which thus is well promoted.

We can now see how, depending on the perspective of the observation and theorization, the positive and negative sides of the music video – as an observed object – change.

An example of a music video where the visual part manages to create another interpretation level, albeit without the support of subtitles deliver-ing lyrics, is the clip for *Revolution 909* by Daft Punk (directed in 1997 by Roman Coppola). In this case the music belongs to the electronic genre, a genre which, as previously indicated, allows for creativity and experimen-tation concerning the levels of narration and direction technique.[2] The visual level narrates the story of a tomato. Before the song starts, we see a rave party which is suddenly interrupted by the police. A girl is stopped by a policeman, but while the officer talks to her she is attracted by something on his chest which, as the following subjective shot shows, turns out to be a sauce stain on the man's white shirt. Then, as the music starts, we see a visual reconstruction of the way the stain came into existence. The visuals thus tell the story of a tomato from the moment it is picked up in the field, to the moment when it is brought to a supermarket and sold. Next, the music video turns into something like a stereotypical TV-cooking show, illustrating the preparation of pasta with tomato sauce. When the dish is completed, the finished pasta is poured into a box which is put into a paper bag. The sequence with the preparation of the meal ends with a detail shot of this bag which then dissolves into a shot where the bag is now standing on the back seat of a police car – obviously there has been a time ellipsis. The policeman from the opening scene takes the bag and starts to eat the pasta, but when he hears a distress call from the rave location on the radio, he stains his shirt with the pasta sauce. Together with his colleague the officer hurries to the place seen at the beginning of the video clip, and ends up facing the girl who watches the stain on his shirt. This action presents us with a circular narrative structure since in this moment we are watching the same image we saw at the beginning of the video: the story starts again, after the long flashback, from the moment where it had started. The policeman follows the girl's glance which diverts his attention from her and enables her to run away.

Another function of images in respect of the music is *to direct the expressivity of the song by creating a specific, guiding atmosphere.* Images can bias the way the expressivity of a song is perceived, pushing its reception in the desired direction. In this context we can take recourse to Chion's notion of the so-called "added value" (Chion 1997: p. 12), according to which music has the power to enrich the informative value of a given image; but the same holds also true the other way round and thus images can influence the way a song is perceived.

A song can be differently interpreted depending on the listening subject. What one person perceives as 'sweet', can be 'sad' for another because the emotional perception varies from individual to individual. Music belongs, in fact, to the sphere of subjectivity. Instead, images, especially when not accompanied by music, are usually more 'objective', and it is hard to interpret them in entirely different ways because we will have a more or less unambiguous interpretation of them. The music video director will rely on the 'objective' image content in order to achieve an audiovisual entity which can be interpreted from the point of view of its content and its 'contained' emotions in accordance with his aim, which is to push the expressivity of the music into the desired direction.

Consider, for example, the music video for *Rabbit In Your Headlight* by U.N.K.L.E. (shot in 1998 by Jonathan Glazer). This video presents dark and gloomy images and creates the claustrophobic atmosphere of a tunnel where a man is walking in the middle of the road. The man gets repeatedly hit by cars, but the drivers do not stop to check the conditions of this man who continues to talk and scream as if he were schizophrenic. All these elements provoke in the viewer a feeling of pain and irritation because of what he sees and hears at the same time: the images accompany a musical development, formed by piano and drums, and completed by the voice of Thom Yorke, which, with its long, moaning-like cantilenas, sounds like the expression of suffering. When trying to describe the music level, one could use words which are the exact opposite of melodious and catchy: some could perceive it even as boring, at times even irritating.

Let us now think about the clip for *Praise You* by Fatboy Slim (directed in 1998 by Spike Jonze), where images contribute to create a joyful and funny atmosphere for the video clip text. Or think about the music video for *All is Full of Love* by Björk (shot in 1999 by Chris Cunningham), where the slow movements of the two robots contribute to create an atmosphere of peace and tranquility. In all these cases we will have an *emotional bubble*, a unique and harmonic atmosphere.

However, images do not always accompany the emotional sphere evoked by the music in a coherent way. Rather, in order to create a further reading perspective, they sometimes deliver something akin to a visual counterpoint. When listening to Coldplay, for example, one could describe some of their songs as 'romantic' and 'sweet'. After having listened to their song *The Hardest Part* one would thus expect a music video in which the visual content evokes the same type of emotions in accordance with the song. Instead, director Mary Wigmore's 2006 video surprised the viewer by using images which trigger a completely different atmosphere in comparison to the one suggested by the song. Although it is possible that the scenes featuring an odd couple – "he is 25 years old and she is 84 years old", as the presenter emphasizes at the beginning of the video – performing an acrobatic dance while wearing bathing suits may create feelings of affection in the viewer, the overall visual value of the video is rather cold and detached, ironic and in any case contrary in tone to what one would expect when listening to the song in the absence of these images. In this case the two levels develop in a counterpoint way, each proceeding in an autonomous direction.

The same can be said for the music video for *Same Mistake* by James Blunt (directed in 2007 by Jonas Åkerlund). The song, dominated by the smooth and melodic processions of guitar and voice, is matched with images of the singer going out at night and having fun. Yet the images are edited in a much faster manner than the development of the music. They appear as images which could work rather well with a rock song, for example. As well, the musical and visual levels develop parallel but independently, thus showing – especially with respect to content and emotions – only a few contact points and a few vertical matches (if we exclude the abovementioned lip-synching). We thus will have a visual field which, in relation to the musical one, can be characterized as 'dissonant'. These kinds of choices reflect the desire to surprise the viewer by creating images that develop independently from the music. This approach also gives a sense of originality, rather than banality, because it differentiates itself from the usual and accustomed pattern of editing suiting images to the music.

Finally images can *create matches with given parts of the song*. This is the most important function, the one which can create the most challenging ideas for the textual analysis.

Almost every music video is sprinkled with synchronization points, i.e. "salient moments of synchronous convergence between a sound and a visual moment: a point where the syncresis effect (...) is more marked, like a more marked chord in music".[3]

The concept of syncresis is, in the end, crucial: it is the "inevitable and spontaneous joint between a sound and a punctual visual phenomenon when these occur simultaneously, regardless of any kind of rational logic".[4] "*Regardless of any kind of rational logic*": this is the most interesting point to explore in a textual analysis, i.e. trying to find the moments where two matters of expression such as images and music, originally so different from each other, manage to get in touch with each other, combining and giving life with surprising results. These moments are the synchronization points, and they can be predictable (for example, I hear the sound of a guitar and at the same time I see the guitar), but also original and unexpected (an electronic sound and a street lamp, a mummy and a drum set). They are needed to give to the music video its own phrasing "just like marked chords or cadence – that is, vertical matches between elements – would do in a music sequence"[5] (Chion 1997: p. 55-58).

Also in the case of music videos we can deal with vertical matches, whereas with vertical we mean the connection between different matters of expression such as music and image, each carried out in a horizontal development, a connection which is very often harmonious, but which can also be dissonant.

## VISUAL LEITMOTIVES

Images can also be linked to specific phrases, to musical developments or to specific instruments: they can work as a *visual leitmotiv* (Adorno/Eisler 1975: p. 22) inside the musical vagueness. In the case of music videos, according to Chion (Chion 1997: p. 48-55), we can assume the presence of a visual leitmotiv when images manage to establish a connection with the music, giving a specific visual theme to specific musical reprises, phrases or musical developments (such as a melody) or refrains. Whereas the musical leitmotiv of a movie offers the opportunity to link key characters or certain aspects of the story with a specific theme, in music videos musical phrases can match the key character, and refrains can match certain visual motives. Due to their repetition, visual leitmotivs enable the spectator to recognize the development of specific images as matching specific musical developments, and they also create expectations. When hearing the repetition of the refrain, for example, if the viewer has already seen a leitmotiv, he or she can expect to see the same images again.

Just as a musical leitmotiv in a movie works to symbolize punctuation, in music videos this role is given to the images.

An example of these concepts can be found in *Come to Daddy* by Aphex Twin (directed in 1997 by Chris Cunningham). In this video, the visual effect of distortion simultaneously corresponds to the acoustic on the musical level. This works as a synchronization point, a vertical match between music and visual level, which are developed horizontally and build a harmonic vertical match. If throughout the music video the distorted sound would have been repeated many times and if each time it would have been linked to the same image of the blue face – itself distorted –, then we would have had a visual leitmotiv.

Such a clear visual leitmotiv can be encountered in the clip for *Come into My World* by Kylie Minogue (directed in 2002 by Michel Gondry). In this video, the circular repetition of the same long take is shown four times, and each take corresponds to the four repetitions of the song's refrain. Each time the refrain begins, the viewer sees the singer in the same place as the last time, repeating similar movements, and each time another image of Kyle Minogue is added so that in the end four of them are acting simultaneously in the same scene. Gondry has thereby combined a specific musical development with a specific visual theme (here represented by the singer and her movements).

To sum up, we can have:

- *synchronization moments* and
- reprises and repetitions of *synchronization moments* which create *visual leitmotives.*

There is a third case, albeit a very rare one, when the music video is made up in its whole by synchronization points, due to a vertical, punctual, constant and continuous link between sound and image. This leads to a situation where this continuous vertical match ultimately erases itself, giving way to – and turning into – one single horizontal development.

The majority of the existing music videos is built on joints, i.e. on vertical links which are created occasionally, momentarily while the other moments are dominated by autonomous and independent developments of music and images (thus not even creating dissonant vertical matches).

The third case of a music video made up entirely by synchronization points, as described above, could instead be defined as a *synchronic continuum.* As we will see, Michel Gondry is the only director who dedicates himself to its development.

## THE FUNCTIONS OF THE MUSIC

Having dealt with the functions of the images in respect of the music (and having omitted deliberately the description and deepening of their promotional and commercial functions), it is now much easier to talk about the functions of the *music* towards the visual part of a music video. Music here has two main duties.

The first one, thanks to its continuous nature, is to "keep the images together", whether they are fragmented or not. Music is, according to Gianni Sibilla, "that textual 'adhesive' which enables the superficial fragmentation of the text and the not verisimilitude of representation".[6] Besides, based on Jost's theory of sincerity (Jost 1987: p. 46) we are inclined to accept that rather an image can be retouched than sound or music. Therefore the musical part of a music video (with the exception of electronic music) is rather connected by the viewer to notions such as 'reality' and 'truth': the music we hear is 'true', while we cannot be sure of the truth and reality of the images we see by now everyday.

In addition, Sorlin states that the oral parts represent the truth concerning television, not because they are truthful in themselves, but because they seem to be stable and reliable, given that a 'television standard' language dominates the microphones. Images, however, are much more malleable. They can be "stretched, deformed, stained and it then becomes irritating"[7] (Sorlin 1997: p. 232).

According to Chion, the most common function of sounds is to unify the flow of the images (despite possible visual cuts) on a time level (this is what he calls the *overlapping effect*) as well as on a spatial level: through the overall and all-embracing contexts of the sounds a general framework for the images is created which achieves the effect that the visual counterpart of an acoustic element gets immersed in a kind of homogenizing fluid (Chion, 1997: p. 46). Here, music plays the role of the "unifying and encompassing element"[8], which makes it transgress the visual element's boarders in time and space. Chion here even explicitly refers to the "clip which, thanks to a musical base which is dominating – and having as duty only to place here and there some synchronization points in order to put together in a soft way images and music – enables images to move as much as they like in time and space".[9]

The second 'duty' of the music in a music video is to determine the choice and the rhythmic configuration of the visual elements. One can here think about the lip-synching mentioned previously, or about the other 'basic' synchronization, the one between the sound of a musical instrument and its image.

We can thus summarize the following:

**1. The 'Duty' of Images towards the Music**
A. Paraphrasing the verbal text of the song
B. Facilitating the comprehension of the verbal text
C. Creating an expanded reading and interpretation perspective of the song
D. Orienting the expressivity of the song by creating a specific atmosphere
E. Creating matches with given parts of the song

**2. The 'Duty' of the Images towards the Images**
A. Keeping the images together
B. Determining the choice and rhythmic configuration of the visual elements.

## MICHEL GONDRY'S CONTRIBUTION

Michel Gondry is a director who, throughout his career, has intensively considered songs as a basis for the creation of the visual part of an appropriate music video. Therefore, the final part of this article is dedicated to a deeper analysis of two of his music videos, *Around the World* and *Star Guitar*. These two music videos have been chosen for analysis because they demonstrate the concepts described above concerning audio-visual matches and configurations, synchronization points and synaesthetic relationships, key concepts for those interested in the relationship between the visual and the acoustic level. But we will see also how the clip for *Around the World* also offers a rich soil for a discussion of different music video genres.

We have thus to emphasize the fact that classifying *Around the World* (produced in 1997 for Daft Punk) confronts us already on the content side with the first troubles. This audio-visual text is not a narrative music video since it does not tell a story; but it is not a purely conceptual video either, if we rely on the definition given by Sibilla according to whom (Sibilla 1999: p. 21/26) this type of music video is characterized as "being made of free associations" which, while developing a general theme, nevertheless fosters a "fragmented language".[10]

We could now forcefully insert the music video for *Around the World* into this genre by arguing that the subject conceptualized by the director is an attempt to create a kind of visual music, i.e. an attempt to create precise matches between the visual and the musical part. However, a brief description of the content of the visual part of the music video is rather easy: the viewer watches a choreography of dancing bodies. But, firstly, the dancing bodies do not belong to the musicians and the performers of the song. Secondly, through a deeper analysis, it will be clear that things are much more complicated than it may at first seem.

There are elements in this music video which make it difficult to classify as purely conceptual, each having to do with the way in which the main action of the clip is developed. Firstly, images are not put together according to a free association, and secondly the structure is coherent rather than fragmented. *Around the World* is characterized by a strict linear structure, both in the relationship between its images and in the connection between images and music. The images in this music video have strong connections with each other and are combined in order to favor a consequential development of the main topic. Thus, *Around the World* can be classified as a conceptual music video in the sense that it deals with its general theme, the visualization of the music. Simultaneously, the music is interpreted through a formal organization of the visual components which is different to the one theorized by Sibilla; i.e. it is an organization which does not proceed through free associations.

We can see, therefore, how this video clip evades the already mentioned genre definitions. But it also escapes the definition of the performance music video: although *Around the World* shows a particular performance, the viewer does not follow the performance of the musicians or group members, but rather – metaphorically speaking – the performance of the musical instruments.

Or to put it differently: in the music video, Michel Gondry has chosen to create a precise correspondence between each of the instruments of the song on the one hand and the visual level of the music video on the other hand. He has linked each instrument with a distinct element of the choreography in a way that enables the viewer to clearly distinguish each element from the others. This is why the director has linked each element to a certain, easily recognizable figure or character. There are five main instruments which create the soundtrack, each of which corresponds to a visual element in the music video:

| bass guitar | very tall characters with a very small head |
|---|---|
| drums | mummies |
| guitars | skeletons |
| synthesizer (the sound reminds us of 80's disco music) | female swimmers dressed up with rhinestone and glitter |
| vocoder (featuring a metallic sound) | robots |

Therefore, if each instrument is visually 'translated' into a character, then it is as if the viewer would 'see' the musical elements performing, even though in an indirect way. Actually, it could be a bit of a hazard to state that the video is a visual performance of the musical instruments, and this brings us to the following: if *Around the World* escapes the existing categories, can it be considered as representing a new genre of the music video?

I would suggest the phrase *choreographic music video* as a label for this supposed new genre which falls into a content–based classification. Here, bodies that are developing a choreographic performance compose the content. These bodies, however, do not belong to the members of the band (for instance, to those of a boyband or a girlgroup) or to the singer; this is the main difference in contrast to a performance music video. By choreography I mean the actions expressed not only through dancing, but also through gestures or movements of the body, for example the representations of bodies swimming, running or working out. Some examples here are the music videos for *Let Forever Be* by The Chemical Brothers (made in 1999 by Michel Gondry), for *Praise You* by Fatboy Slim (directed in 1999 by Spike Jonze), for *Weapon of Choice* by The Chemical Brothers (shot in 2001 by Spike Jonze), for *Black Rocking Beats* by The Chemical Brothers (produced in 1999 by Spike Jonze), for *Nuvole Rapide* by Subsonica (made in 2002 by Luca Merli) or for the previously mentioned *Nightswimming* and for *The Hardest Part* (directed in 2006 by Mary Wigmore). All these videos feature the presence of the human body as the centerpiece of the visual framework. Moreover, in the newly proposed genre of the *choreographic music video* we can assist choreographic performances exhibitions not only by *somebody*, but also by *something* different from the members of the band who have created the song. Examples of this include the clips for *Number One* by Playgroup (produced by the French company Partizan Midi Minuit) where a stereo sound-system is shown dancing to the music in a disco-setting, or for *Fell in Love with a Girl* by The White Stripes (directed in 2002 by Michel Gondry) where the musicians are substituted by their counterfeits, pieced up together from Lego-modules.

In the end, one last clarification: the choreography must not necessarily be the only visual component of the music video, but can be linked to other narrative, conceptual or performance parts.

After having classified the music video, in order to proceed with the analysis it must be pointed out that Michel Gondry has played with different codes which are important for the analysis (Casetti/Di Chio 1989: p. 72-74):

- Iconographic codes:[11] these codes, which regulate the construction of complex images, are strongly conventionalized and have a fixed meaning. Through them, the viewer usually understands from a dress code or a behavior or the physiognomy that the figures he sees have to be identified as for example 'a policeman' or a 'positive hero'. In Gondry's video, the spectator sees women wearing a swimsuit, whom he can thus identify as 'swimmers'; instead, figures which are entirely covered with bandages, have to be recognized as 'mummies'. Only after seeing the video again and again, and with a heightened attention, the viewer will begin to understand that the swimmers actually 'represent' the synthesizer, and that the mummy 'stands for' the drum set.

Besides this, in order to create a tight audio-visual link, the director has made the most of:

- the iconic composition codes[12], which organize the relationships between the different elements in an image. By using the dislocation of images inside the scenography, Michel Gondry has managed to draw the attention of the viewer to one single group of elements of the visual composition at a time. The scenography is based on a symmetric structure which is formed by the composition of different elements: in the full shots, while the camera is filming the entire set frontally, the viewer sees the characters/instruments fully occupying the screen; when instead filming distinct parts of the scene, the camera grants the viewer only glances on individual characters;
- figurative codes[13] which determine how different elements are grouped and displayed on the surface of the image, creating distinctively composed arrangements, i.e. the way in which characters are grouped (for instance, the moment when the swimmers dance back and forward between the skeletons, but also the 'pursuit' between the tall men and the swimmers); the objective here is also to guide the look of the viewer from one element to the other and thereby draw his attention to the musical elements represented by them;
- the codes of image plasticity[14], which enable the viewer to separate components from each other by drawing the attention of the viewer towards them while at the same time making him understand their significance in the context of the whole video; via a strategic use of these codes, Gondry succeeds in having one element of the choreography stand out against every other element. Thanks to the use of close-ups that concentrate on distinct groups and their movements (as opposed to groups that do not move), Gondry manages to guide the viewer's gaze towards elements which are important in that specific moment. By positioning one of these groups closer to the viewer while simultaneously placing others further in the background, he also directs the audience's attention to elements of heightened importance in the music itself.

The director thus wants to direct the attention of the viewer to certain visual elements for the reason which is central to the aim of his music video: in order to achieve a match of everything that can be seen with everything that can be heard. Hence, if in the development of the song there are moments where it is not possible to hear all five instruments at the same time, also on the visual level not all the five characters groups can be seen at the same time. In other words, if the viewer hears only one instrument in the soundtrack, he will see only the group of the characters that represent this instrument; if he hears three instruments he will also see three characters etc. Even when confronted with a higher number of characters, the viewer's attention will be (thanks to the skilled use of the abovementioned codes) guided and focused on the groups which correspond to the instruments which can be heard. As already said, this is achieved through the different handling of the elements within the context of the scenography (by positioning them for example in the background or in the foreground), their immobility or movement, the way they are filmed etc.

Let us, for example, have a closer look at the 'robot' characters, which, even though the viewer may not initially notice them, can be seen from the beginning of the video. Unlike the tall men and the swimmers who are moving, the robots are motionless and stand in the background margins of the shot while the other two groups are centrally positioned. They are thus in a 'faraway' position, whereas the tall men and the swimmers in the foreground are much closer to the viewer; finally, the robots are also in the shade while the other two groups are illuminated. When the presence of the robots is necessary, i.e. especially when the refrain (whose metallic voice they represent) is heard for the first time, Gondry guides the attention of the viewer onto them: they get illuminated, begin to walk and there is also close up of them in a central position.

Michel Gondry has thus not only succeeded in creating audio-visual correspondences of the main elements of the soundtrack, but he has also created some synchronization points between the visual and the musical part for the whole duration of the song. The main features of *Around the World* are the cross-references and 'echoes' between the audio and the visual level. The abovementioned synchronization points, which are happening instantaneously and suddenly in the majority of the music videos, are instead constant, systematic and present throughout the whole duration of the video.

If the author of an audio-visual text is able to create correspondences between such different elements – in this case: a musical instrument and a character – this is due to the syncresis phenomenon. Syncresis, as Chion points out, can also work on 'vacuum moments', i.e. with instantaneous images and sounds which have nothing to do with each other, but which nonetheless are perceived as monstrous agglomerations that we find irresistible and inevitable. The example from Chion is "the syllable fa and the image of a dog; a knock and the image of a triangle".[15] In the same way in our video we have the syncresis between a girl wearing a swim–suit and the simultaneous sound of a synthesizer, between a mummy and a drum set, and so on. Thanks to syncresis, according to Chion, the wittiest and most surprising configurations can arise: *Around the World* is a perfect example of this.

Once the audio-visual correspondences have been established, they can be used throughout the whole duration of the video. The visual leitmotiv, in this case, is established by matching each instrument with a character, in the same way as each key character of a film text is provided with a musical theme which characterizes it.

When proposing a summarizing scheme starting from the analysis of this video, we can list different categories of remarks:

1. *Around the World* is a choreographic music video.
2. *Around the World* is an attempt at music visualization which had already been tried by members of the musicalist wave and vanguard in the 20's (such as Abel Gance, Fernand Léger, Hans Richter, Walter Ruttmann to mention a few).
3. *Around the World* is based on continuous and constant synchronization points (*synchronic continuum*).
4. The main function of the images concerning the music is to create connections with the song. The function of the music concerning the images is to determine the choice and rhythmic configuration of the visual elements; furthermore, the music keeps the images together.
5. In *Around the World* we also have an example of what Michel Chion has dubbed as *mickeymousing*, a concept, used by him in the form of the *"muscial mickeymousing"* in his analysis of the use of sound in cinema (Chion 1992: p. 105), according to which musical phenomena, shown actions and movements can be perfectly synchronized. In our case, however, since the song was in existence prior to the production of the images, we can speak of a reversed *visual* mickeymousing because the characters, shown on the visual level, are accompanying the musical part with synchronous and matching movements.

The viewer of the music video, when following the audio-visual text for the first time, might see only some weird characters, dancing to the rhythm of the music, but after a more accurate view he certainly will notice audio-visual correspondences arising. However, these can be still missed by some members of the audience, especially if they watch the video in an inattentive way. But the interesting side of Michel Gondry's work generally is – this a remark which ideally should be applicable to all music videos – that it even can stand a superficial vision without being boring, and at the same time, it offers to the attentive viewer a densely and richly structured composition which can be analyzed in depth.

The second music video we are going to analyze is *Star Guitar* (2002), also directed by Michel Gondry, this time in order to accompany a song by The Chemical Brothers.[16] As with Daft Punk, the Chemical Brothers produce electronic music. And like *Around the World*, *Star Guitar* features very few lyrics, save for a very short, almost imperceptible sentence. The analytical proposal for this music video is, due to its similar underlying principle, the same as *Around the World*: the clip also attempts to create precise and constant audio-visual connections. In *Star Guitar*, though, this is realized in a different way for two reasons: firstly, the content of the visual part is consisting of one single long take; there are neither editing cuts nor single shots to analyze. Secondly, the audio-visual matches are created between the music and landscape elements, not between specific sounds and the performers of a choreography. However, the basic concept of the two music videos is the same: Gondry wants to create a vertical synchronic and constant relationship between the music and the images. Gondry achieves this in *Star Guitar* by combining the music with an unexpected and surprising visual element, as if he wants to demonstrate the power of the syncresis, its power to link, beyond any rational logic, visual contents to the music.

From a visual point of view, the music video is entirely based on the subjective experience of a train trip. Hence, the camera takes the perspective of a traveler who looks out of a train window in the opposite direction of the journey. Each sound matches, on the visual level, with an element of the digitally formed landscape: silos, lampposts, small houses, fences, bridges, trucks, the passing of another train. If we want to put *Star Guitar* into the classification system proposed by Sibilla, we can define it as a conceptual music video devoted to the theme of travel. As in *Around the World*, however, it is necessary to point out that the way the visual part is conceived transgresses the formal characteristics of the conceptual video. The images are neither fragmented nor associated in a random way, and it is not hard for the viewer to understand the message which the director wants to communicate. The visual content and the theme of this video are, from the outset, clear, immediately understandable and simple: even too simple, as it first seems. Therefore we can begin to wonder if Gondry's message is mainly this one we immediately understand (which means: the depiction of a simple train ride). If we would try to classify *Star Guitar* just as a conceptual audio-visual text which wants to communicate the concept of traveling, we risk being too restrictive. Gondry's choice of such an easy visual subject might indicate that the he wanted to deal more with the technique used to create images and that he wanted to give this technique more importance.

In order to better describe this music video it is necessary to interpret the word 'conceptual' in another way and to try to understand not only the underlying concept of the content but, above all, also the way in which this content is organized. It will then become clear that the main idea of this music video has to be sought not only on the level of its images, but rather in the way these images are part of a language. In fact, the content of the clip seems to be language itself. Seen in this perspective, the director deals with the question of how images can be created and linked to music. By creating a virtuosic visual language, Gondry draws the viewer's attention to his mastery of making music videos. This is why he starts from such a minimal idea as the journey, in order to create a technically complicated text which emphasizes the used code. In this video, as in *Around the World*, the content of these clips also deals with the possibilities of creating and linking images to a song in order to interpret it visually.

This is not the first time Gondry has pursued an idea like this. Rather, this approach is characteristic of his style. Many of Gondry's music videos emphasize technical ability and this acquires more and more importance since in most of Gondry's videos digital technique is shunned. An example is the video for *Lucas with the Lid Off* by Lucas, made by Gondry in 1994 and realized in one, single, long traveling shot in analogue technology. Another example is the small virtuoso masterpiece for *Sugar Water* (1996) by the Japanese duo Cibo Matto.[7] The visual part is formed by two long takes which, thanks to a vertical division of the screen (*split screen*), are simultaneously presented. The images of the sequence on the left part are flowing in chronological order, while those one in the right side are shown in reverse: the perfect accord of the two sequences, showing the mirroring actions of the two Cibo Matto singers, is obtained by a meticulous organization and rehearsal of the two shootings, like in *Lucas with The Lid Off*. In this case, however, to further complicate things, the lives of the two characters played by the two singers are destined to cross in the middle of the video due to a car crash. From this moment on the two sequences switch places: while the one on the left side is shown in reverse, the one on the right now develops normally. Throughout the video Gondry creates contacts and complementarities between the two long sequences (in one scene, for example, a cat enters a mailbox on the left side and leaves immediately on the right side, apparently passing from one sequence to the other). Again, such things will be noticed by the viewer only after having watched the video several times over with care. Interestingly, again, Gondry refrained from making things easier by using digital technology, deciding instead to shoot the two sequences of the video in a 'traditional', analogue way.

The same can be said of the clip for *Protection* by Massive Attack, directed in 1995 in which the visual part presents a single, long sequence and again, as with the shooting of *Lucas with the Lid Off*, each actor and member of the film crew had a precise duty to fulfill and to know what the others had to do during the shooting. The resulting images are deceiving the viewer for what he perceives as a long, vertical shot is actually – thanks to optical illusions and mirror tricks – a long horizontal take.

The way images are connected to the song in *Star Guitar* is the same as in *Around the World*: each sound matches a visual element. At the beginning of the music video the viewer sees the railway track, an electricity pylon and two poles which repeatedly appear at fixed intervals; the soundtrack features a beat which is similar to the one of a drum set (similar since it is not actually coming from a drum set, but is created through sampling), followed by two other beats – in the whole music video the rhythm is given by low-pitched beats, which can be described as drum beats. The above mentioned repetition of the two landscape elements (the electricity pylon and the two poles) thus appear as visual counterparts of these rhythmic elements. The sequence 'one beat–two beats' is repeated four times. Simultaneously, on the visual level, there is the repetition of the sequence 'pylon – poles' for four times. After that, when the musical elements become more complex and features new sounds, the scenography likewise gets more complex because new elements are added in the depth of the landscape. Thus, the same way the beat goes on while new sounds are heard, the railway tracks, the pylon and the poles are repeated while new buildings, such as houses, silos and other poles are added.

Moreover, each time a short, quick sound (such as a drum beat) is heard, the viewer will see a visual counterpart for this, for instance, a passing lorry or a bridge, appearing only for a very short time in the scenery which unfolds in front of the train window. When the soundtrack instead features longer, enduring sounds, the landscape will then also show continuous elements: the length of each visual element thus corresponds to the length of the sound it is connected with.

In the second half of the music video there is a sequence which is worth analyzing – it is a moment in which another train crosses the virtual carriage in which the viewer seems to be sitting at high speed. A sound is then simultaneously heard which, if taken as a mere sound alone, is hard to describe since it is difficult to understand its nature and source. However, the same sound, when connected with the transit of the train, suddenly becomes understandable, because referential – the viewer now can easily refer it to the sound to be heard when he finds himself in the situation presented in the music video: sitting on a train which crosses another train.

This is a typical example for what Chion describes when he writes that in the audio-visual combination one level of perception influences the other (Chion 1997: p. 7): it makes a difference for the perception of a phenomenon if you only hear or if you also see it. It is the concept of the 'added value' according to which in music video an image enriches a given sound with expressive or informative value.

Therefore, in the two pieces I have presented in this essay, Gondry has managed to create very precise vertical audio-visual matches, reaching in his own way – thanks to the *synchronic continuum* – a goal that many artists before him had tried to reach. By making the most of the potential of phenomena such as 'added value', 'synchronism' and 'syncresis', he has managed to create visual matches for music, thus giving referents to what – by definition – is non-referential.

## REFERENCES

**1 |** Adorno/Eisler 1975 for example was already written between 1940 and 1944 and got then first published in English in 1947.

**2 |** See here also the analysis provided by Keazor/Wübbena 2010a.

**3 |** Chion 1997: p. 55–58: "(...) momenti salienti di incontro sincrono tra un momento sonoro e un momento visivo: un punto in cui l'effetto di sincresi (...) risulta più accentuato, come in una musica un accordo più marcato degli altri".

**4** | Ibd.: "(...) la saldatura inevitabile e spontanea che si realizza tra un fenomeno sonoro e un fenomeno visivo puntuale quando questi accadono contemporanea-mente, indipendentemente da ogni logica di tipo razionale".

**5** | Ibd.: "(...) come potrebbero darlo, in una sequenza musicale, gli accordi mar-cati o le cadenze – in breve gli incontri verticali tra gli elementi".

**6** | See Sibilla 1999: p. 29: "La musica è quel 'collante' che permette la frammen-tazione di superficie del testo e la non verosimiglianza della rappresentazione."

**7** | Sorlin 1997: p. 232: "(...) tirata, deformata, macchiata e allora diventa irritante".

**8** | Chion 1997: p. 46: "(...) inglobamento unificante (...)".

**9** | Chion 1997: p. 74: "Il clip che, a beneficio di una base musicale che regna sull'insieme - e avendo come obbligo soltanto quello di seminare qua e là dei punti di sincronizzazione miranti a sposare l'immagine e la musica in maniera morbida -, permette all'immagine di muoversi a volontà nel tempo e nello spazio."

**10** | Sibilla 1999: p. 21: "(...) con il concettuale si sviluppa un tema, un' immag-ine attraverso una struttura associativa più che causale (...)". Ibd., p. 26: "Il lin-guaggio frammentato (...) si basa su una struttura 'concettuale', fatta di libere associazioni (...)".

**11** | Casetti/Di Chio 1989: p. 73: "codici iconografici".

**12** | Ibid., p. 71: "codici della composizione iconica".

**13** | Ibid., p. 72: "codici della figurazione".

**14** | Casetti/Di Chio 1989: p. 72: "(...) codici della plasticità dell'immagine (...)".

**15** | Chion 1997: p. 59: "(...) la sillaba fa e l'immagine di un cane; un colpo e l'immagine di un triangolo (...)".

**16** | See for this also the analysis by Keazor/Wübbena 2010b.

**17** | See for this also the analysis furnished by Keazor/Wübbena 2007: p. 291f.

## BIBLIOGRAPHY

Adorno, Theodor W./Eisler, Hanns (1975): *La musica per film*, Roma: New-ton Compton editori. (original title *Komposition fur den Film*, 1969 Munchen: Rogner & Barnhard).

Casetti, Francesco (1986): *Dentro lo sguardo – il film e il suo spettatore*, Mi-lano: Bompiani.

Casetti, Francesco/Di Chio, Federico (1989): *Analisi del film*, Milano: Bom-piani.

Chion, Michel (1992): *Le son au cinéma*, Paris: Cahiers Du Cinéma/Edi-tions de l'Etoile.

Chion, Michel (1997): *L'audiovisione. Suono e immagine nel cinema*, Tori-no: Lindau. (original title *L'audio–vision. Son et image au cinéma*, 1990 Nathan: Paris).

Gabrielli, Giulia (2003): "Musica e Immagine" (II- III-IV –V). In Fucine Mute (www.fucine.com).

Jost, François (1987): "Approche narratologique des combinaisons audiovisuelles". In: *Les musiques des films, vibrations –Musiques, Médias, Société*, Paris: ed. Privat, p.46.

Keazor, Henry/Wübbena, Thorsten (2007[2]): *Video thrills The Radio Star. Musikvideos: Geschichte, Themen, Analysen*, Bielefeld: transcript.

Keazor, Henry/Wübbena, Thorsten (2010)a: "Spike Jonze: Daft Punk, Revolution 909". In: *See this Sound. An Interdisciplinary Survey of Audovisual Culture*, Cologne: Verlag Buchhandlung Walther König, edited by Dieter Daniels, Sandra Naumann and Jan Thoben, p. 230 (also online under: http://beta.see-this-sound.at/werke/576).

Keazor, Henry/Wübbena, Thorsten (2010)b: "Michel Gondry: The Chemical Brothers, Star Guitar". In: Dieter Daniels/Sandra Naumann/Jan Thoben (eds.) (2010): *See this Sound. Audiovisuology Compendium. An Interdisciplinary Survey of Audiovisual Culture*, Cologne: Buchhandlung Walther König, p. 233 (also online under: http://beta.see-this-sound. at/werke/586).

Metz, Christian (1980): *Cinema e psicanalisi*, Venezia: Marsilio Editori. (original title *Le signifiant imaginaire*, 1977 Paris: UGE).

Sibilla, Gianni (1999): *Musica da vedere. Il videoclip nella televisione italiana*, Roma: Rai, VQPT.

Sorlin, Pierre (1997): *Estetiche dell'audiovisivo*, Scandicci (Fi): La Nuova Italia. (original title: *Esthetique de l'audiovisuelle*, 1995 Nathan: Paris).

# "Sense and Sensibility"

## Two Versions of Rammstein's *Du riechst so gut*

Matthias Weiss

At the request of the editors, this essay analyzes two versions of the music video for *Du riechst so gut* ("You Smell So Good") by the German rock band Rammstein from the perspective of Art History.[1] These two clips are of interest for a number of reasons. First of all, even though they visualize the same song, they differ very much from one another. Secondly, both draw more or less openly on established iconographies, the decoding of which is commonly regarded as the quintessential task of art historical studies. Thirdly, despite their dissimilarity, the two clips deal with the same problem, namely the visualization of a non-visual sensory perception – the sense of smell. Last but not least, their dissimilarities raise the question as to the influence of the song's visualization on the listening experience and on the connected establishment of meaning, which in the case of a video clip, in contrast to a mere listening experience, ensues from the interaction of the auditory and the visual.

### APOTHEOSIS OF THE LIBIDINOUS: THE SONG *DU RIECHST SO GUT*

Released on August 24th 1995, *Du riechst so gut* was the first single of the band Rammstein, which had formed a year earlier. The song, which runs 4:50 minutes[2], etsbalished the band's reputation as *Agent Provocateur*, a status they still maintain.[3] In *Du riechst so gut*, impulsive beats and strong guitar riffs dominate, accompanied by the solemn development of a synthesizer and violin.[4] The lyrics (see appendix), menacingly recited by lead singer Till Lindemann, are about violence, or, more specifically, rape which, however, is not actually named as such but copiously paraphrased: The lyrical 'I', connoted by the singer's deep voice as male, chases his – presumably female – victim, closes in on her, touches her with his hands...

Whether the rape is actually committed or just imagined remains unclear. Its interpretation as a mere fantasy is supported by the fact that the chronology of the criminal act is consistently ruptured by the alteration of the verses and the chorus: while the man seems to reach the woman in the second verse, he appears again to be chasing her by the end of the last chorus. An additional ambiguity may be discussed with regard to the male lyrical 'I', who describes himself as being driven by and at the mercy of his own lower instincts. Within the lyrics, the boundary between victim and offender thus becomes porous, and due to this permeability the double sense of the verb 'to smell' ("riechen") is graspable: On a first glance, the lyrics seem to confirm the notion that the male protagonist actively and deliberately seeks the woman's scent as a kind of track, while his female counterpart passively and involuntarily exudes her scent and thus leaves her trace behind. However, a reverse interpretation is also possible, namely that the woman deploys her scent deliberately as a bait for her defenseless admirer, who then has no choice but to follow her – this, however, a precarious reading of the song which is in no small part responsible for the uneasy feeling that this song might induce to some listeners.

It also seems to be noteworthy that the lyrics deal not just with one, but with four of the five human senses and that the relationship between these four senses is considered as well. As the title suggests, 'to smell' ("riechen") is the verb that dominates the verses as well as the chorus. In most cases, this verb is uttered directly, but in some instants it is exchanged for the word 'to scent' ("wittern") or is paraphrased with 'fresh trail' ("frische Spur") or 'dripping sweat' ("tropfender Schweiß").[5] Another, less frequently mentioned sense is the sense of touch. It is addressed with verbs such as 'to touch' ("fassen", "anfassen") and 'to feel' ("spüren") but also with formulations such as 'warm blood' ("warmes Blut") and 'hunger' ("Hunger"). The same is true for the auditory sense, which is circumscribed with the 'scream' ("Schrei") that both the male and the female protagonist blurt out. It is also no coincidence, that the visual sense is brought up only in its negation, quite literally in the declaration 'I don't see you' ("Ich seh dich nicht") and the question 'Don't you see...?' ("Siehst du nicht...?"), but also in the announcement to wait until it gets 'dark' ("dunkel"). The same counts for the state of being 'blind' ("blind") and the 'sunlight' ("Sonnenlicht") that confuses the mind instead of purging it.

With regard to the storyline, this last-mentioned verse, by turning the common metaphor of light as a means of cognition into its opposite, might be understood as a first indicator, that Rammstein's *Du riechst so gut* is not primarily about intellectual self-reflection, but instead deals with bodily and libidinous sensations in the first place. Its topic is the experience of being completely overwhelmed by a sensation, which might be perceived as lust or agony, and which finds its acoustic equivalent in the morbid industrial drone of the music. This focus on sensation is affirmed by the fact that the lyrics refer back to the traditional hierarchy of the senses. These, however, are reversed: in philosophy, sensuousness and sensual experience are evaluated in terms of their capabilities to advance cognition. Since smell has no instructive power, Imanuel Kant, for example, ranks the sense of smell at the very bottom of their hierarchy.[6] He endorses his view by referring to a number of other reasons. According to him, odor is ephemeral and, moreover, it is more often a source of disgust than one of pleasure. Since it is almost impossible to elude it, odor deprives the human being of his or her personal freedom. Finally, in order to be noticed, odor needs to enter and penetrate the body – a characteristic that endows the sense of smell with a sexual component, and because of this to Kant it is not only highly suspicious, but in his view also completely disqualifies it as a means of cognition.

## EFFEMINATING THE VIEWER AND THE BAND: THE MUSIC VIDEO *DU RIECHST SO GUT* '95

Conforming to the usual business procedures, the music video *Du riechst so gut* '95 (director: Emanuel Fialik)[7] was presumably first aired two weeks before the release of the single. The clip runs for four minutes, which means that the song in the video is fifty seconds shorter than the single-version.[8] The clip is a classic performance video – if not with regard to the instrumental, then with respect to the vocal rendition of Till Lindemann and the other band members, who together with the lead singer perform the chorus lines, without, however, being shown with their instruments. The video begins with a completely white frame, which only a split second later can be identified as the studio background. Already in the first sequence, we meet the entire cast of the clip: a dog (a Doberman pinscher; fig. 1a), several species of flowers (yellow gerbera and chrysanthenum; fig. 1b), the lead singer and the other band members (Richard Kruspe, Paul Landers, Oliver Riedel, Christoph Schneider, and Flake Lorenz; fig. 1c), who most of the time perform with bare chests, covered with oil or sweat.[9]

Figs. 1a–c: Introduction of the cast: the dog, one of the yellow flowers, Rammstein. Stills from the music video by Emanuel Fialik: Rammstein, Du riechst so gut '95, 1995

The focus of the clip lies on the vocal performance of Lindemann. The remaining shots (camera operator: Frank Griebe), mainly close-ups, are charged with suspense achieved by basic means: slow tracking-shots, cross-fading, jump cuts, the sudden reversal into the negative pattern, the interruption of the reduced chromaticity – black, white, flesh tones – by iridescent light reflections and the alternating colors of the blossoms (achieved through special effects), changing from their original yellow color to a luminous red, to pink and finally to a morbid blue.

The clip connects the visual level with the acoustics in different ways. To start with, by formal means: the fast, sometimes breathtaking editing-frequency (film editing: Mathilde Bonnefoy) creates a flickering, which corresponds to the hammering staccato of the music, but overwhelms the eye even more so than the music challenges the ear. In addition, acoustic accents are also visually marked. The drum rolls seem to make the im-age shiver or tremble, for example, while the third, especially dynamic intermediary section is combined with calm, almost motionless images. Furthermore, interconnections can be seen on the level of visual motifs, first of all with regard to the performance and its gestural enhancement. For example, Lindemann swivels his arm sideways while intonating the line 'I follow you' ("Ich geh dir hinterher") and hits his hand and knee with violent fist-strokes. Moreover, one can mention the metal glasses, worn by Lindemann, with their observation slits, limiting the vision of their bearer and thereby making him go 'blind' ("blind").[10] And one has, of course, to mention the dog, an animal which, equipped with a particularly subtle scenting ability, smells in the active sense of the word, as well as one has to mention the flower which, with its fragrance, smells in the passive sense of the word. This context, in combinaton with the editing of the video on the one hand and the grammatical gender of the animal and the plant on the other, initially affirm the interpretation of the dog (in German: "Hund", m) as male and the flower (in German: "Blume", f) as female.

It should also be noted that the chosen motifs comply with the icono-graphy of the sense of smell as established during the second half of the 16th century. First of all, consider Cesare Ripa's *Iconologia* – probably the most influential compendium for the composition of pictorial allegories. According to Ripa, pictorial allegories depict abstract concepts by personi-fying them with the help of various figures; the sex of these personifica-tions is aligned with the gender of the Latin term and is then more closely defined by clothing, attributes, etc. In the 1603 edition of the *Iconologia*[11], the entry to "Odorato" describes odor as a young man, wearing a green garment, decorated with various flowers, and carrying a bouquet of flow-ers in his right hand and a vial in his left hand which stand for the natural and the artificial scents. A hound, which is known for an extremely sen-sitive sense of smell, rests by his feet.[12] As confirmed by the manual of Ripa's allegories, revised and newly published 150 years later in Augsburg by Johann Georg Hertel (fig. 2), some of these motifs have proved them-selves quite persistent – namley the dog and the flower which we also find in *Du riechst so gut '95*.[13]

*Fig. 2: Johann Georg Hertel/Gottfried Eichler jun./*
*Jakob Wangner:* Odoratus. Der Geruch *("The*
*Smell"). Engraving, 195 x 125 mm, circa 1760. Munich,*
*Zentralinstitut für Kunstgeschichte*

Whether these concordances are purposeful recourses to an antiquated repertoire or just a coincidence (the motifs of flower and dog are quite obvious choices), is difficult to reconstruct. But in any case, they seem to be important mainly for one reason: in Ripa's case, both the flower and the dog are attached to the male figure merely as attributes, thus, in the music video, the male protagonist likewise seems to represent a visual equivalent of the sense of smell along with the animal and the plants, albeit in a less subtle and less cultivated manner than in Hertel's version.

When looking at the iconography of the sense of smell from a wider perspective, these considerations become even more plausible. Due to an engraving by Frans Floris and Cornelis Cort (1561) which was circulated roughly at the same time as Ripa's guidelines, the sexual affinity of the allegory of smell seems to have been considered as much less obligatory than that of the attributes. The engraving of the two artists shows a seated woman, wearing a wreath of blossoms while arranging flowers in a basket or a vase. At her feet a dog rests as well, sniffing at the flowers. Later versions of this allegory emphasize the sexual aspect of sensual experiences.

*Fig. 3: Hendrik Goltzius/Jan Pietersz Saenredam:* The Five Senses. The Smell. *Engraving, 170 x 125 mm, 1595. Vienna, Graphische Sammlung Albertina*

*Quamvis floriferus sit gratus naribus hortus,*
*Sæpe tamen dulci fel sub odore latet.*

This becomes evident for example in the image of a couple by Hendrik Goltzius and Jan Pieters Saenredam (1595; fig. 3). As is the case in the video, in their engraving the male and the dog respectively the female and the flower are equated. What makes this composition particularly appealing is the fact that even though it focuses specifically on one of the five senses, it does not neglect their interplay during an erotic experience: the man not only pets the dog und thus feels its fur, but he also touches the woman's dress and her warm shoulder beneath the smooth fabric. Her gaze longingly searches for his, while his eyes rest on the delicate flower that is being presented to him or on the lips of his companion, pursed for a kiss.

Additionally, a homoerotic interpretation of the topic is possible. Following Ripa, Pier Francesco Mola's *Giacinto (Olfatto)* (without date; fig. 4) depicts the sense of smell in the form of a male figure, for example.

*Fig. 4: Pier Francesco Mola:* Giacinto (Olfatto)
*("Hyacinthus [The Smell]"). Oil on canvas, 176 x 105
cm, without date. Ariccia, Palazzo Chigi*

Given the title, the represented youth can be identified as Hyacinthus, who
according to Ovid's *Metamorphoses* (X 162–219) was one of Apollo's lovers.[14]
Mola also tries to interconnect different sensory perceptions. Similar to
some of the Rammstein band members (fig. 5a–c), Mola's recumbent nude
holds a twig with white blossoms to his nose. His bare skin is touched by
heavy drapery and light clouds. In accordance with the traditional motif of
seduction, he gazes over his shoulder towards the spectator.[15] Mola's failure
while trying to convey the sensation of a multi-sensual, synaesthetic experience, however, makes it clear that the aspired interconnection of the senses
in his case remains merely depicted and thus is only visually represented –
meaning that the painting addresses above all if not solely the visual sense
and is not able to achieve an interplay with all the others senses.[16]

*Figs. 5a–c: Like Mola's Hyacinthus, two band members (Richard
Kruspe, Oliver Riedel) are also sniffing at flowers. Stills from the music
video by Emanuel Fialik: Rammstein,* Du riechst so gut '95, *1995*

How does all this play itself out in the Rammstein video? As an audio-visual
medium, the clip initially addresses itself to the eye and the ear, but in addition it also allows for an experience that includes other senses, too: if the
music is loud enough, the beat may be felt on the skin and in the bowels.
The fierce and menacing sound and the morbid lyrics as well as the aggressive performance by Lindemann might give the listener a chill. There is
only one of the senses menitioned in the video that is not directly activated
and that is – the sense of smell. In order to depict this sense, Rammstein

and director Fialik make recourse to established iconographies.[7] However, by inverting the hierarchy of the senses, as formulated by philosophy, they reverse the established images into an apotheosis of the libidinous.

Finally, in what way do these findings help to clearify the identification of the lyrical 'you', which, even though it is addressed directly, is never actually named? And what influence does this have on the (self-)positioning of the audience? As long as heterosexual normativity is left untouched, the recital of the lyrics in combination with the images may still suggest that the indeterminate lyrical 'you' is female. On the visual level it would then be represented solely through the flowers (which does make sense, since the analogy between a woman and a flower is, as seen, a topical one), or it remains a blank space[18], which might – or should – be claimed by the viewer. This interpretation is supported by the central orientation of all band members toward the camera and especially by those shots in which the lead singer Lindemann reaches out or points at his audience (fig. 6a).[19] It remains to be discussed, however, whether the viewer is addressed independently from his or her sex, or whether and inhowfar the approach of the audience in *Du riechst so gut '95* might not be equated with an effiminating of each and every viewer (regardless of his sex) and thus with an attack on their sexual identity.

*Figs. 6a–c: The interplay between thy lyrics and the film image does not constitute a consistent lyrical 'you': One time it can be identified with the viewer, another time with the band members (here: Oliver Riedel, Christoph Schneider), then with lead singer Till Lindemann himself. Stills from the music video by Emanuel Fialik: Rammstein,* Du riechst so gut '95, 1995

The latter interpretation is supported by the fact, that not only the audience, but all the other men in the video might be addressed as the lyrical 'you' as well. The erotic charging of their bodies, achieved by their nakedness, their sweaty appearance, the scrutinizing camera, but most of all a number of cuts and their correlation with Lindemann's performance, might confirm this. Particularly at the beginning of the first chorus and from then on consistently, the changing images may be understood as a parallelization of band members with flowers. The same effect is achieved by shot-reverse shots between lead singer and choir (fig. 6b). In this way, the person who is *not* singing is identified as the lyrical 'you'. Moreover, the band members look almost androgynous in comparison with the brute hypermasculinity embodied by Lindemann.[20] Till Lindemann constructs a male lyrical 'you' in the conventional sense only, when, during his delivery of the title-verse, he lifts his left arm and takes in the smell of his own armpit (fig. 6c). This auto-erotic gesture implies two things: First of all, the lead singer unites the active and the passive concept of smelling in a single individual, and therefore assumes the roles of the victim and offender at the same time. Secondly, the gesture fits into the common staging strategies of a rock star – a position that the singer had not reached at this point of his career, but to which he definitely aspired and which this clip was meant to help him achieve. In that year, however, he did not succeed: *Du riechst so gut '95* did not enter the charts.

## Domesticating the Fantasy of Violence: The Music Video *Du riechst so gut '98*

The second video clip, *Du riechst so gut '98* (director: Philipp Stölzl)[21], was produced for the re-release of the single on April 17th 1998.[22] This new mix of the song is 4:24 minutes long, barely half a minute shorter than the first version.[23] The running-time of the music video, which presumably from the beginning of April on was aired on TV by the music channels, corresponds to that of the single. Due to the repetition of the calm instrumental part, which consists of spherical tones only, this new video is about 20 seconds longer than the one from 1995.

The budget for *Du riechst so gut '98* was much larger than it had been for the earlier one, evident in the polished quality and aesthetics of the images reminiscent of Hollywood-movies, including opulent set design, the advanced use of special effects and last but not least the choice of the image format (widescreen instead of the usual television format, i.e. 16:9 instead of 4:3). The most obvious difference between the two videos, however, is the fact that the later version is constructed as a narration: A tantalizingly beautiful, dark-haired girl, wearing a red coat and a tricorn of the same color, rides through a forest on a black horse. She seems to be on the run. During a short break from her frantic ride, she reaches for her handkerchief and dabs the sweat from her forehead and cleavage (fig. 7a). When she rushes onward, she loses the handkerchief or deliberately lets it fall to the ground. After nightfall, the tissue is found by what seems to be an animal roaming through the woods, but actually turns out to be a young man with flickering red eyes, dressed in white. Having sniffed the handkerchief, the man falls to his knees and follows the trace of the young woman to a castle, where a ball is taking place.[24] He sees the girl through a window. She now wears a red ball dress, a red choker and is decorated all over with red roses. He follows her through the mansion and meets her in the park, where he kneels down in order to restore the handkerchief to her. They kiss passionately and he follows her into her bed-chamber. As they undress, the woman – only initially horrified – sees that wolves are breaking free from her lover's body and ultimately even from his head (fig.

7b). Meanwhile, downstairs the dance continues until the party guests, all dressed in black, shy away from an unfamiliar sight. Dressed in the beautiful girl's red gown and smeared with blood, the young man walks into the hall and collapses. Wolves jump out of the dress and are chased by the other male guests, who have grabbed shotguns out of a gun locker. Meanwhile, the other women look after the young girl who is lying on her bed, seemingly dead. The wolves manage to escape and as they take on human guise again, the young woman opens her eyes, which are now just as red and flickering as those of the wolfmen (fig. 7c).

*Figs. 7a–c: The girl in the red dress (Maja Müller) is chasing on a black horse through the forest. Having guided the man into her bedroom, a pack of wolves bursts out of him. After their lovemaking the eyes of the girl are gleaming as red as those of the wolfmen. Stills from the music video by Philipp Stölzl: Rammstein, Du riechst so gut '98, 1998*

Before analyzing this version of the video, the differences and similarities between this and the other clip should be mentioned. As in the 1995 version, the singing of the vocals is displayed as a performance, but the lead voice is now visually divided among all six band members.[25] Moreover, diegetic sounds such as rolling thunder or the howling of wolves have been added to the soundtrack. Likenesses can also be found concerning the usage of motifs such as the dog (the wolves) and the flower (the embroidered rose on the handkerchief, the silk roses in the hair and on the ball dress of the beauty). One more obvious parallel is to be found in the reduced color palette. The shots (camera operator: Sebastian Pfaffenbichler) are dominated by achromatic colors such as black and white as well as sallow hues of brown and green. A fervent red, which is used for the flowers as well as for the girl's garments, constitutes a strong contrast to this range of colors.

The interconnection of image and sound is achieved through a comparatively unobtrusive adjustment of the movement internal and external to the image with regard to speed, beat and rhythm of the music (film editing: Sven Budelmann). The deviations are much more conspicuous, such as a slow motion image paralleled with a driving beat (when the horse jumps over a barrier) or the usage of time lapse for the increased speed of the third intermediary section. More evident connections may be found with regard to motifs, even though the lyrics and the images are not always synchronized. To name only some examples: the girl wipes off her 'sweat' ("Schweiß"), the red embroidery on the handkerchief evokes stained 'blood' ("Blut"), the man falls to his knees and 'crouches' ("kriecht"), and after the intro, the narration takes place when it has become 'dark' ("dunkel"). Directly matched, however, are lines like 'Now I've caught you' ("Jetzt hab ich dich"), when the man meets the woman at the park; 'Then I touch the wet skin' ("Dann faß ich an die nasse Haut"), when the woman takes hold of the rain-besprinkled hands of the man; 'I touch you' ("Ich faß dich an"), when one of the other female guests touches the seemingly dead girl; and the main line 'You smell so good' ("Du riechst so gut"), when the wolf-man absorbs the scent of the girl.

Dealing with the narration of the video, one can hardly overlook the fact that it refers to the fairy-tale of Little Red Riding Hood[26], which throughout the centuries has been handed down in various versions and adaptions. Charles Perrault's version from 1697 is generally regarded as the earliest written edition.[27] The most well-known however is that of the brothers Grimm from 1812 (1843).[28] Their purpose is to alarm and to warn their audience, which was meant to consist mainly of young girls. In the first case the fairy-tale is directed to the juvenile female aristocrat, in the second one to the adolescent townswoman. However, while Perrault in his moralistic epilogue openly admits that his warning is directed against the persuasiveness of young squires[29], the brothers Grimm are less straightforward. Their Little Red Riding Hood only learns that it should not defy her mother's rules.[30]

Since the middle of the 20th century, the sexual implications, which at least in the Grimm's adaption are merely implicit, became more and more important, especially for psychoanalytics like Erich Fromm or Bruno Bettelheim.[31] This increased interest in the sexual aspects of fairy-tales, especially in the field of psychoanalysis has affected further literary treatments of the narrative. The author Angela Carter, for example, adapts these interpretations and in her short stories *The Werewolf* and *The Company of Wolves* turns them into an emancipatory narration.[32] In the latter, she portrays a fearless Little Red Riding Hood, who only laughs at the wolfman threatening to devour her and in the end falls asleep between the paws of the beast which she has pacified by making love to it.[33] The video clip ties in with this very version of the narrative – not directly, however, but once more mediated through the feature film *The Company of Wolves* (1984, director: Neil Jordan), which itself draws from Carter's short stories. Loose ties with the movie may be observed in the dramaturgy. To name just a few: both plots are set within an imaginary 17th or 18th century (fig. 8a); the baroque party is probably intended as an expression of overambitious cultivation which is overrun by the animalistic, uncivilized, libidinous[34]; both wolfmen are characterized by a gallant demeanor as long as they look like a young man (fig. 8b); both girls are quite curious and open-minded, which means that they seem to fear and at the same time to yearn for the loss of their virginity; and last but not least, they are both finally transformed into beasts. More concrete formal and motific adoptions can be found in the color palette, both within the shots of the staircase through which the wolves race (director of photography: Bryan Loftus), but most notably in the spectacular special effects shot, in which a wolf breaks free from the throat of the man (fig. 8c).[35]

*Figs. 8a–c: The theme, some motifs, the colors, and the special effects are heavily indebted to the movie* The Company of Wolves. *Stills from the film by Neil Jordan:* The Company of Wolves, *1984*

Taking all these observations into account, *Du riechst so gut '98* obviously portrays a less radical, less violent desire, especially since the girl evidently gives her consent to the initial intercourse.[36] Roughly summarized, the pictorial level might be understood as a magically inflated and pompously staged coming-of-age-storyline, which remains attached to a slightly puerile demonization of the sexual, as the last frame showing the sexually affected or rather infected girl might confirm.

In conclusion, two more questions arise when comparing this version of the clip to the one produced three years earlier. First question: what role does the sense of smell, the sense of touch, the auditory, and the visual sense play? The auditory sense, the sense of touch and even the sense of smell that dominates the lyrics are only alluded to in the more recent clip. At the ballroom, the man takes in the scent of one of the female guests (fig. 9a), and in the bed-chamber he absorbs that of the girl. The sense of touch is insinuated by the fierce kissing and the physical contact of the women (fig. 9b). The motif of the lutist (fig. 9c) corresponds to the traditional iconography of the auditory sense.[37]

*Figs. 9a–c: The senses (such as smell, touch and hearing), dealt with in the lyrics, are only hinted at in the more recent clip. Stills from the music video by Philipp Stölzl: Rammstein,* Du riechst so gut '98, *1998*

Primarily, however, this clip deals with the visual sense, the gaze. It is addressed by the mask that hides its bearer from the glances of the surrounding party members, but at the same time draws attention to his or her eyes. But most of all the visual sense is emphasized by the position and the movement of the camera that looks through the mask (fig. 10a), the camera that roams around at the eye-level of the wolf and thereby aligns itself with the animal's body movements, and that adopts or discloses voyeuristic perspectives (fig. 10b–c). Therefore, it is not only the concentration on the visual, necessary in order to comprehend the narration, which provokes that the listening experience is disregarded in favor of the image.

*Figs. 10a–c: The sense of sight is dominating the second clip while the lyrical 'you' is here consistently to be identified with the girl in the red dress. Stills from the music video by Philipp Stölzl: Rammstein,* Du riechst so gut *'98, 1998*

Responsible for this is especially the use of the camera, which makes the music video first and foremost a visual event.

Second question: who may be identified as the lyrical 'you' and what conseqences does this have for the role of the viewer? This question, and along with it the question of the sexes, is solved in this clip quite definitely. Lyrically speaking, the men seem to address the girl in the red dress exclusively.[38] Only the sequence where one of the men is wearing this particular gown becomes ambiguous. Contextually speaking, the sequence does not dissolve the boundaries between the sexes. Rather, it depicts the parallels between devouring and sex itself, which is also immanent in the narrative of Little Red Riding Hood. Just as the wolf was once inside the man, the man now is inside the woman: so completely has he penetrated and absorbed her body, that he has become one with her.[39] This explicit focus of the lyrical 'you' corresponds with the fact that none of the performers ever look directly at the audience. Paradoxically, however, exactly this confirms and attests the primacy of the visual sense, which reigns at least within classical Hollywood-cinema.[40]

Summing up, one could say that the visual level of the music video for *Du riechst so gut '98* doesn't translate and expand the song's strategies of overpowering in the same way the clip for *Du riechst so gut '95* does. Rather, Stölzl's video shifts towards a mainly visual owerpowering of the viewer. Such a shift may have been due to the intention to counter the acoustic opulence of the song with something equivalent on the visual level. This, however, leads nevertheless to a weakening of the listening experience. Or, to phrase it casually, Rammstein and director Stölzl wanted to produce and have produced 'big cinema' – at the cost of making the audience of *Du riechst so gut '98* first and foremost a *watching* audience, whose sexual identity might remain unoffended, but who also remains excluded from a sensual experience that includes more than the visual. The viewers have by all means appreciated this decision: in Germany, *Du riechst so gut '98* reached number 16 on the single charts.

## APPENDIX

Rammstein: *Du riechst so gut* (1995)
Music and lyrics by Richard Kruspe/Till Lindemann/Paul Landers/Dr. Christian Lorenz/Christoph Doom Schneider/Oliver Riedel

> 1. Der Wahnsinn / ist nur eine schmale Brücke / die Ufer sind Vernunft und Trieb / ich steig dir nach / das Sonnenlicht den Geist verwirrt / ein blindes Kind das vorwärts kriecht / weil es seine Mutter riecht / [Ich finde dich] / Die Spur ist frisch und auf die Brücke / tropft dein Schweiß dein warmes Blut / ich seh dich nicht / ich riech dich nur ich spüre dich / ein Raubtier das vor Hunger schreit / witter ich dich meilenweit / REF: Du riechst so gut / du riechst so gut / ich geh dir hinterher / du riechst so gut / ich finde dich / so gut / ich steig dir nach / du riechst so gut / gleich hab ich dich /
> 2. [Jetzt hab ich dich] / Ich warte bis es dunkel ist / dann faß ich an die nasse Haut / verrate mich nicht / oh siehst du nicht die Brücke brennt / hör auf zu schreien und wehr dich nicht / weil sie sonst auseinander bricht / REF: Du riechst so gut / du riechst so gut / ich geh dir hinterher / du riechst so gut / ich finde dich / so gut / ich steig dir nach / du riechst so gut / gleich hab ich dich / Du riechst so gut / du riechst so gut / ich geh dir hinterher / du riechst so gut / ich faß dich an / so gut / du riechst so gut / jetzt hab ich dich / Du riechst so gut / du riechst so gut / ich geh dir hinterher.

The rendition of the lyrics follows the printout which accompanies the album *Herzeleid* (Motor Music GmbH, Hamburg, LC 4909). The additions in the square brackets correspond to the listening experience. The statements concerning the authorship are taken from Rammstein 1999: p. 42.

## REFERENCES

**1** | The titling of the different song versions and of the two music videos is not always consistent. In order to discern them clearly, here the following titles are used: *Du riechst so gut* for the song, *Du riechst so gut '95* for the music video from 1995 (director: Emanuel Fialik) and *Du riechst so gut '98* for the music video from 1998 (director: Philipp Stölzl).

**2** | The album *Herzeleid* was released exactly a month later. There, the duration of the song is given as 4:49 minutes. The difference of one second presumedly is due to technical reasons.

**3** | To this already the name of the band refers: it stands for a bollard, used in front of entrances and exits, but at the same time it hints upon the city of Ramstein in Rheinland-Pfalz which hosts as an American military base. In 1988, due to an accident during a military air show, 70 people were killed and hundreds injured. The spectacular and cruel incident then caused an immense stir and was also thematised in the lyrics of the song *Rammstein* which also features on *Herzeleid*.

**4** | For the notation see Rammstein 1999: p. 42-49. Musically, Rammstein is counted among the representatives of the "Neue Deutsche Härte" ('New German Harshness') which developed during the 90's. Their characteristics are German lyrics, extremely low vocal range, a rolling intontation of the letter "R" and a mix of electronic and hard rock music with a heavy emphasis on rhythm. A clear differentiation from other forms of rock music is, however, difficult.

**5** | Remarkable in this context is the fact that both nouns are also used in the language of hunters: The "Spur" ('trail') is here referring to the imprints of hoofless game animals, "Schweiß" ('sweat') to the blood flowing from the bodies of all game (and hunting dogs). Both, "Spur" as well as "Schweiß" make the pursuit of the prey possible. Stinglwagner/Haseder 2004: p. 623, lemma "Schweiß"; p. 645, lemma "Spur" and the following composites.

**6** | Kant 2000: p. 42-61, esp. p. 47-50; Kant 2006: p. 45-60, esp. p. 49-51. Kant treats olfaction and taste in the same subchapter, for him they are on the same level.

**7** | These remarks are based on the version on the DVD *Lichtspielhaus Rammstein* (Motor Music GmbH 2004).

**8** | This among other due to the forgoing of a repetition of the Intro.

**9** | How close the relationship between the sound carrier and the music video is can be seen by the fact that the sleeve designs of both the single and the album (photography by Parler; sleeve design by Dirk Rudolph) closely resemble the visuals of *Du riechst so gut '95* concerning motifs and formal style: the cover of the single is dominated by the picture of a yellow gerbera flower against a pale blue background. The booklet for *Herzeleid* shows the members of the band with bare chests in front of a giant chrysanthemum flower, portraits and a gerbera flower.

**10** | The glasses are a stage accessoire, used in order to protect the singer from injuries during the pyrotechnical interludes.

**11** | This was the second edition. The first one had been published in 1593.

**12** | Ripa 2000: p. 448, lemma "Odorato".

**13** | Hertel 1979: p. 114. The edition of the *Iconolgia* from 1603 was the first one which was illustrated. However, there is no illustration for the entry "Odorato".

**14** | According to Ovid Hyacinthus was so badly injured during a mutual discus game that he died – he was then transformed by Apollo into a flower which still today carries Hyacinthus' name. Ovid 1999: p. 50-53; Naso 2004: p. 488-493.

**15** | Concerning this aspect of seduction in a shoulder-portrait ("rittrato di spalla") see Krüger 1995: p. 153-154.

**16** | Other than in the examples, referred to by Krüger (see note above), Mola's failure does not seem to be due to an elaborate interplay of establishing and infringing of illusion, but rather to a lack of technical skill.

**17** | Also the chosen species make clear that the flowers are supposed to merely represent scent in general since – other than for example roses and jasmine – they have no characteristic fragrance. Instead, the radiant colors of the flowers, shown in the video, could be understood as a visual equivalent for the signalling effect of scents.

**18** | This would mean that *Du riechst so gut '95* not depicts the object of desire, but desire itself whose target can't be represented. This would correspond with a psychoanalytical interpretation in the wake of Lacan, according to whom 'desire' ("désir") results from a 'lack' ("manqué") which can't be articulated or compensated. Evans 1996: p. 35-39, p. 95-96; Evans 2002: p. 53-58, p. 181-182.

**19** | The direct addressing of the viewer is considered a typical trait of muscial films or TV formats such as advertisment. Casetti 1998. Both – musical film and TV-advertisment – had an impact on the genesis of the music video. Weiß 2007: p. 17-22.

**20** | Almost during the entire duration of the video gradually different forms of masculinity are hence staged and – depending from the interpretation as offenders or victims – separated. Only at the end, when the entire band forms a chorus, all members are marked as a collective of offenders.

**21** | The basis for the following analysis is again the version on the DVD *Lichtspielhaus Rammstein* (Motor Music GmbH 2004).

**22** | The reason for this second production might have been that Rammstein wanted to break into the music market of the United States of America as well. The fact that director David Lynch had used the two songs *Rammstein* and *Heirate mich* ("Marry Me") for the soundtrack of his film *Lost Highway* (1997) had caused quite a stir in the United States.

**23** | The cover (photography by Parler; sleeve design by Dirk Rudolph) corresponds to the one of the earlier single release, but it is entirely kept in hues of white, grey and silver.

**24** | Locations were Schloss Babelsberg near Potsdam and Schloss Schönhausen in the Berlin district Pankow.

**25** | The monster appears in the form of one single wolf and as six wolves. This is due to the fact that by request of the band in every music video not only all of their members have to be heard, but to be seen. At the same time this can be understood in the way that the clip does not deal with the encounter of a specific man with a specific woman, but rather with a generic meeting. See for this also the making-of for *Du riechst so gut '98* on the DVD *Lichtspielhaus Rammstein* (Motor Music GmbH 2004).

**26** | In the production of music videos the reference to fairy tales is not unccommon: the clip for Rammstein's *Sonne* (*Sun*, 2000, director: Jörn Heitmann) for example refers to *Sneewittchen* (*Snow White*) by the Grimm-brothers respectively the animated film by Walt Disney which was released under the title *Snow White and the Seven Dwarfs* (1937, director: David Hand). Brüder Grimm 1971: p. 297-308; Brüder Grimm 1983: p. 184-191. More subtle references to Disney's film can be traced in the clip for Madonna's song *Hollywood* (2003, director: Jean-Baptiste Mondino). See Weiß 2006a.

**27** | Charles Perrault: "Le Petit Chaperon Rouge", in: Perrault 2002: p. 132-137; Perrault 2008: p. 32-39.

**28** | Brüder Grimm: "Rotkäppchen", in: Brüder Grimm 1971: p. 174-180; Brüder Grimm 1983: p. 98-101.

**29** | "Mais hélas! qui ne sait que ces loups doucereux, / De tous les loups sont les plus dangereux." Perrault 2002: p. 136. "[B]ut alas! everyone knows that these soft-spoken wolves / are the most dangerous wolves of all." Perrault 2002: p. 137. "Doch ach, ein jeder weiß, gerade sie, die zärtlich werben, / gerade diese Wölfe locken ins Verderben." Perrault 2008: p. 39.

**30** | "Rotkäppchen aber dachte 'du willst dein Lebtag nicht wieder allein vom Wege ab in den Wald laufen, wenn dirs die Mutter verboten hat'". Brüder Grimm 1971: p. 179. "[A]nd as for Little Red Cap, she said to herself: 'Never again will I leave the path and run off into the wood when my mother tells me not to.'" Brüder Grimm 1983: p. 101. Thus this version of the fairy tale ends. Directly attached to it, a second version tells that the girl had learned her lesson. With the help of the grandmother she then takes care that the wolf falls into the well and drowns.

**31** | Fromm 1951: p. 235-241; Fromm 1982: p. 157-160; Bettelheim 1976: p. 166-183; Bettelheim 1977: p. 158-173. Bettelheim mentions *en passant* that with the questions of Little Red Cap after the ears, eyes, hands and the mouth of the wolf also the four senses of hearing, seeing, feeling and tasting are addressed.

**32** | Angela Carter: *The Werewolf*, in: Carter 1981: p. 108-110; *Der Werwolf*, in: Carter 1982: p. 173-175; Angela Carter: *The Company of Wolves*, in Carter 1981: p. 110-118; *Die Gesellschaft der Wölfe*, in: Carter 1982: p. 177-190.

**33** | "See! sweet and sound she sleeps in granny's bed, between the paws of the tender wolf." Carter 1981: p. 118. "Sieh nur! Lieblich und wohlauf schläft sie in Großmutters Bett, zwischen den Pfoten des zärtlichen Wolfs." Carter 1982: p. 190.

**34** | The coloring of the clip is also pointing into this direction. As mentioned, the people at the court are wearing black garments which in fairytales mostly stands for the evil and dishonest. The wolfman, instead, is all dressed in white, thus he could stand for the good and virtuous.

**35** | Other things are taken from the movie *Bram Stoker's Dracula* 1993, director: Francis Ford Coppola): the dark, loose and put up hair and the strikingly red dress of the girl show obvious similiarities to the appearance of Mina Murray (Winona Ryder) during one of her amorous encounters with the title character (costume design: Eiko Ishioka). In order to sleep with Lucy Westenra (Sadie Frost), an easy-going girlfriend of Mina, Dracula (Gary Oldman) repeatedly transforms into a werwolf-like creature which is described by Lucy as red-eyed. Every time Dracula approaches Lucy's manor, the camera (director of photography: Michael Ballhaus) transfers the audience into the viewpoint of the monster. Dracula then brings death to the young woman, waiting for him in bed, in the shape of a wolf. Raecke 2003: p. 77, footnote 214. The folly of the scene during the ball and the appearance of an unbidden guest, then chased by the celebrating people, is instead reminiscent of *Dance of the Vampires* (1967, director: Roman Polanski).

**36** | This is not only suggested by the behavior of the girl, but also by the fact that she is strewed with roses.

**37** | Ripa suggests in one of the two variants on how to depict auditory a lute-playing woman, accompanied by a hind. Ripa 2000: p. 448, lemma "Udito". Especially the attribute of the lute established itself. Concerning the gender allocation of the person playing the instrument the artists didn't commit themselves. One can here also refer to what has been shown especially concerning the male *Lute players* by Michelangelo Merisi da Caravaggio (painted shortly before 1600): in these paintings the depiction of contemporary performance practice is closely interconnected with an allegoric representation of hearing (respectively of also other senses in the case of the lute player in the Eremitage, St. Petersburg) and the erotic bias of both themes. See Posner 1971; Trinchieri Camiz 1991. Such an interconnection can be also discerned in *Du riechst so gut '98*. The here appearing lute player serves on the one hand as a visual reference to the musical and thus the audible elements of the music video, on the other hand his appearance and his attention towards one of the female guests anticipates the encounter of the wolfman and the girl.

**38** | The operating of the camera and the costume design are thus constituting a visual regime which filmmaker and theorist Laura Mulvey, proceeding from Sigmund Freud's remarks on scopophilia (or scoptophilia: voyeurism), has grasped with the concept of the "male gaze". According to Mulvey the viewing situation in the cinema is adjusted in a way that the woman is installed as an image or spectacle, that simultaneously is looked at and displayed. The position of the man, instead, is that of a spectator or bearer of the look. However, one can't assume that *Du riechst so gut '98* (as a sort of counterdraft to its precursor three years before) is aiming at an explicit masculinization of the audience. Although the subjective camera shots, the view through the mask and the wolf-like roaming close to the ground are offering an identification with the lyrical 'I' (implicitly marked as male), the conventionality of these viewpoints on the one hand and the atrociousness of the seen on the other hand are countering a consistent identificaction and rather put the viewer into the position of an observing third party. Laura Mulvey: "Visual Pleasure and Narrative Cinema", in: Mulvey 1989: p. 14-26, esp.

p. 19-21. For the subversion of the "male gaze" in Madonna's music video *Open Your Heart* (1986, director: Jean-Baptiste Mondino) see Weiß 2006b.

**39** | This is also the only moment in the clip which could be described as a transient collapse of the lyrical 'I' and the lyrical 'you' into one.

**40** | In order to sustain the illusion of a closed cosmos, the classic Hollywood film usually renounces a direct addressing of the viewer. See Allen 1995; Cassetti 1998. Concerning the question of the position of the viewer in the cinema see Mayne 1993; Stokes/Maltby 2001.

## BIBLIOGRAPHY

Allen, Richard (1995): *Projecting Illusion. Film Spectatorship and the Impression of Reality*, Cambridge: Cambridge University Press.

Bettelheim, Bruno (1976): *The Uses of Enchantment*, New York/NY: Knopf; transl. Liselotte Mickel/Brigitte Weitbrecht: *Kinder brauchen Märchen*, Stuttgart: Deutsche Verlags-Anstalt, 1977.

Brüder Grimm (1971): *Kinder- und Hausmärchen. Vollständige Ausgabe, mit einer Einleitung von Hermann Grimm und der Vorrede der Brüder Grimm zur ersten Ausgabe von 1819*, München: Winkler; transl. Ralph Manheim: *Grimm's Tales for Young and Old. The Complete Stories*, New York/NY: Anchor, 1983.

Carter, Angela (1981): *The Bloody Chamber and Other Stories*, London: Penguin; transl. Sybil Gräfin Schönfeldt: *Blaubarts Zimmer. Märchen aus der Zwischenwelt*, Reinbeck bei Hamburg: Rowohlt, 1982.

Casetti, Francesco (1998): *Inside the Gaze. The Fiction Film and Its Spectator*, Bloomington/IN: Indiana University Press.

Evans, Dylan (1996): *An Introductory Dictionary of Lacanian Psychoanalysis*, London: Routledge; transl. Gabriella Burkhart: *Wörterbuch der Lacanschen Psychoanalyse*, Vienna: Turia und Kant, 2002.

Ferino-Pagden, Sylvia (1996): *Immagini del sentire. I cinque sensi nell'arte*, Milano: Leonardo Arte.

Fromm, Erich (1951): *The Forgotten Language. An Introduction to the Understanding of Dreams, Fairy Tales, and Myths*, New York/NY: Holt, Rinehart and Winston; transl. Liselotte und Ernst Mickel: *Märchen, Mythen, Träume. Eine Einführung in das Verständnis einer vergessenen Sprache*, Reinbeck bei Hamburg: Rowohlt, 1982.

Hertel, Johann Georg (1970): *Des berühmten italiänischen Ritters Caesaris Ripae allerley Künsten und Wissenschaften dienliche Sinnbilder und Gedancken*, Augsburg [circa 1760]. Reprint Munich: Fink.

Kant, Immanuel (2000): *Anthropologie in pragmatischer Hinsicht*, hg. von Reinhardt Brandt, Hamburg: Meiner; transl. Robert B. Louden: *Anthropology from a Pragmatic Point of View*, Cambridge: Cambridge Univerity Press, 2006.

Krüger, Klaus (1995): "Der Blick ins Innere des Bildes. Ästhetische Illusion bei Gerhard Richter". In: *Bruckmanns Pantheon. Internationale Zeitschrift für Kunst* LIII, p. 149-166.

Mayne, Judith (1993): *Cinema and Spectatorship*, London: Routledge.

Mulvey, Laura (1989): *Visual and Other Pleasures*, Bloomington/IN: Indiana University Press.

Naso, Publius Ovidius (2004): *Metamorphosen*. Edited and translated by Gerhard Fink, Düsseldorf: Artemis & Winkler.

Ovid (1999): *Metamorphoses IX–XII*. Edited with an introduction, translation and notes by D. E. Hill, Warminster: Aris & Phillips.

Perrault, Charles (2002): *The Complete Fairy Tales in Verse and Prose. L'intégrale des Contes en vers et en prose. A dual language book*. Edited and translated by Stanley Appelbaum, Mineola/NY: Dover; transl. Ulrich Friedrich Müller: *Contes de Fées. Märchen*, Munich: Deutscher Taschenbuch Verlag, 2008.

Posner, Donald (1971): "Caravaggio's Homo-erotic Early Work". In: *The Art Quarterly* XXXIV/3, p. 301–324.

Stinglwagner, Gerhard K. F./Haseder, Ilse E. (2004): *Das Große Kosmos Jagdlexikon*, Stuttgart: Franckh-Kosmos.

Stokes, Melvyn/Maltby, Richard (2001): *Hollywood Spectatorship. Changing Perceptions of Cinema Audiences*, London: British Film Institute.

Raecke, Anika (2003): *Cultural Studies und Populärkulturanalyse. Die Rezeption von Rammstein*, M.A. thesis Universität Lüneburg.

Rammstein (1999): *Rammstein Liederbuch*, London: Wise.

Ripa, Cesare (2000): *Iconologia. Overo descrittione di diversi imagini cavate dall'antichità, et di propria inventione*, Rom 1603. Reprint Hildesheim: Olms.

Trinchieri Camiz, Franca (1991): "Music and Painting in Cardinal del Monte's Household". In: *Metropolitan Museum Journal* 26, p. 213-226.

Weiß, Matthias (2006a): "'Spieglein, Spieglein an der Wand ...' – Anmerkungen zur Verweispragmatik des Musikvideos am Beispiel von Madonnas 'Hollywood'". In: Nicole Kallwies/Mariella Schütz (eds.), *Mediale Ansichten. Dokumentation des 18. Film- und Fernsehwissenschaftlichen Kolloquiums. Universität Mannheim 2005*, Marburg: Schüren, p. 113-119.

Weiß, Matthias (2006b): "Peepshow und Panopticon: Madonnas 'Open Your Heart'". In: Birgit Mersmann/Martin Schulz (eds.), *Kulturen des Bildes*, Munich: Fink, p. 305-324.

Weiß, Matthias (2007): *Madonna revidiert. Rekursivität im Videoclip*, Berlin: Reimer.

## Photographic Sources

Figs. 1a-c, 5a-c, 6a-c, 7a-c, 9a-c, 10a-c: *Lichtspielhaus Rammstein* ℗: © 2004 Motor Music GmbH. Licensed exclusively to Universal Records, a division of UMG Recordings, Inc. (DVD).

Fig. 2: Hertel 1970: p. 114.

Figs. 3, 4: Ferino-Pagden 1996: p. 118, 169.

Figs. 8a-c: *The Company of Wolves* © 2001 Concorde Home Entertainment GmbH. (DVD).

of music videos. A very recent example is the video for Julian Casablancas' song *11th Dimension*, directed by Warren Fu in December 2009, where different kinds of visual effects, props, and make up were used to place the singer in a surrounding reminiscent of the Eighties, and thereby intentionally link the genre of his music with the era.

The audio-visual complexity of these forms calls for a careful consideration about the semiotic tools to apply when analysing them. First of all we need to start from the concept of audio-visual syncretism: Semiotics conceives syncretism as the merging of two or more different languages into one which gains an expressive autonomy and specific features, different from the mere sum of the pre-existing ones. In this sense the audio-visual language is indeed a syncretic one.

The strategic practice upon which every kind of audio-visual syncretic text is built, is filmic enunciation. On the one side, enunciation takes shape through editing processes, which, in this case, mean the practice of selecting and combining different elements originating from different languages. Enunciation, on the other hand, becomes the object of *a mise en scène*: many of the most recent music videos are built upon constant references to a fake, recreated backstage area, or to fictitious production context where the conflict between the stars and the music industry is staged.

The aim of this metatextual process is to renegotiate the relationship with the spectator, offering him the illusion to be part of a secret and the logic behind the successful construction of the star.

Consequently, the performer's body now also shows the once hidden marks of his construction. The aim is no longer to be perfect, but to appear as "authentic". Paradoxically this is achieved by unveiling the effects of a physical or digital manipulation towards such a "perfection".

Departing from this scenery, our hypothesis is that a semiotic analysis of the audio-visual complexity of a music video, combined with a study of the visual manipulations of the performers' bodies seen in the clip, will be particularly useful in the examination of the aesthetic of music videos.

## CELEBRATING THE STAR.
## THE BODY OF MUSIC ICON AS A SEMIOTIC DEVICE

As a "text within the text", the body is essential to understand the semiotic nature of the music video. The performer's figure is flexible and like clay can be constantly shaped, transformed, and transfigured in accordance with the soundscape. The body is twisted, decomposed, multiplied, and reworked in a process of a manipulation that addresses the viewer, while at the same time unveiling hidden and probably even unusual details of the performer's icon. Seen in this perspective, the aesthetics of the music video force the viewer to be a part of the star's celebration. By allowing the fan's gaze to come very close to the mythical body of the performer, he is concurrently seduced as a consumer for whom the music video suggests possible models of identity, both original and mysterious, and designed to remain in the hit list of fans' preferences. In recent productions of music videos, the mutation and manipulation of the performer's figure is even more explicitly emphasized and used as a metaphor for the tempting possibility to create oneself a new identity. Given the fact that the process of de- and reconstructing is clearly shown and demonstrated as such, the audience's initiative is encouraged and the viewer is invited to engage in reconstructing the meaning of the whole marketing strategy (see Peverini 2001): In Jean-Baptiste Mondino's music video for Madonna's song *Hollywood*, directed in 2002, the pop icon exposes herself during some aesthetic interventions by playing with the rumours and stereotypes she's surrounded with.

In music videos, therefore, different kinds of re-semantization of the body are enacted, not only in order to give the star a new seducing skin, but also in order to visualize an ironic or polemic process, a repertory of clichés about the star's exterior appearance. In this way, an endless and unpredictable auto-reflexive mechanism is set into motion (see Pozzato 2006): Consequently, in Vaughan Arnell's music video for Robbie Williams' song *Rock DJ*, released in 2000, the performer is literally stripped to the bones, throwing his flesh ironically at an audience of adoring young girls.

The star's image must be constantly renewed in order to endure the challenge of the constantly changing media languages and formats. Reality shows such as castings shows (like for example *American Idol* or *Pop Idol*) that deal with continuous backstage revelations, have made the public increasingly competent about the process of designing and manufacturing a star. Thus, in the music videos sleek faces are replaced or overlapped with clear signs of the manufacturing process, initiating a never ending self-reflexive game. Seductiveness itself is even a value when it is revealed as the result of an artificial process, the consequence of a fragile dialectic between the performer and the music industry.

Emerging bands and pop stars need to establish themselves as icons with an identity that is on the one hand original, but extremely familiar and playing along the rules of the game on the other: both disruptive maverick and aligned stock character at the same time. In the context of such a process, the Cultural Industry is often represented as an infernal machine, a steamroller that overwhelms single identities in an ever ending process of banalization.

The conflict between the star, the industry, and the audiences leaves signs on the body of the star. Manipulations of his identity are often visually represented as distortions and scars, evidence of the effects the tension between his distance and his affiliation with the industry have upon him. Given that these artificial signs usually involve make up, the star improves his value while exhibiting his authenticity with the help of a forgery (see Peverini 2004 and Peverini 2005).

Starting from this complex scenery through some videos analysis, I will construct an axis, going from the simple performance *mise en scène* to a total metamorphosis of bodies up to their strategic disappearance which presents a new challenge for the competence of the fans.

How can we approach the analysis of the aesthetics of the music video while trying to overcome overrated dichotomies such as indie/mainstream or narrative/non narrative?

Given that record companies and TV channels are facing a medial, economic and social revolution which contributes to the transformation of any kind of text, I will focus on some of the aesthetic effects of the global change that affect music videos in the Web 2.0 while trying to retain some methodological topics. If we state that the aesthetic effectiveness of media texts is based upon their languages and their relations with the audience: what happens then when we face an object such as the music video which continuously changes its strategies and forms under the spell of new digital effects and ever changing editing techniques?

Many authors from Andrew Goodwin to Neil Feineman agree that the development of any kind of categorization is impossible and even useless:

"Although videos may all look alike to the disdainful critic, they come in all sizes, shapes, and colors (...) Music video directors must tailor each video to the song and have far less room to move than they would with a longer, more modulated feature-film script, so they don't have the same luxury of fully developing distinctive visual signatures. But video directors have compensated by becoming extremely good with the time they have. Despite the compressed format, they have managed to stamp their videos with personalized styles, looks, and themes. In the process, they are increasingly treated as true auteurs." (Feineman 2000: p. 24)

From a socio-semiotic perspective, the only way to explore what seems to be the core of the problem – this type of superficial vagueness –, is to first survey the industrial and cultural context in which music videos are produced and distributed, and then dismantle the textual levels, that is: to reconstruct, according to Michel Chion, the relationship between sounds, images, noises and words. From my point of view this is just the first step in the process of an analysis. Understanding semiotic procedures that empower the surface of music videos, unveiling the secrets behind the rhythm and studying lyrics is just a preliminary stage for the focus on the strategies of visualizing the performance, the *mise en scène* of the body.

My hypothesis in particular is that the production of music videos has now reached a technological peak. Even if digital effects are more and more realistic and the manipulation of images is incredibly refined, the audience has at the same time become increasingly competent and even accustomed to read, interpret and decode the style of the particular directors.

Does this automatically mean that music videos have lost all their astonishing power? Not at all. It means that if we actually strive to understand the mutations and changes behind these dynamics, we'll have to move ahead.

Nowadays digital effects are so common that they can be considered an established rhetoric. As a result we now have to deal with very codified styles which, far from the original experimental efforts, are now constituting almost a manneristic system of practices.

In our social network era, the music star, as a system of images, is multiplied inside a cross-medial labyrinth into which new spectators venture to come. One could even say that the most advanced users, such as groupies and official fans, are as a matter of fact helping to build this labyrinth.

Semioticians conceive of a text as strategic space where a reader's interpretative skills are practiced. To capture the attention of the fans, music videos are located at the center of this intricate net. At the core of this complex mechanism we detect the star, his image, his body. The performer's identity is at the same time an instrument and the target of the audience's interpretative effort.

The success of music videos is not only a matter of rhythm and audio-visual syncretism. The complex relations between the music, the images and the lyrics, the editing and the visual effects are just parts of the whole content. This means that if we aim at reconstructing the composite logics on which the aesthetics of this audio-visual phenomenon is based, we have to dissect the texts, focusing on different levels.

## First Level: The Audio-Visual Surface

The first, flexible level that can be examined is the surface of a text, the place where sounds and images get in touch with each other. Since the images for music videos are always produced by starting from the structure of the music, we must reconstruct how actors, figures, shapes, and colors 'visualize' sounds. In other words, the audio-visual aesthetics of this level involve translation between different languages (such as for example from 'audio' to 'video' - see Spaziante 2007).

Focusing on this plane, we can state that a music video relies first of all on the aesthetics of photography and secondly on the aesthetics of the moving image. We have to admit that every effort at categorization is incomplete and temporary because the surface of the music video, being strategically built in order to catch the spectator's eye, relies on different ephemeral factors such as the ever changing styles and codes of fashion, the atmospheres evoked by the lyrics of the song, and the references to musical or the cross-over of cinematographic genres.

But even if we can't classify the nature of every single image, we can at least identify a visual continuum concerning the ways in which the star is (re)presented and which encompass extremes such as for example sleek, glossy figures vs. 'lo-fi', indie-style icons.

In the first case the surfaces of music videos are related to the visual codes and figures of the fashion system: the images are neat, the colors are bright, and the composition of the frames is well balanced. In the second case the music videos imitate home made short movies and footage, the style of direction aims at reproducing the maximum grade of 'realism': colors, camera movements, post production effects are all deliberately unprofessional. We are here facing an important topic about the ambiguous and uncertain nature of the music video suspended between mannerism and radical linguistic innovation.

## Second Level: The Visual Effects

This level concerns the editing and the postproduction. From a historical perspective, music videos have always been a strategic testing ground where visual effects were widely experimented. As Christian Metz stated in his fundamental essay *The Impersonal Enunciation or The Site of Film*, the success of music videos exasperates visual codes, rhythms, and narrative strategies, shocking with special effects, which are bombing the surface of texts, stepping over any kind of experimentation concerning meanings (see Metz 1991: p. 67).

In the golden era of the music video, experimentation with rhythm was an essential issue: Chris Cunningham invented a new, very condensed way of representing the beat by creating a non narrative editing style, based primarily on sounds. At the opposite end we find the formal slowness which characterizes the whole video production of Sigur Rós. Both approaches served the same purpose: to capture the viewer's attention, hooking him to the screen and to the constantly changing flood of televised images which can be easily surfed by using the remote control. Now, that television has lost its supremacy, music videos are living in a wider cross-medial space where rhythm still has a leading role in the effectiveness of the music videos, but it is certainly difficult to conceive other experiments that transcend the radical innovations of both Cunningham and Sigur Rós concerning the audio-visual rhythm.

However, a margin of innovation can still be found in some music videos which ironically play with their digital texture, simulating and emphasizing a feigned technical imperfection: the clip for Chairlift's *Evident Utensil*, directed by Ray Tintori in 2009 (fig. 1), uses digital effects in order to simulate the sort of loss of definition which is usually due to the high compression of a video when it is uploaded on the web.

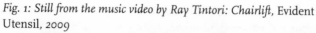

*Fig. 1: Still from the music video by Ray Tintori: Chairlift*, Evident Utensil, 2009

In this way the music video shows its 'maturity' by demonstrating its awareness of the heightened importance of the Internet distribution for audio-visual media. In the case of the Chairlift-video low-definition images are pushed to their boundaries in order to enable a kaleidoscopically flowing sequence of portrait shots: the images of the band members are in fact time and again melting into streams of colors, seemingly ruined by their low fidelity and deconstructed into pixels, in order to reappear then as recomposed into a new shot. As Luke Lewis stated in the British musical magazine NME: "It's sort of like the moment a Magic Eye image starts to jump put of the page, crossed with the semi-transparent 'heat sensor' effect in the 'Predator' films. Only utterly modern and not two decades out of date as both those examples suggest. (...) The same effect can be seen in Kanye West's new video, 'Welcome To Heartbreak'. The future? Who knows, but it looks damn cool" (Lewis 2009).[1]

## Third Level: The Content of the Music Videos

Issues of narrativity are nowadays still at the center of the debate along with issues of metatextuality. Trying to find some coherence in the narrative structure of a music video is a thorny and muddled operation. In most cases the content of a video is the result of the overlapping of different elements, among which narrativity often is not predominant. As Carol Vernallis writes:

"Music videos obscure narrative as they build up a history. The video often begins with the establishment of a ground and with a sense of stability and coherence. Although I cannot immediately understand the movement from one shot to another, the music begins to give me some feel for it, and the lyrics help me to piece it together. Once the music video starts developing a sense of history, however, and once the musical, visual, or lyrical elements begin to draw upon what the video has presented thus, far, I note that I cannot find these sources from earlier in the video" (Vernallis 2007: p.119).

Nowadays, considering the new cross-mediatic context, we can observe an important, brand new topic: with an ever growing frequency a new kind of audio-visual material started to appear alongside the official music video. We're not talking about fans produced videos here, but about a coherent strategy according to which the official video, conceived to promote a new album or single, is now just a part of a wider set of materials which (such as diaries or videoblogs) are documenting the making of an album, the recording sessions, the backstage action, the life on tour and every other kind of extra activity of the stars. Their content transcends the single official video and widens the boundaries of the mediatic space where the stars reveal themselves to their audience.

## Fourth Level: The Representation of Performer's Body

The aesthetic of the music video and of the portrayal of the performer are indissoluble. Let's not forget here that these video clips are a promotional form designed not only to sell a mere object, the album, but also a more immaterial object of value: the star. At this point, we can say that the new issue is about the new ways to create the myth of a star. The expressive potential for innovation transcends mere technical innovations and focuses more on experimentations concerning the performer's body and generally the star. Music videos, or better, their producers and directors, have the power to create new mythologies, thus celebrating the stars in ever new ways. The collaboration of the British musician Damon Albarn and the British comic book artist and designer Jamie Hewlett concerning the drawn pop group Gorillaz is a neat example of this trend (see for this and its history Keazor/Wübbena 2007: p. 395-397). The purpose of music videos is to install and to illustrate an adoration at the same time. Even if a crisis might affect the economics, it won't necessarily affect devotion and thus the power of music to create identification and the longing of the fan to reach the mythical pop star. Seen from this point of view, star identity isn't a static condition, but a process.

In my book *Il Videoclip. Strategie e figure di una forma breve*, I identified the four phases a performer's body passes through from a historical point of view (Peverini 2004: p. 173).

## Phase One: Body *Mise en Scène*

Here we talk about the representation of a performance. Settings are the only variable parameter. Bodies are shown in the foreground in all their splendor. Musical genres such as R'n'B and Hip-hop constructed all of their imaginary in this way.

## Phase Two: Body Manipulation

Radical forms of manipulation and mutation are very common issues in contemporary videos. Floria Sigismondi's music video for Marilyn Manson's song *Tourniquet*, directed in 1996, is a clear example of this tendency to constantly mould a body, not only in order to shock the viewer, but also in order to present a physical deformation as a metaphor for the complexity and dynamism of an artistic identity.

## Phase Three: Manipulation of the *Mise en Scène*, Metatextuality and Backstage Revelation

Stars are not only staging their conflict with the music industry, but they build complex narrative worlds upon that and forge a new complicity with their fans through that. Michel Gondry's music video for Björk's song *Bachelorette*, directed in 1997, which narratively followed the principle of a chinese box, stages the struggle of an artist against the star system and the logic of consumerism The rise and the fall of a music star is represented as a story within the story, a complex *mise en abyme*, where the dramatic experience of the loss of identity appears to recur infinitely.

## Phase Four: Simulacra *Mise en Scène*

This is a decisive phase. Playing with identities is a more and more popular practice. Making recourse to alter egos, masks, camouflages, multiple identities is the way to spread the performer's body throughout the web, to get his voice more widely heard. The most ambitious and complex project in this cross-mediatic phase is, without doubt, that of Gorillaz. This virtual band, composed of four animated musicians, is at the centre of a fictional narrative world that uses the logic, practices, and tools of communication in order to interact with their fans: on Twitter or on Facebook the audience can find not only the band's official tweets, but also Murdoc Niccals' (self-proclaimed 'leader' of the band) ill-humoured anticipations about the new album and flippant remarks about the star system.

In our cross-medial era we are not witnessing a fifth phase, but rather a recombination of the four phases listed above which are often drastically taken to their extremes. But if we consider masterpieces such as Chris Cunningham's celebrated video, *Come to Daddy* (directed in 1997), we could hardly imagine what can be done further.

A recent example: the greatest iconic androgynous body of the 80's, Grace Jones, made a return in 2008 with a new video, *Corporate Cannibal*, directed by Nick Hooker. Even if we can easily appreciate its sophisticated style, we can also state that from a semiotic point of view, it doesn't add anything new to the logic behind the representation and valorization of the body in music videos. The video develops a vision which, seemingly inspired by David Cronenberg's horror movie *Videodrome* (1983), doesn't appear as a prophecy anymore, but simply follows a tendency that has been explored all throughout the last decade: the audience is by now well used to morphing effects and to electronic transfigurations of the body (fig. 2).

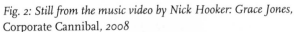
*Fig. 2: Still from the music video by Nick Hooker: Grace Jones,* Corporate Cannibal, 2008

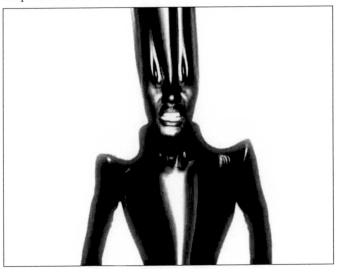

Though, of course this video in the end really fulfills its purpose: Jones looks terrifying, ferocious, vampiric, she demonstrates how an electronic body can still appear as so carnal.

If the music video directed by James Frost for Radiohead's song *House of Cards* (2008) and Michel Gondry's clip for Björk's song *Hyperballad* (1996) have taught us that electronic bodies are rather intangible, dematerialized, purer in a certain way, Jones insists upon her goal to dominate everything in a very physical and sensual way. She plays the role of a capitalistic vampire, an expression of Corporates she represents. She sings: "I'll consume my consumers, with no sense of humour."

In this new perspective, the aesthetics of music videos is faced with two different and opposed combinations of elements, two ways of representing the star. And the here resulting dichotomy is based upon the antithesis between the high grade of realism vs. the extreme fake.

The process of gaining the loyalty of an audience unavoidably passes through a choice: even though the end result must be the same maximum level of credibility towards the audience, this goal can be achieved in two ways:

## 1. Maximum Level of Fake

The music video deals with the artificiality of the music industry and is based on the creation of simulacra, playing with metatextuality, with constant cross-references between the text and its own context.

Spreading these new elements means creating noise, a buzz around the star, letting the treasure hunting of the fan become richer and richer. Building a story, a complex world around a star, means to build a labyrinth in which fans can playfully get lost. And it means for the performer to subtract him- or herself from the spotlight, to maintain privacy, to concentrate him- or herself on the creative work, to let simulacrum do the dirty job.

In this respect, the music video for Gnarls Barkley's song *Smiley Faces* (directed by Robert Hales in 2005) is a little masterpiece of video-musical experimentation. It doesn't simply play with the elegant recombination of musical footages. Rather, by cutting and pasting music icons and fragments of history, it sustains the claim of the two musicians for an original identity by paying homage to all the stars who had an influence on their music style.

The video opens with two weird characters, the phantasmal music historian Milton Pawley (interpreted by Dennis Hopper) interviewing Sven Rimwinkle, owner of the fictitious label A&R Fantaboulous Records. They introduce the spectator into a properly metatextual labyrinth where the existence of 'Gnarls Barkley' (here not considered as the band's name but as a real person) is at stake. Following the interview, a brief text "from the archives of Milton Pawley" introduces the video's first sequence which reveals itself as a proper video-musical mockumentary: the plausible (re-) construction of a fake music industry myth (fig. 3).

*Fig. 3: Still from the music video by Robert Hales: Gnarls Barkley, Smiley Faces, 2005*

Like new incarnations of Woody Allen's homonymous protagonist from his film *Zelig* (1983), the two musicians are crossing the whole history of pop music in a sequence of footage where they're digitally inserted next to icons such as Lou Reed, David Bowie, The Clash or Michael Jackson. From a semiotic point of view it is crucial to underline how this editing technique is strictly related to the music played by Gnarls Barkley which is structurally also based on samples and loops: the musical technique of the 'cut & paste' is thus metaphorically represented on a visual level.

As Maureen Turim writes:

"Many of the most intriguing music videos acknowledge a grand debt to historical avant-garde and progressive (in the usual sense of this term) art movements in all media. This debt is often acknowledged through citation. In other words, the past of the creative arts is not just 'appropriated' but also is reworked, and often it is clearly marked as intertextual reference, thus inviting viewers to make connections between the art making at present and its history." (Turim 2007: p. 89)

### 2. Maximum Grade of Authenticity

The video is supposed to be used as a sort of shop window in which the performance simple takes place without any added meaning. This is the case of most indie rock acts. Their credibility, their indie-cred, is communicated via a bare stripped execution. The music video here is back to its primary function: to document the performance and let the audience get familiar with the singer's face.

The Good the Bad and the Queen is a supergroup formed by Damon Albarn (Blur–Gorillaz), Paul Simonon (The Clash), Tony Allen (Fela Kuti), and Simon Tong (The Verve). In the music video for their song *Kingdom of Doom* (directed in 2007 by Giorgio Testi), they expose themselves in a very peculiar performance. Set in a small kitchen in West London, the musicians prepare a full English Breakfast, following instructions by a TV cooking program. The video, trying to provide the highest grade of realism, uses camera footage cut together with film images from Paul Simonon's mobile phone. Such a music video, so far from the usual clichés, allows these rock celebrities to boast their everyday life, celebrating paradoxically their own aura by undressing from their star garments (fig. 4).

*Fig. 4: Still from the music video by Giorgio Testi: The Good the Bad and the Queen,* Kingdom of Doom, *2007*

Authenticity is not an absolute truth. It is the result of a textual strategy, a simulation where all the elements contribute to recreate an effect of reality. Stars interact, interfere, and play with these materials, make fans feel involved, important, necessary. No matter if they (and their labels) decide to show themselves as a bare naked – honest – transparent band/performer, or if they decide to manufacture a whole fictional world to demonstrate how sincere they are concerning their own history.

New forms of devotion are more and more individual: fans can build up their own simulacra, play with props and objects, submit their own music videos, produce mash-ups, write fictions the star will then read.

Let's consider the so called 'mash-ups', ranging from fan generated videos which are becoming even more popular than the official versions of the music video, up to the "Mtv videoremixer", a new tool MTV provides for their online-users in order to easily combine video clips, still images, and effects into a unique video creation based on a popular music video. A proper contact between the star and the fan in real life is an utopia. But we have now many more tools in order to simulate such a contact and many levels in order to visualize this impossible interaction.[1]

At the end of this essay, let's try to answer the crucial question: is the music video in an aesthetic crisis?

Here, we can say that in the best examples an ideal balance between language experimentation and promotional strategies has been reached. Music videos became a strictly codified form. At the end of a long process the relationship between fans, musicians and record labels is redefined under a new rhetoric which is based on the illusion of a collective promotion: fans are thus asked to give their contribution to a strategy that is, however, unavoidably mediated by music industry business logics.

Probably in the future aesthetics will be characterized by micro changes, very subtle variants within a range of proofed effects and tested strategies.

Paradoxically, at the same time, the real margin of innovation won't be found in videos themselves, but outside, in the manifold media strategies videos will be involved in. Even if we start by stating that the budgets for the production of music videos will never be the same as in their golden age, and even if we state that we saw the end of the predominance of music television, we must not forget that music videos are the supplies the fans are asking for in order to be able to watch their idols, to be seduced by images and to be included in the star's fictional universe.

Music videos are increasingly becoming a form of dialogue, a means of a relationship between a star and his audience, a game where the star launches some clues and the fans reconstruct their sense and thus feel more and more involved, appreciated, powerful.

The band Nine Inch Nails literally involved their fans into a new entertainment form, an alternate reality game entitled *Year Zero*, named after their 2007 concept album and created by 42 Entertainment, the same group who designed the popular videogame Halo2. The game, expanding the album's storyline, provided fans with clues initially hidden on tour merchandise and then spread via websites, voicemail messages, murals, fliers and other real-world media. Fans were introduced into a network of fictitious, in-game messages from a futuristic, Orwellian setting. A treasure hunt led people to find USB drives hidden at NIN concert venues in Lisbon and Barcelona, containing the real prize, unreleased songs from the album.[2]

Fans can search the bands they like directly; they can vote and click and voice their own opinions; they can remix and mash up, they can take part in competitions, they can submit their own videos and finally they can reopen the music video semiotic structure.

This new path has been lead by seminal bands such as Radiohead and Nine Inch Nails with their fan-committed videos: for the promotion of their album *In Rainbows* in 2008, Radiohead launched a video contest in collaboration with the animation website AniBoom, inviting fans to create animated videos for any of the songs on the band's album.[3] Similarly, in the same year, Trent Reznor, the lead singer of the band Nine Inch Nails, announced a YouTube contest for fan-generated visuals in order to accompany his experimental album *Ghosts I-IV*.[4]

Therefore we face new strategies, borrowed from the viral and buzz marketing, based on the dynamics of word-of-mouth recommendation: the music video by Mathew Cullen for the song *Pork and Beans* by the band Weezer, produced in Spring 2008, is the first video which premiered exclusively not on a TV channel, but on YouTube, and the clip stars YouTube- and Internet-celebrities together with the band.[5]

The music video for *My Drive Thru*, a song commissioned by the shoe company Converse for their centennial "Three Artists, One Song" campaign from Julian Casablancas (The Strokes), Santigold and Pharrell Williams (The Neptunes), directed by Marie Hyon and Marco Spier and issued in July 2008, is the next step, where the promotional goal of such clips is clearly uncovered and openly exposed: a music video is financed by an iconic brand such as Converse, featuring a supergroup of three "All Stars" (a pun on Converse's most famous shoes name) which has been assembled for the occasion (fig. 5).

*Fig. 5: Still from the advertisement by Marie Hyon and Marco Spier: "Three Artists, One Song", My Drive Thru, 2008*

This video had a very strong impact (it is said to have been one of the top ten shared videos in its first day of release, with over 750,000 streams, and since it was also used afterwards in shortened versions for 30-second and 60-second cinema and television advertisements, it reached an even bigger audience: see Wikipedia-entry), certainly also achieved by the fact that here three famous and iconic musicians from different genres collaborated under the sign of an even stronger, uniting icon: a pair of shoes. The inherent metatextuality of the whole project is made evident in the music video by, for example, presenting the musicians (in tune with the general Converse-campaign's paper doll chain theme, where people were connected by their Converse shoes) as cut-out paper dolls (fig. 5). As fakes, in other words.

At the present the aesthetic of music videos is more than ever an open debate: it involves not only technologic innovation and digital dreamscapes, but also deeper dynamics where the body of the performer and the gaze of the viewer/reader collide, like two moving figures on a changing chessboard.

Let's have a look at a last example.

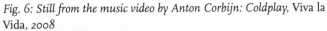

*Fig. 6: Still from the music video by Anton Corbijn: Coldplay,* Viva la
Vida, 2008

In summer 2008 the British band Coldplay accompanied their song *Viva la
Vida* with two music videos. Whereas the first, "official" video was directed
by Hype Williams, the musicians also ordered a second, alternate version
from Anton Corbijn.[6] Although coming from two different directors, both
videos are connected: Williams depicts the band performing in front of
blurred details from Eugène Delacroix' painting *Liberty Leading the People*
(1830; Paris, Louvre) which was also used for the cover image of the album
*Viva la Vida or Death and All His Friends*; the images of the music video
seem to have a cracked surface, similar to an old painting, and at the end of
the clip, the band members are shown, seemingly dissolving into flakes of
paint peeling off of their bodies. Corbijn's version also features the Delacroix-painting, but uses it in a different way – the video actually represents
a first-time-experiment insofar as a musician, Coldplay-leadsinger Chris
Martin, asked a famous director such as Corbijn, to do something no one
had ever done before: to (as the band clearly states on their website where
the music video can be seen) undertake the "attempt at a video cover version".[7] The music video covered here "out of love for Depeche Mode and
the genius of Anton Corbijn" (as the band states on their website) is the
famous clip for *Enjoy the Silence*, shot by Corbijn in 1990. While there Dave
Gahan was shown, dressed in a royal robe and wearing a crown, a deck-
chair under his arm, Martin in the video-cover is presented in the same
attire (fig. 6), wandering around in the surroundings of The Hague, but
now carrying the Delacroix-painting under his arm. Ultimately, both videos
represent an ironic, somewhat modern re-interpretation of Ernst H. Kantorowicz' seminal study on *The King's Two Bodies* where the author showed
that in medieval times the monarch was thought to have two bodies – an

ordinary mortal one, and another one, infused with a divine right that separated him from other mortal beings (Kantorowicz 1957).

## REFERENCES

**1** | See for this also the contribution by Jegl/Wetzel in this volume.
**2** | See http://en.wikipedia.org/wiki/Year_Zero_(game) (last access 12.1.2010).
**3** | See http://www.aniboom.com/Radiohead (last access 12.1.2010).
**4** | See http://www.youtube.com/group/ninghosts (last access 12.1.2010).
**5** | See for this also the introduction in this volume, p. 7.
**6** | Both videos can be viewed under http://www.coldplay.com/vivavideo1.php and http://www.coldplay.com/vivavideo2.php (last access 12.1.2010).
**7** | http://www.coldplay.com/vivavideo2.php (last access 12.1.2010).

## BIBLIOGRAPHY

Feineman, Neil (2000): "Introduction". In: Steven Reiss/Neil Feineman: *Thirty Frames per Second: The Visionary Art of the Music Video*, New York: Abrams p. 10-29.

Kantorowicz, Ernst H.: *The King's Two Bodies*, New Jersey: Princeton University Press 1957.

Keazor, Henry/Wübbena, Thorsten (2007²): *Video thrills the Radio Star. Musikvideos: Geschichte, Themen, Analysen*, Bielefeld: transcript.

Lewis, Luke (2009): 'Evident Utensil' - Chairlift's Mindblowing HD Video (20.2.2009). http://www.nme.com/blog/index.php?blog=121&title=chairlift_s_mindblowing_new_video&more=1&c=1&tb=1&pb=1 (Last assessed 2.1.2010).

Metz, Christian (1991): *L'énonciation impersonnelle, ou le site du film*, Paris: Klincksieck.

Beebe, Roger/Middleton, Jason (2007): "Introduction". In: Roger Beebe/Jason Middleton (eds.): *Medium Cool. Music Videos from Soundies to Cellphones*, Durham: Duke University Press, p. 1-12.

Peverini, Paolo (2001): "Il videoclip. Un'analisi dei dispositivi enunciativi". In: Isabella Pezzini (ed.): *Trailer, spot, clip, siti, banner. Le forme brevi della comunicazione audiovisiva*, Roma: Meltemi, p. 67-109.

Peverini, Paolo (2004): *Il videoclip. Strategie e figure di una forma breve*, Roma: Meltemi.

Peverini, Paolo (2005): "Ritmi e forme di un'audiovisione alterata". In: Gianfranco Marrone (ed.): *Sensi alterati. Droghe, musica, immagini*, Roma: Meltemi, p. 65-84.

Pozzato, Maria Pia (2006): "La pittura di Francis Bacon nel videoclip *Radio*. Lyrics, immagini, musica tra sincretismo e traduzione intersemiotica". In: Nicola Dusi/Lucio Spaziante (eds.): *Remix-remake. Pratiche di replicabilità*, Roma: Meltemi, p. 241-257.

Spaziante, Lucio (2007): *Sociosemiotica del pop*, Roma: Meltemi.

Turim, Maureen (2007): "Art/music/video.com". In: Roger Beebe/Jason Middleton (eds.): *Medium Cool. Music Videos from Soundies to Cellphones*, Durham: Duke University Press, p. 83-110.

Vernallis, Carol (2007): "Art/music/video.com". In: Beebe Roger, Middleton, Jason (eds.): *Medium Cool. Music Videos from Soundies to Cellphones*, Durham: Duke University Press, p. 111-151.

Wikipedia-entry "My Drive Thru": http://en.wikipedia.org/wiki/My_Drive_Thru (Last assessed 2.1.2010).

# Liquid Cosmos

## Movement and Mediality in Music Video

LAURA FRAHM

Music videos generate a liquid cosmos out of light reflections, fluid movements, and transformations of colors; they create visionary worlds that
expand and transcend our conceptions of temporality and spatiality. Any
attempt to grasp the specificity of music videos, then, has to part from
these assumptions; it has to take into account that music videos, above all,
are premised on the idea of *transformation* – of a transformation, however,
that is intrinsically linked to what I will call 'medial movement.' In my
paper, I will explore the interlinkages between mediality and movement
in music videos by focusing on three different aspects of 'medial movement.' In turning my view on the work of three music video directors
– Anton Corbijn, Chris Cunningham, and Floria Sigismondi –, I will highlight the potential of conceiving music videos through its reflecting, fluid,
and transformative forms of movement that, in their interplay, allow us to
reconsider the relationship between the mediality and the intermediality
of music video.

The transformability of music video, its potential to move beyond established spatiotemporal coordinates and to overcome the boundaries of
representation that is clearly addressed in these first assumptions, has
been discussed – sometimes explicitly, sometimes implicitly – from the
first essays on music videos through to the most recent publications, exhibitions, and television series on music videos.[1] Yet these initial observations on the transformability and self-reflexivity of music videos can even
be further developed. In my article, I will build on recent positions in the
discussion on the intermediality of music video in order to turn my view
on the question of music video's mediality. In other words: I will shift my
perspective from a notion of music video that is primarily defined by its
embeddedness into preexisting forms of artistic expression towards a perspective that defines music video as a medium in its own right.

If we look at the theory and history of music videos, we can observe
that scholars have always tended to extensively *compare* music videos to

other media and arts; particularly when attempting to define music video, the focus is often on a line of argument that links it to other media and arts – or more precisely, points to the interrelations and correspondences with feature films and short films, with art and video art, with comics and advertising that validate music video's inherent intermediality.[2] The definition of music video, then, seems to be intrinsically linked to the question of how it positions and articulates itself within the context of other media and art forms.

This perspective on the intermedial exchanges and interdependences of the video has been highly fruitful and opened up new ways of 'looking at music.'[3] In the following, however, I will explore and sound out the potential of another perspective, of an opposing line of argument that rather focuses on music video's specific mediality, that's to say, on those forms of (what I will call) 'medial movement,' that is, the unique configurations of image, text, and sound in which the video reflects on its own medial conditions. The works of Anton Corbijn, Chris Cunningham, and Floria Sigismondi, as I will argue, develop their potential precisely from this dual movement, drawing both on the complex interactions with other arts and media, and on the video's own medial expressions. In their videos, the reference to other media and artistic forms is always visible – from photography to video installations to painting; yet at the same time they develop distinctive, singular forms of 'medial movement.' In their videos, they explore a liquid cosmos that is constantly transformed by its own specific movements; they explore singular worlds that are composed out of light reflections, fluid movements, and transformations of colors, thus stimulating new visions and, what is more, raising a new awareness of the transformability and self-reflexivity of music video.

## I.   FAMILIAR WORLDS? OBSERVATIONS ON THE INTERMEDIALITY OF MUSIC VIDEO

The medium video initially originated from a complex multimedia system, which is crucial to understanding its inherent dynamics and especially its high degree of interdependency with other media. The medium video emerged and developed during a period of media history that is largely characterized, according to Yvonne Spielmann, "by processes of linking, mixing, and layering".[4] This aspect is crucial, because these external processes of linking, mixing, and layering are in turn deeply incorporated into the music video, in a way that they are articulated both *inward*, in its threefold substructure of image, text, and sound, and *outward*, in its continuous referral to other forms of arts and media.

As a result, recent research on music video has proceeded to treat image, text, and sound as equally essential elements of music video analysis, while at the same time claiming an increasing attentiveness of video's complex associations, references, and recursiveness (see in this respect

Keazor/Wübbena 2007; Weiß 2007; Vernallis 2004). Yet this balanced, considerate approach was by no means self-evident in the history of music video research. On the contrary, the wide range of early essays on music videos in fields like music journalism, early media studies, and (critical) cultural theory in fact bear witness to a rigorous questioning or even irretrievable negation of this new form of audiovisual expression (for some representative examples see Neumann 1983 and Rauh 1985), rightly subsumed by Ulrich Wenzel under the category of the so called 'deficit hypothesis:' "Especially absences are attributed to music video, like the absence of narrative coherency and continuity, or the inconsistencies between the song text, musical form, and film-aesthetic realization."[5] In contrast to this reduction of music video to a mere play with different narrative strands and visual fragments, some scholars – primarily in the field of postmodern theory – have markedly embraced and elaborated on the possibilities of music video's intermediality, highlighting its potential to combine and to reassemble the most diverse forms of artistic expression.[6]

Intermedial theory has always formed a crucial part of scholarship on the music video. Most importantly, it provided the opportunity to explore the many-layered historiography of the music video, dating back to the very first attempts at visual music and spreading out to the heterogeneous precursors of music television, from the sound slides of the 1890s to the Scopitones of the 1960s and 1970s.[7] Intermedial theory shaped the basic conditions of the video, and at the same time, it raised an awareness of its complex references and correlations. At least since the early 1990s, several publications on music video show the effort to emphasize the video's intermedial aspects: on the one hand, by constantly relating music to its visual aspects, to a 'visual sound' (see Moritz 1987 and Hausheer/Schönholzer 1994) and, on the other hand, by gradually introducing a 'musicology of the image'.[8]

Yet the concept of intermedia is even more complex than these first explorations of music video's referentiality might suggest, because the notion of intermediality incorporates distinctive levels and phenomena. Following remarks by Irina O. Rajewsky, we can distinguish three different phenomena of intermediality: The first is the phenomenon of *media combination*, which is "based on the addition of at least two medial systems conventionally perceived as distinct".[9] The second is the phenomenon of *media shift*, which refers to the "production process of the media product, that is, the process of transformation of a media-specifically fixated 'pre'-text resp. 'text'-substrate into another medium",[10] and the third phenomenon is that of *intermedial references*, indicating a referential process within the interpretation structure, where a medial product establishes a connection to another medium *via* the system.[11] These three characteristic traits of intermediality all come together, in varying degrees and consequences, in the music video: firstly, in its combination of elements from film and video art, from comics and advertising; secondly, in its visualization of the constant shift between its different referential sources; and, closely interlinked with that, thirdly, in its intermedial references to particular media and art forms. As a result, music videos emerge from a vivid process of media mixing and layering, most basically enhanced by its intermedial substructure of image, text, and sound.

Against the backdrop of this multilayered intermediality, it is impossible to conceive the relationship between the music video and other arts and media as mono-directional or even hierarchical. As Henry Keazor and Thorsten Wübbena have pointed out in *Video thrills the Radio Star*, it is about time – given the recent developments in music video production – to renounce "the often postulated model (...) according to which the small, quick, and dirty music video is sister to and inspiration for the bold innovations of its brother, the big, ponderous, and expensive feature film".[12] The parasitic relationship between 'cannibal' (as attributed to music video) and 'victim' (as attributed to its cultural sources) has meanwhile reversed or become increasingly indistinguishable (see Keazor/Wübbena 2007: p. 318 and Keazor/Wübbena 2006) while, at the same time, a special emphasis is placed on music video's mutual reciprocity and interaction with its medial and cultural references.

Positioning the music video thus in the middle of a highly differentiated media system is very productive, inasmuch as it foregrounds video's own complexity and heterogeneity. Nevertheless, the prevalent process of defining music video *in relation to* other arts and media, that's to say, the overall premise of *comparison* also runs the risk of coming to a halt, of reaching its inherent limits. Because, pointedly worded, the only thing we will encounter, at the end, are the 'familiar worlds' of intermedia, that is, the well acquainted system of medial traits and complex allusions, reassuring the music video's affiliation with and embeddedness into the system. To be more precise, comparing music video in such a way will provide us with manifold and fruitful insights on its similarities and differences to other arts and media – yet as much as the video can be understood from this perspective, and as much as there is a desire to define it by comparing it to those media and art forms to which it is, without any question, recurrantly referring to, the specific *medial quality* of the music video remains elusive, which is articulated, as I will argue in the following, particularly by its reflexive figures of 'medial movement.' And it is exactly this 'elusiveness' of video that points to a crucial aspect of the video, as Thomas Mank has once observed: The category 'video' virtually eludes any classification, because "at closer consideration, the concept of 'video' reveals the vexing quality of actually not conforming to any connotations and definitions."[13]

## II. Moving Spaces and the Mediality of Music Video

In order to grasp the elusive category of the video, it is most promising, as I have argued earlier, to start with the idea of *transformation*. In the following, I will suggest an approach to music video that adapts some of the most basic assumptions in new media theory and media philosophy to the question of the mediality of music video. To be sure, turning the back on the question of intermediality in order to accentuate the mediality of music video is by no means a negation of the productive aspects of music video's intermediality. On the contrary, the intermedial aspects will serve as an inevitable basis and as a starting point as I shift my perspective towards the mediality of the video, or more precisely, to those reflexive images, in which music videos not only point at other media but rather reflect on their own medial potentials of transformation, of 'medial movement.'

This shift of perspective towards the mediality of music video draws on a basic axiom in new media theory; it proceeds on the assumption that videos, like all media, obtain "their status as a scientific object – that is, an object that can be systematized – precisely because they store, process, and convey under conditions they themselves create and are."[14] As a consequence, any access to the mediality of music video is to be found exclusively under these self-generated, inherent medial conditions. It is most important to note, however, that this focus on mediality does not aim at any kind of ontology of the music video. On the contrary, scholars in the field of new media theory have most convincingly shown in recent years that there 'are' no media, that is, a fixed concept of media that is capable of defining the 'essence' or the 'nature' of media.[15] Instead, media are conceived as complex configurations of practices and processes, or, as Eva Horn puts it, they fully unfold their potential as they invoke the concept of 'becoming' media: "Theorizing media thus means not so much analyzing a given, observable object, as engaging with processes, transformations, and events" (Horn 2007: p. 8.).

In the context of music video, the key concepts of process and transformation – being two of the most advanced concepts not only in media theory in general, but also in the fields of media philosophy, cultural history, and spatial theory[16] – are inextricably linked, as I will show, to the question of 'medial movement.' Yet the concept of movement, again, is manifold and polysemous in view of the music video. On a most basic level, we could say that music videos perform 'movements in space,' encompassing a broad range of movements such as the *rhythmic movements* of the dancers and performers, the *animated movements* of figures and objects, and the *abstract movements* of lights and colors. Yet, music videos are not only able to produce certain 'movements in space,' but rather they have the potential to generate self-reflexive, relational images and transitions, converting these 'movements in space' into genuinely 'moving spaces.'[17] In other words, the idea of movement – be it rhythmic, animated, or abstract – is deeply inherent to the concept of the music video.[18] Yet these ideas can even be further developed, because if we take a closer look at the broad range of music videos, we cannot only detect, from time to time, the emergence of genuinely 'moving spaces,' but beyond that there seem to be different layers of 'medial movement,' which transcend the actual movement, or more precisely, which closely interlink the idea of movement with the epistemic question of mediality.

In order to delineate and to specify these unique 'medial movements' of the music video, it is most useful to return to Yvonne Spielmann's statements about the video as a medium. Because the video, according to Spielmann, can be understood as a fundamentally reflexive medium in that "unlike traditional visual media, it processually unfolds both dimensionality and directionality and produces transformative forms of imagery."[19] Thus, Spielmann emphasizes the reflexive, the processual, and the transformative as three key characteristics of this particular medium.[20] As a matter of fact, Spielmann develops these concepts in view of video art and video installations; however, applied to the field to music video and the concept of 'medial movement,' these three traits – in their interplay – seem to reveal something of music video's specific mediality. For the singular 'world of the music video'[21] is permeated by manifold nuances of movements: by reflecting and glowing, by flashing and sparkling, by shifting and fluctuating movements that emanate from its most basic, threefold structure – the processual development of music, the progress of and reference to the lyrics, the dynamics and rhythmic of the visual.[22]

Taking up and enhancing these ideas, I will distinguish three specific, distinct forms of 'medial movement.' The first movement is a *reflexive and reflective movement*, which plays with the composition of light and light reflections, most basically alluding to its origins in the moving light picture. We might find this reflective movement of light in music videos that involve light performance shows, like for example Lenny Kravitz' *Are You Gonna Go My Way* (Mark Romanek, 1993) or Audioslave's *Cochise* (Mark Romanek, 2002), which show a continuous play with light figures and formations, adding up, especially in the case of *Cochise*, to a visual excess of flickering lights and bursting fireworks. Yet apart from these performance videos, there also exists a most remarkable series of music videos that reveal an iridescent, shimmering light, which is flowing, twisting, and turning all through the setting, as put into effect, for example, in the music videos by LynnFox[23] for Björk's *Nature is Ancient* (2002) and, even more notably, for Björk's *Oceania* (2004), where the shimmering pinpoints of light are unfolding under the surface of the water, surrounded by corals and jellyfishes while vividly streaming all across the ocean.

Especially with regard to *Oceania*, it is almost impossible to draw the borderline to the second facet of 'medial movement,' that is, a *processual, fluid movement*, which does not only refer to the actual display of water – although music videos often seem to be pervaded by dropping waters, sparkling sea surfaces, and ever-expanding oceans –, but also alludes to a certain fluid quality of the moving elements in the video. The immanent fluidity of music video, its potential to simultaneously enact formations and transformations of fluid material, is certainly most strikingly performed in Busta Rhymes' and Janet Jackson's *What's it Gonna Be* (Hype Williams, 1999). Yet there are also other facets of fluidity in the video, ranging from the actual capacity of water to exceed space, like the giant rising 'M' emerging from the ocean in Missy Elliott's *She's a Bitch* (Hype Williams, 1999), through to a total abstraction of fluid movement that is most purely performed by a couple of floating lines in a black environment, like in Björk's *Unravel* (LynnFox, 2003), most basically alluding to lines in a stave set in motion and hovering through an impalpable space.

The third facet of 'medial movement' in the video is a *reshaping, transforming movement*, which refers to the potential of music video to completely transcend time and space, creating new worlds of colors and abstractions, but most importantly: to visualize the very process of its own transformation. The interlinkage of color and transformation is a crucial aspect in the music video; because on the one hand, we often find a monochrome imagery that generates unprecedented settings, relocating the performer within an 'otherworld.' Such a monochrome imagery characterizes, for instance, Mark Romanek's music videos, with probably the most memorable examples being Janet Jackson's *Got 'Til It's Gone* (1997) and, above all, Johnny Cash's *Hurt* (2002).[24] Yet the transformative power of color, on the other hand, can also be enacted through abstraction of colors that are pulsating and varying according to the rhythms of the music, ranging from Daft Punk's famous *Around the World* (Michel Gondry, 1997) to Beck's *Mixed Bizness* (Stéphane Sednaoui, 2000), from Kylie Minogue's *It's in Your Eyes* (Dawn Shadforth, 2002) to Coldplay's *Speed of Sound* (Mark Romanek, 2005), where we find a vibrant spectrum of movements, oscillating between the nuances of light and the nuances of color.[25]

These three forms of 'medial movement' in the video – light movements, fluid movements, and color movements – will be examined in more detail in the following sections where I will explore the video works of three different music video directors. The music videos by Anton Corbijn, Chris Cunningham, and Floria Sigismondi, which I would like to highlight in this context, could be regarded as essential and highly influential variations on the reflexive, the processual, and the transforming movement of music video, as each of them centers on a specific quality of movement that is condensed into particular figures – into figures, whose specific value largely derives from the overall attempt of subtly balancing the possibilities of intermediality that, at all times, remain visible in their videos. Yet at the same time, they show the decided effort to go beyond intermedial references in order to generate new, unique forms of expression, thus accentuating and foregrounding the potential of 'medial movement' in the video.

## III. ANTON CORBIJN: MOVEMENTS OF LIGHT, REFLECTIONS OF LIGHT

Anton Corbijn's videos, to start with, can be interpreted as a variation on the reflective and reflexive movement of music video. In his continuous reference to photography, with which Corbijn started his career in the early 1970s (see Görner 2003: p. 66-76), his videos unremittingly experiment with the qualities and modalities of light. The grainy black-and-white aesthetics and the monochrome colors lend his videos a particular, identifiable visuality.[26] In his music videos, he often creates a succession of moving light images that, at all times, sustain their tangible reference to the photographic medium. This technique becomes most basically evident in one of his early video works, David Sylvian's *Red Guitar* (1984), because here, we find two overlapping spatial orders of motionless individual figures on the one hand, which are scanned and encircled by the camera, while on the other hand, the surrounding clouds and mist are continually moving – sometimes slowly, sometimes rapidly – all through the setting, thus contrasting the two qualities of movement: halted motion and continued motion. In Corbijn's music video for Depeche Mode's *Barrel of a Gun* (1996), to give a second example of his playing with the medial differences between photography and film, the visible, circular frame of the camera constantly alludes to a photographical camera lens, while at the same time oscillating between the unbound movement of film and the arrested movement of photography.

Corbijn's explorations of the music video, his experiments with the sounding and moving image, always reveal a glimpse of photography,[27] while his photographic work, in turn, possesses cinematic qualities to the extent that his photos always seem to represent a rhythmic segment that has been extracted from an overarching movement.[28] The borders between photography and video are fluid in Corbijn's work; they enter into a productive exchange, as both media influence each other and change each other's characteristic traits. Moreover, in Corbijn's photography as well as in his video work, both halted motion and continued motion are always manifested as a play of light and a movement of light. Yet while in his photographs, the nuances of light, as Brian Eno emphasizes in his essay on Corbijn's photographical series *Star Trak*, "create an enchanted sculptural stillness – like in those Maya Deren films where time seems to have become viscous" (Eno 1996, without pagination), his videos by contrast create a particular form of 'medial movement,' which exceeds the boundaries of (animated) photography. Instead, they reveal a reflective and reflexive movement that reaches beyond the difference between halted motion and continued motion, as I will show in the case of U2's *Electric Storm* (2002).

In Corbijn's videos the reflective and the reflexive quality of light are closely intertwined and cannot be conceived separately. Especially in the case of *Electrical Storm*, these two facets of light are constantly intersecting. In the narrative passages of this video, telling the love story between a mermaid and a young man, the imagery is utterly imbued with light reflections and modulations of light (fig. 1).

*Fig. 1: Still from the music video by Anton Corbijn:*
U2, Electric Storm, 2002

In the glitter of light reflecting on the surface of the water, in the continual flickering of lamps in sparsely lit archways, and in the subtle reflections of light on the faces of the figures, space seems to break down gradually. Moreover, in the process of this continuous variation on the (moving) qualities of light, space itself ultimately becomes a fraction of light that culminates, at the end of the music video, in the fireworks above the ocean's horizon, where the young man returns the mermaid to her natural surroundings. In this process, the constant oscillation of light between its own luminance and its potential to generate light reflections leads to a reflection on the potential of the video to generate its own, singular moving spaces of light.

In *Electric Storm*, Corbijn utilizes the entire spectrum of light, which pervades many of his videos, being a core element of his ingenious video aesthetics. His videos often seem to completely dissolve into light figures and light reflections that are variegated in the most different ways, as for example in the theatrical, stage like arrangement in Mercury Rev's *Opus 40* (1999), where the band is endued with luminous clothes and astronaut suits, reflecting the light sources, installed at the edge of the stage. But certainly the most impressive and memorable figure of Corbijn's light images is the light bulb suit in Depeche Mode's *Barrel of a Gun*, which condenses his reflections on the moving quality of light into a certain, tangible form (fig. 2).

*Fig. 2: Still from the music video by Anton Corbijn: Depeche Mode, Barrel of a Gun, 1996*

In Anton Corbijn's videos, to sum up, light is subject to a continuous variation, while at the same time, his videos reflect on their own preconditions as a medium, as moving light images – since here, light appears not only as light design or light sculpture, but as a polymorphic movement of light that reveals the intrinsic potential of the video to create light rhythms and light reflections. Corbijn continually explores the possibilities of music video in stretching its inherent boundaries towards a moving space of light that transcends and defies any established spatial coordinates. In his imaginative video aesthetics, he reshapes the music video in introducing new forms of reflective movements that form a vital part of the liquid cosmos of music video.

## IV. CHRIS CUNNINGHAM: FLUID MOVEMENTS, FLUCTUATING WORLDS

A specific, recurrent form of medial movement also characterizes Chris Cunningham's videos. Yet in contrast to Corbijn's work, Cunningham's videos do not primarily revolve around the constant play with the shifting trias of light, reflection, and movement, but rather with the aesthetics of water and fluids. His video works can be conceived as a permanent reflection about a world that is in a state of endless flux. He creates unique settings that are ever shifting and ever changing, relentlessly reshaping our conceptions of space in foregrounding its potential of transformation, while, at the same time, most precisely orchestrating the movements according to the music.[29] Thus, examining the qualities and potentials of fluid movement is a core element in Cunningham's work and can be regarded as a line connecting his music videos and his video installations.[30] Especially in his music videos, fluid movements can assume the most diverse shapes. Firstly, the movements can be related to the entire spatial composition, creating an environment of flux and fluidity, as I will explain using the example of the video *Only You* by Portishead (1997). Secondly, fluid movements can condense into liquids that are spreading out and flowing all through the space of the music video, such as in *All is Full of Love* by Björk (1999). Thirdly and finally, fluid movements can be abstracted and related to a certain quality of movement as they are assigned to presumably fixed, immovable objects, as I will discuss regarding Madonna's video *Frozen* (1998).

In *Only You*, fluidity is inscribed in and performed through the entire spatial environment. Here, the tight, sparsely lit gap between the two houses seems to be strangely filled with water.[31] The figures – a young, twelve-year old boy and Portishead's singer Beth Gibbons – move through a spatial vacuum as if moving through water. *Only You* creates a peculiar world, where any spatial causality is undermined as the video unfolds in strange, impossible movements within a limitless, watery space. Moreover, the motion of the figures is repeatedly slowed, stretched, and extended, creating an uncanny, trance-like atmosphere. Sometimes following, sometimes crisscrossing the interrupted rhythm of the music, the slowed down motion in this video unites the two figures in an enigmatic, elegiac dance. In this context, *Only You* most clearly bears reference to Cunningham's installation *flex* (fig. 3), which formed part of his exhibition at the Venice Biennial in 2001 (see Keazor/Wübbena 2007: p. 320).

*Fig. 3: Still from the video installation by Chris Cunningham:* flex, *2001*

Because in *flex*, we find a similar setting of water, where two figures – a man and a woman – are utterly intertwined and floating through a fluid space. Yet in contrast to *Only You*, the fluid movements in *flex* are carried to an extreme, unleashing an excessive acceleration and increasing violence of the bodies' movements.

Whereas the water in *Only You* and *flex* gains its strange, unsettling quality because it leaves no visible trace, it takes on a very different quality in Björk's award-winning video *All is Full of Love*.[32] Because in the latter, the water is no longer dim, lit only here and there, spreading to fill the entire space, but rather, it coagulates into a milky, thick, and opaque fluid. It flows over the equipment and hinges, penetrates the machine's windings, and drips onto the milky white floor. Moreover, the fluid in *All is Full of Love* develops a processual quality, being directly and visibly incorporated into the scenario of the post human creation of two androgynous androids played simultaneously by Björk (fig. 4).

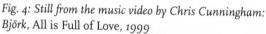

*Fig. 4: Still from the music video by Chris Cunningham: Björk,* All is Full of Love, *1999*

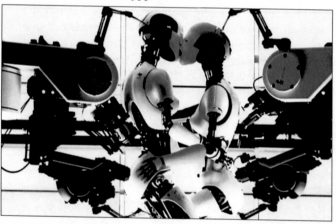

Advancing and abstracting this idea, we could say that the fluid movement in *All is Full of Love* refers to an overarching process of transformation, which the video both engenders and performs, while at the same time logics of motion are subverted and reduced to absurdity since a closer inspection reveals that all of the fluids are actually flowing backwards.

Fluid movements in Cunningham's work, as these first examples illustrate, are not confined to simply displaying fluidity or the fluid quality of movement, but rather, Cunningham tends to carry them to their limits: on the one hand, in slowing down movement to its (potential) stagnation, and on the other hand, in reversing and counteracting its immanent nature of flowing. Yet there exists a third aspect to fluid movement in Cunningham's work: a movement that both generates and distributes its own processual, transformative quality. As we can already observe in *Only*

*You*, individual elements – such as a shoelace or a scarf – begin developing their own qualities of movement, as they seem to be led through the water by a ghostly hand. In Madonna's video *Frozen*, however, the large panels of cloth that gather and wind around Madonna gain an even more obvious independent movement quality, or, as Keazor and Wübbena have put it, "the black fabric that flows in folds over the floor oscillates between a stable and a fluid state."[33] This transition from stability to fluidity is crucial, because it demonstrates that in this video even solid, presumably fixed materials and objects are always, at any given moment, being related to a fluid movement; every new formation, to carry on these thoughts, of the flowing fabric as well as every (human or animal) transformation that is performed in this video, only define a momentary, transitional state that will soon be subject to the next, completely reshaping transformation.

In conclusion, both Chris Cunningham's video installations and music videos perform the most different facets of fluid movement; yet they are all converging in the fact that their movements are seemingly endless, suspending any absolute endpoint. Because in their fluid quality they always refer to the processual, to the emerging, and to the 'becoming,' as their elements only gain a momentary state of fixation. Thus, fluid movements in Cunningham's work accumulate to an overall fluctuating, liquid world, which is permeated by those transformative, self-reflexive images that immediately arouse a reflection on the processual quality of the medium video.

## V. FLORIA SIGISMONDI: TRANSFORMATIVE COLORS, TRANSFORMATIVE WORLDS

In Floria Sigismondi's videos, to close the circle, we find a third aspect of 'medial movement,' which possesses a shaping and reshaping, a transformative quality. But transformation, according to Sigismondi's work, unfolds in two distinct, yet closely interlaced directions. The first type addresses the shape of figures, that is, of those transformed and transformative bodies that pervade all of Sigismondi's work, as can be seen, on the one hand, in her photographic works collected in the volumes *Redemption* (1999) and *Immune* (2005). Yet on the other hand, the mutation and transformation of bodies is also a recurring topic of her music videos, with probably the most memorable examples being the deformed creatures disfigured by equipment and clamps in the videos of Marilyn Manson *The Beautiful People* (1996) and *Tourniquet* (1996).

These traits of bodily transformation reveal much of Sigismondi's aesthetics – both in her videos and in her photography, which are deeply influenced by the aesthetics of painting, sculpture, and theatrical settings.[34] As Steve Reiss and Neil Feineman have pointed out, in her work, Sigismondi "pulls theatrical and dramatic imagery from Italian opera and Greek mythology, saturates it with color, and then builds what she calls 'entropic underworlds inhabited by tortured souls and omnipotent beings'" (Reiss/Feineman 2000: p. 234). In the following, I will turn my attention to another type of transformation present in her work that addresses her ingenious, creative, and sometimes even disturbing use of color: the bright, dusty, and shimmering palette of colors undeniably characteristic of Sigismondi's videos, both evoking and modifying the vigorous colorfulness of her photography.[35]

In the video for the group Sigur Rós' *Untitled I (Vaka)* (2003), every natural color palette seems to be discarded. Like a scene of creation, the clip begins with a bright red sky littered with falling stars and comets, as if the world was being completely recreated in the colors of red and black. For the world presented in *Untitled I (Vaka)* is an uncanny universe of grotesque colors that begins with a seemingly innocent scene of children playing in a kindergarten. Yet, already at this point of the video, there arises an underlying and pervasive sense of otherness: black blood flows across the floor as the children are inspected by their guardians, and when they look out the window, they see a world that is completely immersed in luminescent red (fig. 5).

*Fig. 5: Concept/production photo footage from the music video by Floria Sigismondi: Sigur Rós, Untitled I (Vaka), 2003*

The moment they go outside, the children turn into strange figures that frolic through a black, dusty, and powdery snow wearing gas masks and triggering off their violent play of car destruction, which ends with the death of one of the children, while the black snow and the red sky above are evolving into the most bizarre, disturbing color scenario.

While the world in *Untitled I (Vaka)* bursts into strong contrasting colors that seem to completely dissolve spatial coordinates, the color in Martina Topley Bird's *Anything* (2003) is totally eradicated (fig. 6, right). And out of this negation of color, there arises a pitch-black world where the only source of illumination is the light reflecting off the body of the singer, being entirely covered with shimmering diamonds. In subtle accordance with the fluttery rhythm of the music, the black shiny pieces of fabric blow with the wind through the sky and gather around her body like a dense cocoon – markedly alluding to the ever-flowing movement of fabric in Madonna's *Frozen* – as the transformation of color is developing into a meticulous modulation of black. In *Anything*, Sigismondi creates an iridescent scenario, where the entire spectrum of color shadows and color formations originates from one single color: from the color of black.[36]

The specific quality of Sigismondi's videos is that she interlinks the notion of processuality with a processual use of colors; of colors, which are not simply 'there' – whether they are alienated or not – but whose *transformation* is visualized in the course of video. In *Untitled I*, the window-panes in the kindergarten are gradually and visibly turning into red as the children look out for the black snow. And in Christina Aguilera's *Fighter* (2003) we can observe a threefold transformation of the color scheme. At first, there is the black world of the cocoon, where strange black figures balance themselves on stilts, until the environment gradually turns into a white, fluttering dustiness.

*Fig. 6: Concept/production photo footage from the music videos: Christina Aguilera,* Fighter *(left), and Martina Topley Bird,* Anything *(right), both 2003*

In this second, transitory state, we follow the transformation of the cocoon into a butterfly, being attached to a giant white lattice at the wall and surrounded by white butterflies (fig. 6, left), while, at the end of this transformation, we return to the black setting that starts to be intermittently covered with red fields and red layers of color.

The transformative potential of color, to sum up, is a crucial aspect in Sigismondi's videos; and maybe it is most impressively revealed in her music video for Tricky's *Makes Me Wanna Die* (1997), where the different layers of vibrant color are split up, multiplying and distorting the figures that, as a result, are suddenly overlapping within an uncanny space of constant mutation. This aspect is crucial, because what these examples most clearly show is that in contrast to Floria Sigismondi's photography, her music videos reveal the potential of transferring the *play* with different colors into a visible and processual *transformation* through color movement, which affects both the figures and the entire environment, thus reflecting on the potential of transgressing and transforming color images to fundamentally reshape the liquid cosmos of music video.

## VI. CONCLUSION: THE LIQUID COSMOS OF MUSIC VIDEO

The world of music video is a world of rhythmic, pulsating, and vibrant movements. It is a liquid cosmos that is continually transformed by its own particular configurations of image, text, and sound; by configurations, however, which are first and foremost articulated through forms of movement. Yet the concept of movement, as I have pointed out in this article, has to be specified, because music videos do not only display the most diverse forms of rhythmic, animated, or abstract movement, but they produce a distinct, multi-layered quality of 'medial movement' that differs significantly from other arts and media. In other words, the processual development of music, the progress of and reference to the lyrics, and the dynamics and rhythmic of the visual are generating – in their interplay – certain forms of 'medial movement,' each of them combining a specific aspect of the videos's mediality with a specific aspect of movement: the reflexive movement of light, the processual movement of fluids, and the transformative movement of color. This trias of 'medial movement' is crucial, because if we sharpen our view on these three particular movements of the video, we will find the liquid cosmos of music video to be virtually overflowing with light reflections, fluid movements, and transformations of color.

The music videos by Anton Corbijn, Chris Cunningham, and Floria Sigismondi that I have examined in more detail are decisive in this context in as much as they not merely display light movements, fluid movements, and color movements, but rather entangle the display of movement with a reflection on their mediality. That's to say, the continuous light reflections in Corbijn's videos, the fluids in Cunningham's work, and the color transformations in Sigismondi's videos can be interpreted in terms of their singularity and inventiveness; yet, at the same time, they reveal the inherent linkage between movement and mediality in the video. They refer to the video's potential to generate visible *transformations* that emerge from the *processual* quality of the video, while at the same time initiating an overall *reflection* – via the reciprocal production of image, text, and sound, via the reflection of the transformative potential of lights, fluids, and colors, and, not least, via balancing the tension between the intermediality and the mediality of the music video.

The shift of perspective towards movement and mediality in the music video that is articulated, as I have argued, by those transformative, self-reflexive images where the video reflects on its own medial conditions as a medium, can be considered as an attempt to further develop and to expand the question of intermediality. Needless to say, the ideas and assumptions presented in this article are only a few starting points for the overarching question of the mediality of music video that still need further elaboration. Nevertheless, the forms of producing light, of movements of fluids and the flowing, and the transformations of color already reveal a glimpse of these singular moments of medial reflection in the video. They reveal different layers of 'medial movement,' which transcend the actual movement in closely linking the idea of movement with the question of mediality. Yet most crucially, these aspects of 'medial movement' may pave the way towards defining music video as a medium in its own right – of a medium that, above all, constantly reflects on its own potential of transformation.

## REFERENCES

**1** | In this context, the television series *Fantastic Voyages* (Christoph Dreher and Rotraut Pape, ZDF/3Sat 2000) was crucial in exploring the unique 'cosmos' of this medium, like in "A Cosmology of Music Video," "Wonderful Worlds" and "Space is the Place". As to the early publications on music videos, Rainer Winter and H. J. Kagelmann summarize four main characteristics that are prevalent in early music video research, all of which are underlining the video's high degree of aesthetic complexity: (1) acceleration, (2) associative images, (3) self-referentiality, and (4) postmodern art form; see Winter/Kagelmann 1997: p. 210-211.

**2** | In the past years, especially music video exhibitions took up on the question of the intermedial exchanges between video, art, and commercials; see for example the video exhibition at the NRW Forum Düsseldorf, January 1–April 18, 2004; catalogue: Poschardt 2003.

**3** | See in this context the recent exhibition at MoMA, New York, *Looking at Music. Media Art of the 60s* (August 13, 2008–January 5, 2009) curated by Barbara London, which points at the dynamic relations between early 'mixed media' works and visual music from the mid-1960's to the mid-1970's.

**4** | Spielmann 1998: p. 8: "(...) durch Prozesse der Koppelung, Vermischung und Überlagerung (...)".

**5** | Wenzel 1999: p. 45: "Vorzugsweise *Abwesendes* scheint man aus den Clips herauslesen zu können, etwa die Absenz von narrativer Einheit und Kontinuität, oder auch Inkonsistenzen zwischen gesungenem Text, musikalischer Form und filmästhetischer Umsetzung."

**6** | Already in the mid-1980's, Bódy and Weibel have addressed music video as an independent art from; see Bódy/Weibel 1987; for postmodern theory and music video, see Frith/Goodwin/Grossberg 1993, especially the articles by Straw 1993 and Grossberg 1993; the question of a postmodern 'anti-aesthetic' is addressed in Kaplan 1987: p. 33-48; for a reasoned critique on postmodern theory and music television, see Goodwin 1992, especially chapter 7: "Aesthetics and Politics in Music Television: Postmodernism Reconsidered", p. 156-180.

**7** | See Beebe/Middleton 2007, Krüger/Weiß 2008, Keazor/Wübbena 2010, especially the articles by Glöde 2008 and de la Motte-Haber 2008.

**8** | See Goodwin 1992: p. 49-71. In his book, Goodwin conducts a considerate approach to this question in that he highlights the importance of a "*musicological* analysis of visual imagery" (p. 50) on the one hand, while on the other hand conceding that there is also a "prior visual moment that demands some investigation: this is the phenomenon of *synaesthesia*, (...) when one pictures sounds in one's 'mind's eye".

**9** | Rajewsky 2002: p. 15: "(...) *Medienkombination* (...) Addition mindestens zweier, konventionell als distinkt wahrgenommener medialer Systeme (...)."

**10** | Rajewksy 2002: p. 16: "*Medienwechsel* (...) den Produktionsprozeß des medialen Produkts, also den Prozeß der Transformation eines medienspezifisch fixierten Prätextes bzw. Textsubstrats in ein anderes Medium (...)."

**11** | Rajewksy 2002: p. 17: "*Intermediale Bezüge*".

**12** | Keazor/Wübbena 2007: p. 248: "(...) jenes gerne postulierte Modell (...), demzufolge die kleine, schmutzige und schnelle Schwester Musikvideo dem großen, behäbigen und teuren Bruder Spielfilm die kühnen Innovationen einhaucht."

**13** | Mank 1994: p. 21: "(...) (b)ei näherer Betrachtung offenbart der Begriff 'Video' die verwirrende Eigenschaft, sämtliche Konnotationen und Definitionen eigentlich nicht zu sein."

**14** | Engell/Vogl 2002: p. 10: "(...) ihren Status als wissenschaftliches, d. h. systematisierbares Objekt gerade dadurch (gewinnen), daß sie das, was sie speichern, verarbeiten und vermitteln, jeweils unter Bedingungen stellen, die sie selbst schaffen und sind".

**15** | See the special issue of the *Grey Room* on 'New German Media Theory,' especially addressed in the introduction Horn 2007.

**16** | For the field of media philosophy, see Deleuze 1997a, 1997b; Engell 2003; for a discussion on processual (spatial) concepts in cultural techniques, see Siegert 2003; and for the concept of transformation in recent spatial theory see Günzel 2007; Döring/Thielmann 2008.

**17** | As to the distinction between 'movement in space' and 'moving spaces' as well as its implications in recent (sociological) spatial theory, see Löw 2001: p. 33-34; 65. For a more detailed discussion of relational vs. absolute space in the context of the music video, see my recent book: Frahm 2007, especially p. 27-48.

**18** | Gerhard Bühler, too, defines movement as "the essence of the genre of music video" (Bühler 2002: p. 208: "[...] 'Bewegung' [...] macht [...] Essenz der Gattung Musikvideo aus"); yet his observations differ significantly from my approach in that he confines movement to the classical topoi of cinematic movement: to the actions in front of the camera, to the actions with the camera, and to the dynamics of cutting and montage; see ebd.: p. 208-209.

**19** | Spielmann 2005: p. 14: "(...) in Unterscheidung zu herkömmlichen Bildmedien sowohl Dimensionalität als auch Direktionalität prozessual entfaltet und transformative Formen von Bildlichkeit (...) hervorbringt."

**20** | See Spielmann 2005: p. 14. Most notably, Spielmann develops her hypotheses at first "within the relational system of media" and thus with reference to film, television, and computer; see Spielmann 2005: p. 7-32.

**21** | With the concept of the 'worlds' I am alluding to an influential essay by Roberto de Gaetano on 'cinematographic worlds,' where he delineates – following the film philosophy of Gilles Deleuze – the possibilities of substituting the concept of the 'auteur' with the concept of 'cinematographic space;' see de Gaetano 1999, especially "The works and the worlds," p. 183-190.

**22** | Weiß strikingly describes the 'dancing images' of the music video as "flowing and flickering, trembling and pulsating, becoming and vanishing, rearing and collapsing": Weiß 2008: p. 19 ("fließende und flackernde, erzitternde und pulsierende, werdende und vergehende, sich aufbäumende und wieder in sich zusammensinkende [...] Bilder"). Gerhard Bühler, instead, focuses on the role of the music in saying: "Music videos are creating a combination of music and images that redefines the audiovisual relation of image and sound in the medium television. In music videos, images are usually generated both temporally and technically a f t e r the musical material; the basis, the focus of the clip normally is the music" ("Musikvideos schaffen eine Kombination von Musik und Bildern, die die audiovisuelle Beziehung von Bild und Ton im Medium Fernsehen neu definiert. In den Clips entstehen die Bilder in der Regel zeitlich und produktionstechnisch n a c h der musikalischen Vorlage, das Wesentliche, der Schwerpunkt der Clips liegt in aller Regel auf der Musik"), Bühler 2002: p. 160, while Kevin Williams attributes the rhythm of music video to the overall 'flow' of the television (Williams 2003: p. 77-90), describing the 'intersections, bifurcations, and integrations' of other media within the music video as "*rhizomatic*" (p. 39).

**23** | This is the working name of the directors Bastian Glassner, Chris McKenzie and Patrick Chen.

**24** | In their book on music video directors, Steve Reiss and Neil Feineman are quoting Janet Jackson's presentation speech for Mark Romanek: "[Romanek's] videos lure you into a believable otherworld, where natural, supernatural, provocative, and surreal images exist and evoke a wide range of reactions, the same way dreams often leave you with feelings words just cannot describe." Reiss/Feineman 2000: p. 213.

**25** | From these three 'medial movements,' one might draw a line back to the early filmic experiments with light, color, and abstraction within the avant-garde and experimental films of the 1920's and 1930's; yet the reference to short films like Fernand Léger's and Dudley Murphy's influential *Ballet Mécanique* (1924), Ralph Steiner's *H20* (1929), and László Moholy-Nagy's *Lichtspiel Schwarz-Weiß-Grau* (1930) is to be seen more, as I would argue, in a line of *experimentation* with the medium's own preconditions, that is, of testing and challenging its specific mediality than in the line of intermedial reference and imitation.

**26** | A very precise description of Corbijn's photographic aesthetics with relation to the aspects of 'isolation' and 'iconic images' discusses Bangs 2003; Steve Reiss and Neil Feineman, instead, underline his "preference for dense black-and-white images that balance a religious feel and dark romanticism with unexpected touches of humor." Reiss/Feineman 2000: p. 65.

**27** | David Kleiler and Robert Moses define Corbijn's videos as 'photographic videos' (as opposed to the prevailing 'cinematic videos') and they go on explaining: "If cinematic videos are narrative, or tell a story visually using the fundamentals of film grammar, photographic videos are overtly non-narrative and rely less on traditional film syntax. Treatments for these videos describe the photography, the color, the motion, the backdrops — the look rather than the story line." See Kleiler/Moses 1997: p. 28.

**28** | See, for example, the statements of Zdenek Felix concerning the photo exhibition *Star Trak* of Anton Corbijn: "The moment of motion and the fixed image that has been extracted from a fraction of time, are flowing into each other; the photo seems to be a rhythmic fragment of the moving whole, a part of an action that has been interrupted, only for some seconds": Felix 1996, without pagination; as examples of his 'animated photography' we could mention the portraits of *Bruce Cockburn* (Toronto, 1991), of *Frank Sinatra* (Palm Springs, 1993), and of *Courtney Love* (Orlando, 1995).

**29** | As Reiss and Feineman point out: "Cunningham prefers to think of his aesthetic (...) as one that captures the truth behind the music. 'I react strictly to the music,' he says. 'With some music, the emotional impact is so strong that you're busy experiencing the emotion and not seeing pictures. But other tracks put images in your head and almost have a sequential quality to them. I try to translate the emotional resonance of those songs into pictures.'" Reiss/Feineman 2000: p. 70.

**30** | See Wagner 2004, without pagination.

**31** | The conditions of producing this video as well as the complex relations between the 'fluid aesthetics' of the video and its instrumental track, described as "crackling and rustling from vinyl, with slow scratching effects", are addressed in Heiser 2004, without pagination.

**32** | According to Olaf Karnik, Björk's *All is Full of Love* is, without any question, crucial in its visualization of a post-human scenario of creation, because "neither before nor after Cunningham's masterpiece has any clip succeeded in portraying this utopia. For this reason, *All Is Full of Love* continues to retain its status as the best music video of all time." Karnik 2004, without pagination.

**33** | Keazor/Wübbena 2007: p. 422: "(...) changieren die über dem Boden dahingleitenden Falten des schwarzen Tuchs dabei zwischen festem und flüssigem Zustand (...)". See also Weiß 2007: p. 113-140.

**34** | In an interview with Floria Sigismondi, Adriana de Baross writes: "She incorporates early film and painterly aesthetics. She creates hypersurrealism based on the figure, using images derived from hallucinatory dream-states. Her video stills mix with her photography series, and her photographic images translate naturally into sculptural and mixed-media forms. Poetic and often macabre, Floria's images exist in a theater environment that is both narrative and starkly visual." See de Barros, without pagination.

**35** | See, for example, her famous *Self Portrait with Cat* (Toronto, 1995), the portraits of *Marilyn Manson* (Toronto, 1995) and of *David Bowie* (Toronto, 1997), all collected in Sigismondi 1999, while Sigismondi 2005 shows a mix of her photography and stills from her music video for Marilyn Manson, Tricky, and Sigur Rós.

**36** | Here, a parallel might be drawn to the transformations of color in the video installation produced by LynnFox for the live performance of Incubus' *Here in My Room* (2004), where the whole world is shaped and reshaped from the color of red, with the most peculiar objects emanating from red-shaped elements.

## BIBLIOGRAPHY

Bangs, Alan (2003): "Splendid Isolation". In: Veit Görner (ed.): *Anton Corbijn: everybody hurts*, Munich: Schirmer/Mosel, p. 132-144.

de Barros, Adriana (no publication year): "Floria Sigismondi". In: *Scene 360. The Film and Arts Online Magazine*, also online under http://www.scene360.com/ARTdirect_Sigismondi.php.

Beebe, Roger/Middleton, Jason (eds.) (2007): *Medium Cool: Music Videos from Soundies to Cellphones*, Durham: Duke University Press.

Bódy, Veruschka/Weibel, Peter (eds.) (1987): *Clip, Klapp, Bum: Von der visuellen Musik zum Musikvideo*, Cologne: DuMont.

Bühler, Gerhard (2002): *Postmoderne, auf dem Bildschirm, auf der Leinwand: Musikvideos, Werbespots und David Lynchs "Wild at Heart"*, St. Augustin: Gardez!

Deleuze, Gilles (1997a): *Das Bewegungs-Bild. Kino 1*, Frankfurt/M.: Suhrkamp.

Deleuze, Gilles (1997b): *Das Zeit-Bild. Kino 2*, Frankfurt/M.: Suhrkamp.

Döring, Jörg/Thielmann, Tristan (eds.) (2008): *Spatial Turn. Das Raumparadigma in den Kultur- und Sozialwissenschaften*, Bielefeld: transcript.

Engell, Lorenz/Vogl, Joseph (2002): "Vorwort." In: Claus Pias et al. (eds.): *Kursbuch Medienkultur: Die maßgeblichen Theorien von Brecht bis Baudrillard*, Stuttgart: DVA, p. 8-11.

Engell, Lorenz (2003): *Bilder des Wandels*, Weimar: VDG.

Eno, Brian (1996): "Intro". In: *Anton Corbijn: Star Trak*, Munich: Schirmer/Mosel [without pagination].

Felix, Zdenek (1996): "Der fliegende Holländer". In: *Anton Corbijn: Star Trak*, Munich: Schirmer/Mosel [without pagination].

Frahm, Laura (2007): *Bewegte Räume. Zur Konfiguration von Raum in Videoclips von Jonathan Glazer, Chris Cunningham, Mark Romanek und Michel Gondry*, Frankfurt/M.: Peter Lang.

Frith, Simon/Goodwin, Andrew/Grossberg, Lawrence (Eds.) (1993): *Sound and Vision. The Music Video Reader*, London/New York: Routledge.

de Gaetano, Roberto (1999): "Kinematographische Welten". In: Lorenz Engell/Oliver Fahle (eds.): *Der Film bei Deleuze/Le cinema selon Deleuze*, Weimar: Universitätsverlag, p. 182-197.

Gehr, Herbert (ed.) (1993): *Sound & Vision. Musikvideo und Filmkunst*, Frankfurt/M.: Deutsches Filmmuseum.

Glöde, Marc (2008): "Farblichtmusik". In: Klaus Krüger/Matthias Weiß (eds.): *Tanzende Bilder. Interaktionen von Musik und Film*, Munich: Fink, p. 51-68.

Görner, Veit (2003): "Authentic". In: ibid. (ed.): *Anton Corbijn: everybody hurts*, Munich: Schirmer/ Mosel, p. 66-94.

Görner, Veit/Wagner, Hilke (eds.) (2004): *Chris Cunningham. Come to Daddy*, Hannover: Kestner-Gesellschaft.

Goodwin, Andrew (1992): *Dancing in the Distraction Factory. Music Television and Popular Culture*, Minneapolis: University of Minnesota Press.

Grossberg, Lawrence (1993): "The Media Economy of Rock Culture: Cinema, Postmodernity and Authenticity". In: Simon Frith/Andrew Goodwin/Lawrence Grossberg (eds.): *Sound and Vision. The Music Video Reader*, London/New York: Routledge, p. 185-209.

Günzel, Stephan (ed.) (2007): *Topologie. Zur Raumbeschreibung in den Medien- und Kulturwissenschaften*, Bielefeld: transcript.

Hausheer, Cecilia/Schönholzer, Annette (eds.) (1994): *Visueller Sound. Musikvideos zwischen Avantgarde und Populärkultur*, Lucerne: Zyklop.

Heiser, Jörg (2004): "My Head is Ablaze". In: Veit Görner/Hilke Wagner (eds.): *Chris Cunningham. Come to Daddy*, Hannover: Kestner-Gesellschaft [without pagination].

Horn, Eva (2007): "There Are No Media". In: *Grey Room*, Fall 2007, No. 29, p. 6-13.

Kaplan, E. Ann (1987): *Rocking Around the Clock. Music Television, Postmodernism, and Consumer Culture*, New York/London: Routledge.

Karnik, Olaf (2004): "Transhuman Bodies and Images Like Beats". In: Veit Görner/Hilke Wagner (eds.): *Chris Cunningham. Come to Daddy*, Hannover: Kestner-Gesellschaft [without pagination].

Keazor, Henry/Wübbena, Thorsten (2006): "'Kulturelle Kannibalen'? Videoclips in Kunst und Alltag". In: *Forschung Frankfurt*, 1, 2006, p. 44-47.

Keazor, Henry/Wübbena, Thorsten (2007[2]): *Video thrills the Radio Star*, Bielefeld: transcript.

Keazor, Henry/Wübbena, Thorsten (2010), Chapter and entries for "Music Video". In: Dieter Daniels/Sandra Naumann/Jan Thoben (eds.): *See this Sound. An Interdisciplinary Survey of Audovisual Culture*, Cologne: Buchhandlung Walther König, p. 223-233.

Kleiler, David/Moses, Robert (1997): *You Stand There. Making Music Video*, New York: Three Rivers Press.

Krüger, Klaus/Weiß, Matthias (eds.) (2008): *Tanzende Bilder. Interaktionen von Musik und Film*, Munich: Fink.

Löw, Martina (2001): *Raumsoziologie*. Frankfurt/M.: Suhrkamp.

Mank, Thomas (1994): "Im Mahlstrom der Bilder. Absoluter Film und Medienkultur". In: Cecilia Hausheer/Annette Schönholzer (eds.): *Visueller Sound. Musikvideos zwischen Avantgarde und Populärkultur*, Lucerne: Zyklop, p. 14-25.

Moritz, William (1987): "Der Traum von der Farbmusik". In: Veruschka Bódy/Peter Weibel (eds.): *Clip, Klapp, Bum: Von der visuellen Musik zum Musikvideo*, Cologne: DuMont, p. 17-52.

de la Motte-Haber, Helga (2008): "Bild und Ton. Das Spiel der Sinnesorgane oder der Film im Kopf". In: Klaus Krüger/Matthias Weiß (eds.): *Tanzende Bilder. Interaktionen von Musik und Film*, Munich: Fink, p. 69-76.

Neumann, Hans-Joachim (1983): "Stromlinienförmiger Edelkitsch. Auskunft über ein neues Medium: Videoclip". In: *Medium*. Nr. 7, p. 33-38.

Neumann-Braun, Klaus (ed.) (1999): *Viva MTV! Popmusik im Fernsehen*, Frankfurt/M.: Suhrkamp.

Poschardt, Ulf (ed.) (2003): *Video – 25 Jahre Videoästhetik*, Ostfildern: Hatje Cantz.

Rajewsky, Irina O. (2002): *Intermedialität*, Tübingen/Basel: Francke.

Rauh, Reinhold (1985): "Videoclips, Bilderflut und audiovisuelle Geschichten". In: *Medien und Erziehung*, Nr. 4, p. 210-217.

Reiss, Steve/Feineman, Neil (2000): *Thirty Frames per Second. The Visionary Art of the Music Video*, New York: Abrams.

Siegert, Bernhard (2003): *Passage des Digitalen. Zeichenpraktiken der neuzeitlichen Wissenschaften 1500–1900*, Berlin: Brinkmann & Bose.

Sigismondi, Floria (1999): *Redemption*. Berlin: Gestalten Verlag.

Sigismondi, Floria (2005): *Immune*, Berlin: Gestalten Verlag.

Spielmann, Yvonne (1998): *Intermedialität. Das System Peter Greenaway*, Munich: Fink.

Spielmann, Yvonne (2005): *Video. Das reflexive Medium*, Frankfurt/M.: Suhrkamp.

Straw, Will (1993): "Popular Music and Postmodernism in the 1980s". In: Simon Frith/Andrew Goodwin/Lawrence Grossberg (eds.) (1993): *Sound and Vision. The Music Video Reader*, London/New York: Routledge, p. 3-21.

Vernallis, Carol (2004): *Experiencing Music Video: Aesthetics and Cultural Context*, New York: Columbia University Press.

Wagner, Hilke (2004): "Chris Cunningham. Clip-Art and Art-Clips". In: Veit Görner/Hilke Wagner (eds.): *Chris Cunningham. Come to Daddy*, Hannover: Kestner-Gesellschaft [without pagination].

Weiß, Matthias (2007): *Madonna revidiert. Rekursivität im Videoclip*, Berlin: Reimer.

Weiß, Matthias (2008): "Tanzende Bilder – eine Einführung". In: Klaus Krüger/Matthias Weiß (eds.): *Tanzende Bilder. Interaktionen von Musik und Film*, Munich: Fink, p. 9-19.

Wenzel, Ulrich (1999): "Pawlows Panther. Zur Rezeption von Musikvideos zwischen bedingtem Reflex und zeichentheoretischer Reflexion". In: Klaus Neumann-Braun (ed.): *Viva MTV! Popmusik im Fernsehen*, Frankfurt/M.: Suhrkamp, p. 45-73.

Williams, Kevin (2003): *Why I [Still] Want My MTV: Music Video and Aesthetic Communication*, Cresskill: Hampton Press.

Winter, Rainer/H. Jürgen Kagelmann (1997): "Videoclip". In: Herbert Bruhn/Rolf Oerter/Helmut Rösing (eds.): *Musikpsychologie. Ein Handbuch*, Reinbek: Rowohlt, p. 208-220.

## Photographic Sources

Fig. 6: Floria Sigismondi: *Immune*, Berlin: Gestalten Verlag 2005: © dgv – Die Gestalten Verlag GmBH & Co. KG, Berlin, 2005

# Who Cares about the Music in Music Videos?

Toward a Multiperspectival Pop Cultural Study
of Music Videos

CHRISTOPH JACKE

## 1. INTRODUCTION

Madonna, the transnational superstar of music television, has turned fifty;
traditional musical television is having big problems fulfilling its original
function and is mutating into youth television without music; new media
technologies are supposedly leading to a devaluation of pop music: there
are enough reasons in 2010 to reexamine fundamentally the role of the
music video in our media society. *Video Killed the Radio Star* sang the Buggles on the American music television station MTV's first broadcast in
1981. Since then there has been a lot of discussion about whether videos
signified the end of pop music radio, whether music television has replaced the record store on the corner and the music cinema, whether the
DVD has superseded the videotape, and above all whether the new technologies such as MP3, iPod, and the Internet unite all previous media in
the new form of a super medium and thus make them superfluous – that
is to say, 'Internet Killed All the Other Stars.'[1] In the last case, 'killing' can
be understood to be very integrating and accommodating. The same could
be said of the visualization of pop music. For whether it is the good old
LP album cover, the music (video) clip, or a band's presentation of itself
on the Internet via its own home page or MySpace, visualizations of pop
music neither disappear nor are they replaced, they change their media
platform. Clearly, we still need images to go with the sounds in order to
create a comprehensive sound image of pop music in the truest sense of
the phrase.

In my essay, I would like to examine critically – in a kind of rereading –
my own program[2] and more recent research on music videos to assess the
extent to which above all media studies and musicology in German-speaking countries are concerned with videos as everyday visualizations of pop

music between art (e.g. the Oberhausen International Short-Film Festival, which has an award for the alternative music video of the year) and commerce (e.g. Beigbeder's description of music videos as 'whores'[3]). To that end, in the second section I will take another look at and update my assessment of the extent to which the visual and sound worlds of music videos are treated in media studies and musicology. Then in the third section I will present a more comprehensive concept of media and will modify it to expand the broad field of investigation and show which elements are left out of the account by concentrating on certain areas. Moreover, to get ahead of myself a little, many detail studies lack such an explicit concept of media. In the fourth section, the use of this concept of media in the analyses of videos will be illustrated briefly by using the specific example of Britney Spears' 2007 music video *Gimme More*; finally, the fifth section will draw provisional conclusions.

## 2. VISUAL AND SOUND WORLDS IN MEDIA STUDIES AND MUSICOLOGY

Not long ago, in the "Digitale Evolution" (digital evolution) interview series of the pop culture journal *Spex*, probably the most famous theoretician of pop music writing in Germany, Diedrich Diederichsen, commented on the connection of images and pop music as follows:

"In my view, pop music only comes into being when the visual, the publicly performative, and the music come together in certain cultural formats, both in its production and reception. In pop music, it is always very much a matter of developing one's relationship to society, to the public, to seeing and being seen in an exploratory way. That is done with *Vorbilder* (models) and specifically with *Vor-Bilder* (pre-images) in the truest sense of the word."[4]

Popular music, or pop music for short, has always been dependent on images as part of its media offerings.[5] Whereas at first this meant the cover and inner sleeves of LPs and singles, soon came music magazines and their reports as well as the first performances of pop music stars on television. Whereas at first the fans could only construct images in their heads based on still images in the form of photographs or the famous "Starschnitte" (star cuts)[6] in the latest edition of *Bravo*, in the 1960's and 1970's there were special shows dedicated to pop music on German television, such as *Beat-Club*, *Rockpalast*, and *Disco*, whose moving images of performances, studio interviews, and even the first short films supposedly made the stars seem more authentic, close, and alive. It soon became clear to the makers of music television that it was simply too expensive and risky to have live performances in their studios by bands such as Kiss, the masked monster hard rockers from the United States, The Who from the United Kingdom, as no stage (or equipment) was safe from destruction during their shows. So they thought of ways to broadcast the stars via television to their watching fans without the stars having to be present in the television studio: the birth of the music video. In Germany in the 1980's and 1990's, the use of small, usually three-minute visualizations manifested itself most prominently on the pop music show *Formel Eins*, which also had studio guests and showed charts but was primarily dedicated to playing back videos with moderation. Diederichsen again: "In the magnificent fold-out cover, on the one hand, and the music video, on the other, pop music had indeed found forms that were very compelling, that were right in the sense that they brought something together that had always been trying to get together, so to speak."[7]

These short films were by no means just inexpensive substitutes for personal appearances, as is demonstrated by the legendary video for the song *Thriller* by Michael Jackson, which was shot in 1983 and first shown on MTV. The video was fourteen minutes long, cost about 500.000 U.S. dollars, and resembled a short horror movie. With *Thriller*, Jackson transcended limits on both form – in this case time and money – and content, which is why the video is still part of pop cultural memory and serves as illustration of the referential character of videos (to horror, pop, and Michael Jackson himself) and their visual possibilities.

In the two decades since then, the supply of music videos has become increasingly differentiated: in addition to pure performance videos, there are narrative short films, artistic experiments, and above all more hybrid forms that cross over all these categories.[8] Despite this immense thematic and formal expansion of the visual worlds of videos, their presence in the media or more specifically on television has become less important when, as a consequence of the retreat from music television with the merging of MTV and VIVA under Viacom's roof, the remaining programs have increasingly developed into youth television dominated by series and reality television.[9] Only very rarely are elaborate and expensive videos like Jackson's *Thriller* still produced. Yet videos have neither disappeared completely nor been replaced by other visualizations. On the contrary, they are simply diffused in other formats and above all via other media.[10]

It is thus all the more astonishing that studies on the culture and communications of the media, in Germany too, have only gradually begun to address the connections among media, music videos, and pop culture. Moreover, in these and related disciplines there is a deficit of both theories and empirical research in the area of visual communication, which are also essential when it comes to analysing moving images such as videos. Thomas Knieper has called for stronger "visual competency"[11] in communication sciences with a sociological orientation. Joachim Paech has observed that in media studies with a cultural studies orientation "images are only observable 'as images' if they are seen not only in terms of *what* they depict with regard to their medial conditions, but also in terms of *how* they depict".[12] Both aspects, in his view, still receive too little analysis *per se* but especially too little integrating analysis. Even the visual studies *par excellence* – aesthetics and art history – neglect competencies that make the politics of media positions visible when it comes to more recent developments. Tom Holert has remarked on this: "The fundamental visual quality of such states and processes makes it necessary to study technologies and practices that lead to this visuality of the social that they shape and make it possible to experience".[13] For advertising studies, a combination of the study of communication, culture, and marketing that is highly relevant to pop music research, Thomas Schierl has acknowledged: "Our society communicates cultural techniques primarily through systems of linguistic symbols – reading and writing – and criminally neglects visual literacy. Both audiences and communicators (via images) often lack pictorial competence."[14] Finally, to complete the circle of prominent complainants, the sociologist of space Martina Löw believes we have a lot of catching up to do in our schooling to see public images:

"If we consider that visual memory is quite good while at the same time the ability to read images for interpretive patterns is underdeveloped in our culture, the persuasive effect of images is very clearly revealed. Viewers of images are, as a rule, satisfied when they can identify individual objects; they rarely ask themselves what communicative intention is associated with an image."[15]

And the desideratum for scholarship becomes even more intense when we consider the most recent developments, such as computer gaming communities, MySpace profiles, and castings of all kinds in pop culture and above all pop music.[16] At a time of increasing potential for self-representation in everyday media – as pop culture and pop music have shown us – we have to concern ourselves ever more intensely with the necessary platforms and technologies. The French literary theorist Jean-Pierre Dubost stated as early as 1994: "The remarkable thing about our current situation is that the bemoaning of a world that has become too impenetrable might cause us to overlook that our world is more visible than ever."[17]

In order to be able to analyze fully the various levels of visualizations of pop music in media and in particular music videos, I would like to define suitably a concept of media.

## 3. MEDIA: VISUAL CONSTRUCTIONS AS VIDEOS IN THE PROCESS OF MASS COMMUNICATION

If we want to model and state more precisely the concept of media in its full complexity, and if this is to be done for a concept of mass media, which is what music videos are, then one compact concept of media suggests itself that has been discussed in the context of media research by Siegfried J. Schmidt in 2002 and 2007.[18] In that view, media function as "instruments for constructing reality"[19] on various levels of the process of mass-media communication: production, distribution, reception/use, reprocessing (of videos, in this case – that is, sound-image offerings).

On all of these levels, music videos are constructed by actors in diverse roles in pop culture and music – for example, music producers, directors, or stars on the level of production; promotion and advertising employees and PR agents on the level of distribution; and fans and general audience members on the level of reception/use; and music journalists and critics on the level of reprocessing which implies that new media offerings are being produced and depicted.

Media as instruments for constructing reality can be divided in turn into four components that work equally on all four levels of the communication process of music videos:

1. *Instruments of Communication*: Material facts that are capable of functioning as symbols and can be used for socially regulated, enduring, repeatable, and socially relevant structural coupling of systems in the spirit of the production of meaning in question. Schmidt sees spoken, natural language as the prototype for instruments of communication, because since the emergence of language the fundamental principle of the aforementioned semantic coupling of systems by means of significant materialities (and not only in meanings) has become exemplary for all subsequent instruments of communication (writing, image, notation, and so on).

2. *Media Technologies*: According to Schmidt, the technical apparatus enduringly influences – indeed, conditions – any production, distribution, reception, and reprocessing of media offerings. For only something appropriate to the current state of development of a technology can actually be employed by users as a scheme for dealing with media offerings if they have technical access and competence in media technology. For dealing with such media technologies is something that has to be acquired in a socialized way and made a standard part of the competencies of actors. Through routine practice, these competencies generally become a matter of course, becoming invisible and hence neither capable of nor subject to consciousness.

3. *Organizations of Social Systems*: The social acceptance of an instrument of communication, the structure of a media technology necessary for that, and the opportunities for socialization and competence are tied to developing the social institutions that support them (organizations and their departments, such as editorial staffs, publishing houses, television stations, record companies, and institutions such as schools, academies, and universities), whose position in society requires in turn the solution of economic, legal, political, and social problems. Schmidt emphasizes that this component of the social system is by no means external to the instruments of communication and media technologies; rather the framework of relationships between the components must be considered self-organizing.

4. *Media Offerings*: With this component, too, it is clear that it is entangled in the framework of relationships just mentioned. The three other components have an effect on the production, distribution, reception/use, and reprocessing of media offerings. Media offerings are the professionally and institutionally produced media for texts of all kinds (videos, lead stories, features, tracks on a CD, advertising spots, posters, homepages, etc.) that make them available to the market and hence above all the recipients – that is to say, they offer them.

These components influence one another against the backdrop of very specific sociohistorical backgrounds and can only be analyzed separately. Nevertheless, this comprehensive concept of media has proved to be a sensible foundation for research, because it takes into account the entire field of study for media and communication studies and can also help to integrate quite distinct concepts. If we contextualize this concept of media ourselves once again, the result is a highly complex but also flexible model[20]:

*Fig. 1: The Media Culture/Media System (following Schmidt and Zurstiege 2007: p. 67)*

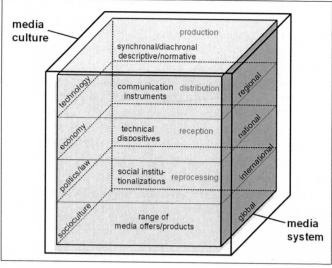

In this complex concept of media, we find the various roles of actors in media and hence in music videos as well. At the same time, the networking is revealed between the steps of the process of mass media communication consisting of production, distribution, reception, and reprocessing.[21] This cube of the media system, designed by media and communication studies experts Siegfried J. Schmidt and Guido Zurstiege, is at once flexible and static and can be applied to diverse media texts and contexts.[22] In the following section we will break down the model using the concrete example of a music video.

## 4. FROM PRODUCTION TO REPROCESSING AS REPRODUCTION: THE EXAMPLE OF BRITNEY SPEARS AND *GIMME MORE* (2007)

If we divide the process of music as a form of mass media communica-tion into the above-mentioned levels of production, distribution, recep-tion, and reprocessing, there are considerable changes in the way actors operate on all dimensions as a result of new technologies. The focus here will be on pop music and especially the music video because it reacts espe-cially quickly and sensitively – indeed, almost seismographically – to large developments.[23]

The production of pop music is simplified in several respects by new, especially digital technologies: it becomes cheaper, easier to learn, and hence more quickly and less ponderously usable. For some time now, anyone with a certain potential in terms of money, time, and space can become a producer of pop music and hence of music videos, if only for fif-teen minutes, to recall Andy Warhol's famous statement. This Everyman as producer of pop music videos by no means replaces elaborate, expen-sive videos like the one director Jake Sarfaty did shoot for Britney Spears in 2007: *Gimme More*, which will serve here as a brief example. The desktop production studio is at least theoretically possible, especially in the world of electronic music, and it has been employed a million times between "Cubase" and "Magix". In part thanks to these new technological possi-bilities, pop music has become increasingly differentiated in styles and subgenres, which raises the question which large, comprehensive style of pop music is entirely new since techno and hip-hop and whether all of to-day's styles and movements are not 'merely' borrowings from earlier mu-sic. The answer is: they are, and they are as trivial as any bad cover band at a county fair and as highly complex as wild bastard pop or mash-up techniques demonstrate. Neither has the fetishization of technology led to pop music being washed up in terms of content, nor do we observe daily unexpected explosions of innovation. The MP3 format no more represents the death of music, as the famous German media theorist Friedrich Kittler recently (2008) declared in another part of the "Digitale Evolution" (digital evolution) series in *Spex*, nor can the qualitative loses in the comparison between vinyl and MP3 that Kittler laments be entirely denied.'

Let's take a brief look at the video *Gimme More* by Britney Spears as an example for the construction of images in music videos. Here it seems clear, that agents of production and distribution like the director or the artist herself offer an image that is already self-reflexive: Britney, in *Gimme More*, is no longer the school girl she used to be in the early videos as in *...Baby One More Time* (directed in 1998 by Nigel Dick) or *Oops! ... I Did It Again* (shot in 2000 also by Dick). In the meantime she, or, better to say, the media constructed image of Britney Spears, has realized that she has become a woman, and has become more 'sexy', 'bitchy' (the words

"It's Britney, bitch... ", can be heard during the opening of the song), and now is dancing in a twilight kind of bar. We do not exactly know what the director and the artist wanted to offer, but we can read a kind of self-reference in this clip, because the Britney presented here has developed and has obviously reacted to the public opinion. That is to say that professional production of a music video has obviously reflected on reception and public opinion and now uses the results of this reflection to produce new media offers and to change the image of a pop music star like Britney Spears, even within the lyrics of the song. "Here again we encounter a reflexive process"[24]:

> "Cameras are flashin', while we were dirty dancing,
> they keep watchin', keep watchin',
> feel's like the crowd was sayin'
> [CHORUS]
> Gimme gimme more..." [25]

*Figs. 2-3: Stills from the music video by Jake Sarfaty: Britney Spears, Gimme More, 2007*

On the other side of production and distribution, one very important area in the process of mass communication of pop music and videos is that of the 'extreme reception and use' that makes possible new media offerings, on whose heels, in a sense, the music video follows reproductively as a process of mass communication. When new offerings result in the process (for example, when a fan or antifan of Britney Spears parodies her music video and uploads these new videos to Tubemix or YouTube, when a DJ cobbles together entirely new tracks from existing material, for example, in remixes or visual mash-ups), they are creative actions based on competencies that lead to new, sometimes even artistic products. Such methods existed in the previous century too, of course, but they were often invisible and remained private, except perhaps in the case of fanzines, the magazines that fans produced about their favorite musicians. In the age of the Internet and an increasing visibility of everyday life, including its pop music, things are naturally related to one another, cited, recycled, and new things created from the old ones. As the art theorist and music journalist Mercedes Bunz has put it: "The adaptation of material takes the place of producing original material: 'cultural trash' is, so to speak the means of production of the future."[26]

Such adaptations are well equipped in the digital age in terms of their necessities – that is, the availability of materials and technologies. Nevertheless, it requires actors who know there way around and are willing to produce something new from trash.[27] These new products, in the form of videos or other pop music and media offerings, can be commercial and professional, but they can also remain in the gray area of the amateurish, lying about on some platform in the Internet or simply getting deleted.[28] In the former case, mass communication can begin its circular process again.

Let's take a look at an example of the reprocessing and reproduction of the Britney Spears-video *Gimme More*, which a fan/anti-fan (Chris Crocker, in this case) put on the Web, using Tubemix as his platform almost parallel to the original release of the video in 2007. Chris Crocker as an agent – no matter, if he is a fan or anti-fan – is using the original music video and the images created to reprocess the image of Spears, plays with it and finally (re-)constructs it in a different way which can be read as a parody or pastiche. While doing this, Crocker is producing a new music video, a new media offer, which here, at least, leads to a certain fame.

*Fig. 4-5: Stills from the video by Chris Crocker,* Britney, this is for you, 2007

It is clear that a pure analysis of the sound or marketing of Britney Spears' song and video *Gimme More* hardly does justice to this complex medium. Detailed analyses of specific videos, directors, and musicians, and fans, as practiced by Michael Altrogge (2000), Henry Keazor and Thorsten Wübbena (2005) or more recently Laura Frahm (2007) and Matthias Weiß (2007), are, of course, necessary and praiseworthy, if one wants to learn to read them as media texts at all. Thanks primarily to the works just mentioned, that step has finally been taken even in the German-speaking world. But if videos, as seismographic pop cultural media offerings, as, in the words of Helmut Rösing, "image worlds of sounds, sound worlds of images"[29], tell us a lot more about the media society in which we live and learn, then analyses that are (more) comprehensive and integrating will be necessary. Which brings me to my summary.

## 5. SUMMARY: MULTIPLE PERSPECTIVES AND TRANSDISCIPLINARITY: DON'T FORGET THE MUSIC IN A WORLD OF MEDIA AND IMAGES!

In conclusion, I would like to return to the beginning of my essay, to its title: "Who Cares about the Music in Music Videos?" was and is the cynical question raised by the absolutely necessary consideration of the various levels and stages of the music video as medium and communication process. Music videos have since begun to attract attention and analysis even among German-speaking scholars, from art history to marketing research. Nevertheless, overarching or rather fundamental systematic studies remain rather rare. The conclusion to be drawn from a historical musicologist's helplessness in the face of marketing or the same behavior from a constructivist media studies scholar in the face of musical analysis can only be that theory and analysis has to be conducted even intense by inter- and transdisciplinary teams of researches, as Henry Keazor and Thorsten Wübbena (2005), for example, have shown for several music videos.[30] As we suggested in the case of *Gimme More*, the music should not be forgotten in the process, but sound as an instrument of acoustic communication is often overlooked in analyses in communications and media studies[31], which shows that there is plenty of work to be done in the productive field of the analysis of music videos.

To put it another way, it should not be 'solely' about the analysis of forms of popular music and culture and their texts – "why do songs have words?", to quote the musicologist and cultural sociologist Simon Frith (1987). A comprehensive study of pop music calls for social and media contexts to be central, without forgetting the texts; not least because this society and its media are responsible for observing and describing popular music and culture. Why do words have songs? Such contextualization and systemization can be achieved by a multiperspectival pop music studies. Only thus can we, in the German-speaking world as well, do justice to the urgent call for pop music analysis that the American musicologist Sheila Sumitra recently expressed in the *Journal of Popular Music Studies*: "[I]t is impossible to adequately consider any topic in popular music without engaging with a variety of other disciplines (...) it reflects and/or engages with its environment in some way that allows for popular acceptance and reception."[32]

# References

**1** | For an introducing synopsis on the meaning and change of music clips see Jacke 2008a, 2008d.

**2** | See Jacke 2003.

**3** | See the title "Werbevideos sind Nutten" of Beigbeder's (2003) cynical text in the exhibition catalogue "Video – 25 Jahre Videoästhetik".

**4** | Diederichsen 2007: p. 63: "Meiner Ansicht nach entsteht Popmusik überhaupt erst darüber, dass das Visuelle, das öffentlich Performative und die Musik in bestimmten kulturellen Formaten zusammenfinden, sowohl bei der Produktion als auch bei der Rezeption. Bei Popmusik geht es immer sehr stark darum, sein Verhältnis zur Gesellschaft, zu Öffentlichkeit, zum Sehen und Gesehen-werden probehandelnderweise zu entwickeln. Das passiert anhand von Vorbildern, und zwar Vor-‚Bildern' im wahrsten Sinne des Wortes."

**5** | For some basic considerations on pop music and media see Jacke 2008b.

**6** | These are multipart posters in German music magazines, to be collected week by week and ultimately to be assembled and glued together, so that the readers in the end come close to the life-size likeness of a pop musician.

**7** | Diederichsen 2007: p. 63: "Mit dem prächtigen Fold-out-Cover einerseits und mit dem Musikvideo andererseits hat die Popmusik in der Tat Formate gefunden, die sehr triftig sind, die stimmen, in dem Sinne, dass sie etwas zusammenbringen, was sozusagen schon immer zusammenstrebte."

**8** | For a recent history of the music video see Austerlitz 2007, for a semiotical approach on music videos between avantgarde and advertising see Peverini 2004.

**9** | For a detailed survey see Neumann-Braun and Mikos 2006 as well as the contribution by Neumann-Braun and Schmidt in this volume.

**10** | See in this context the interviews within the series "Digitale Evolution" in the journal *Spex – Magazin für Popkultur*, issue 310, 311 (both 2007), issue 314, 315 (both 2008), and issue 318 (2009) as well as articles in the monthly journal *DeBug. Elektronische Lebensaspekte*, at last for example on sustainability and digitality in issue 121 (2008).

**11** | Cf. Knieper 2005: p. 49.

**12** | Paech 2005: p. 81: "Bilder sind 'als Bilder' nur beobachtbar, wenn sie über das hinaus, *was* sie darstellen, hinsichtlich ihrer medialen Bedingungen, *wie* sie darstellen, gesehen werden".

**13** | Holert 2005: p. 234: "Die fundamentale Bildhaftigkeit sozialer Zustände und Prozesse macht das Studium der Techniken und Praktiken erforderlich, die zu dieser Visualität des Sozialen führen – die sie gestalten und erfahrbar machen." Concerning the politics of visibility and the visual studies see Holert 2000, who comes to a quite similar conclusion: "An analysis of visual culture ought to investigate the logic of visual processes. In a commercial culture the nature of the image is less interesting than the knowledge of the economy of the accesses to images." (Holert 2000: p. 33: "Eine Analyse [sic!] visueller Kultur sollte die Logik visueller Prozesse erkunden. In einer kommerziellen Kultur ist das 'Wesen' des Bildes weniger interessant als ein Wissen um die Ökonomie der Zugänge zu Bildern" [Original emphases removed, C.J.]).

**14** | Schierl 2005: p. 309-310: "Unsere Gesellschaft vermittelt primär Kulturtechniken im Umgang mit dem sprachlichen Symbolsystem – Lesen wie Schreiben – und vernachlässigt sträflich die *visual literacy*. Es fehlt den Rezipienten ebenso wie auch den (Bilder verwendenden) Kommunikatoren häufig an piktorialer Kompetenz."

**15** | Löw 2008, unpaginated: "Berücksichtigt man, dass es zwar ein ausgesprochen gutes Bildgedächtnis, aber gleichzeitig eine kulturell nur gering ausgeprägte Fähigkeit gibt, Bilder auf Deutungsmuster hin zu lesen, so zeigt sich die persuasive Wirkung von Bildern sehr deutlich. BetrachterInnen von Bildern begnügen sich in der Regel damit, die einzelnen Objekte zu identifizieren, sie stellen sich jedoch selten die Frage, welche kommunikative Absicht mit einem Bild verbunden ist."

**16** | Regarding the artistic self-marketing of pop musicians in the Internet see Ahlers and Vogel 2008. Referring to image politics within pop music see Jacke 2008c.

**17** | Dubost 1994: p. 12: "Das Bemerkenswerte aber an unserer jetzigen Situation ist, dass das Jammern über eine unübersichtlich gewordene Welt uns gerade übersehen lassen könnte, dass unsere Welt sichtbarer denn je ist".

**18** | In the following I am paraphrasing and quoting Schmidt's deliberations (2002: p. 56-57, 2007: p. 71-85) and already have applied this concept of media to music clips (cf. Jacke 2003); For further reading see also Schmidt 2000: p. 70-279 as well as Schmidt and Zurstiege 2007: p. 63-70.

**19** | Schmidt and Zurstiege 2000: p. 170: "(…) Instrumente der Wirklichkeitskonstruktion (…)."

**20** | Cf. Schmidt and Zurstiege 2007: p. 63-70.

**21** | Generally in this connection compare Schmidt and Zurstiege 2007. Concerning the popcultural and popmusical field see Jacke 2004.

**22** | Among others Rösing 2003, Keazor and Wübbena 2005, Wenzel 1999, Wulff 1999, Bergermann 2003 and Jacke 2003 thematise a stronger contextualisation of this kind.

**23** | See Jacke 2006.

**24** | Schmidt 2007: p. 75.

**25** | http://www.azlyrics.com/lyrics/britneyspears/gimmemore.html (last access 1.3.2010).

**26** | Bunz 2006: p. 280: "Die Bearbeitung von Material tritt an die Stelle seiner alten originären Herstellung – 'Kulturschutt' ist sozusagen das kommende Produktionsmittel."

**27** | Cf. Jacke and Zierold 2008 and Jacke and Meinecke 2008.

**28** | Even that is simpler and faster than in the days of the audio cassette, for example.

**29** | See the title of Rösing 2003: "Bilderwelt der Klänge – Klangwelt der Bilder".

**30** | Regarding the transdisciplinary 'thinking outside the box' compare basically Mittelstraß 2003, Gumbrecht 2004 and in particular for analyses of media cultur, communication and music Rösing 2003, Schmidt and Zurstiege 2007, Jacke 2007.

**31** | See the contributions in Schulze 2008.

**32** | Sumitra 2007: p. 110.


# BIBLIOGRAPHY

Ahlers, Michael/Vogel, Tobias (2008): "Selbst ist die Band. Konzepte, Beispiele und Reaktionen auf die künstlerische Selbstvermarktung im Internet". In: *Musik und Unterricht. Das Magazin für Musikpädagogik*, issue 91, p. 30-39.

Altrogge, Michael (2000): *Tönende Bilder: interdisziplinäre Studie zu Musik und Bildern in Videoclips und ihrer Bedeutung für Jugendliche*, vol. 1-3. Berlin: Vistas.

Austerlitz, Saul (2007): *Money for Nothing. A History of the Music Video from the Beatles to the White Stripes*, New York/London: Continuum.

Beigbeder, Frédéric (2003): "Werbevideos sind Nutten". In: Ulf Poschardt (ed.), *Video – 25 Jahre Videoästhetik*, Ostfildern-Ruit: Hatje Cantz, p. 96-99.

Bergermann, Ulrike (2003): "Videoclip". In: Hans-Otto Hügel (ed.), *Handbuch Populäre Kultur. Begriffe, Theorien und Diskussionen*, Stuttgart/Weimar: J.B. Metzler, p. 478-482.

Bunz, Mercedes (2006): "Instabil. Musik und Digitalität als Momente der Verschiebung". In: Christoph Jacke/Eva Kimminich/Siegfried J. Schmidt (eds.), *Kulturschutt. Über das Recycling von Theorien und Kulturen*, Bielefeld: transcript, p. 271-281.

Diederichsen, Diedrich (2007): "Es ist die Wiedergeburt des autonomen Künstlers im alten Sinne", (Digitale Evolution. Teil 1. Interview mit Martin Hossbach und Jan Kedves). In: *Spex. Magazin für Popkultur*, issue 310, p. 62-65.

Dubost, Jean-Pierre (1994): "Vorwort". In: ibid. (ed.), *Bildstörung. Gedanken zu einer Ethik der Wahrnehmung*, Leipzig: Reclam, p. 9-13.

Frahm, Laura (2007): *Bewegte Räume. Zur Konstruktion von Raum in Videoclips von Jonathan Glazer, Chris Cunningham, Mark Romanek und Michel Gondry*, Frankfurt/M.: Peter Lang.

Frith, Simon (1987): "Why Do Songs Have Words?". In: ibid. (2007): *Taking Popular Music Seriously. Selected Essays*, Aldershot/Burlington: Ashgate, p. 209-238.

Gumbrecht, Hans Ulrich (2004): "Auf der Suche nach einem neuen Wahrheitskriterium. Fortschritt in einer Welt von 'Beobachtungen zweiter Ordnung': Wie wissenschaftlich müssen Geisteswissenschaften sein?". In: *Frankfurter Rundschau*, no. 142, 22.06.2004, p. 18.

Holert, Tom (2000): "Bildfähigkeiten. Visuelle Kultur, Repräsentationskritik und Politik der Sichtbarkeit". In: ibid. (ed.): *Imagineering. Visuelle Kultur und Politik der Sichtbarkeit. Schriftenreihe Jahresring* vol. 47, Köln: Oktagon, p. 14-33.

Holert, Tom (2005): "Kulturwissenschaft/Visual Culture". In: Klaus Sachs-Hombach (ed.): *Bildwissenschaft. Disziplinen, Themen, Methoden*, Frankfurt/M.: Suhrkamp, p. 226-235.

Jacke, Christoph (2003): "Kontextuelle Kontingenz: Musikclips im wissenschaftlichen Umgang". In: Dietrich Helms/Thomas Phleps (eds.): *Clipped Differences. Geschlechterrepräsentationen im Musikvideo. Beiträge zur Popularmusikforschung*, vol. 31, Bielefeld: transcript, p. 27-40.

Jacke, Christoph (2004): *Medien(sub)kultur. Geschichten – Diskurse – Entwürfe*, Bielefeld: transcript.

Jacke, Christoph (2006): "Popkultur als Seismograph. Über den Nutzen wissenschaftlicher Beobachtung von Pop." In: Christoph Jacke/Eva Kimminich/Siegfried J. Schmidt (eds.): *Kulturschutt. Über das Recycling von Theorien und Kulturen*, Bielefeld: transcript, p. 114-123.

Jacke, Christoph (2007): "Popkulturanalyse als transdisziplinäres Projekt. Ein medienkulturwissenschaftlicher Vorschlag". In: Florian Hartling/Sascha Trültzsch (eds.): *Siegener Periodicum zur Internationalen Empirischen Literaturwissenschaft (SPIEL)*, vol. 23, no. 2 (2004), p. 268-284.

Jacke, Christoph (2008a): "Ende oder Beginn? Oder mittendrin in der Veränderung? Was die Digitalisierung von Popmusik für die Mediengesellschaft und unser soziales Verhalten bedeutet". In: *Musikforum. das Magazin des deutschen Musiklebens*, no. 3, p. 14-17.

Jacke, Christoph (2008b): "Keine Musik ohne Medien, keine Medien ohne Musik? Pop(-kulturwissenschaft) aus medienwissenschaftlicher Perspektive". In: Christian Bielefeldt/Udo Dahmen/Rolf Grossmann (eds.): *PopMusicology. Perspektiven einer Popmusikwissenschaft*, Bielefeld: transcript, p. 135-152.

Jacke, Christoph (2008c): "'Same, Same But Different': Zur Bedeutung und zum Wandel von Image in der Popkultur postmoderner Mediengesellschaften". In: Daniela Münkel/Lu Seegers (eds.): *Medien und Imagepolitik im 20. Jahrhundert. Deutschland, Europa, USA*, Frankfurt/M./New York: Campus, p. 247-269.

Jacke, Christoph (2008d): "Wer killt denn nun wen? Kein Pop ohne Bilder: eine aktuelle Bestandsaufnahme zur popkulturellen Bedeutung von Musikvideoclips". In: *Musik und Unterricht. Das Magazin für Musikpädagogik*, issue 92, p. 10-14.

Jacke, Christoph/Meinecke, Thomas (2008): "Vorübergehende Vergegenwärtigungen in der Popkultur. Ein Gespräch über das Sprechen über und das Erinnern von Pop". In: Christoph Jacke/Martin Zierold (eds.): *Populäre Kultur und soziales Gedächtnis. Theoretische und exemplarische Überlegungen zur dauervergesslichen Erinnerungsmaschine Pop. Popular Culture and Social Memory: Theoretical and Empirical Analyses on The Oblivious 'Memory-Machine' Pop. Siegener Periodicum zur Internationalen Empirischen Literaturwissenschaft* vol. 24, no. 2 (2005), p. 239-256.

Jacke, Christoph/Zierold, Martin (2008): "Pop – die vergessliche Erinnerungsmaschine". In: Christoph Jacke/Martin Zierold (eds.): *Pop-

*uläre Kultur und soziales Gedächtnis. Theoretische und exemplarische Überlegungen zur dauervergesslichen Erinnerungsmaschine Pop. Popular Culture and Social Memory: Theoretical and Empirical Analyses on The Oblivious 'Memory-Machine' Pop.* Siegener Periodicum zur Internationalen Empirischen Literaturwissenschaft vol. 24, no. 2 (2005), p. 199-210.

Keazor, Henry/Wübbena, Thorsten (2005): *Video thrills the Radio Star. Musikvideos: Geschichte, Themen, Analysen*, Bielefeld: transcript.

Kittler, Friedrich (2008): "MP3 ist der Tod der Musik". (Digitale Evolution. Teil 3. Interview mit Max Dax und Martin Hossbach). In: *Spex. Magazin für Popkultur*, issue 314, p. 64-68.

Knieper, Thomas (2005): "Kommunikationswissenschaft". In: Klaus Sachs-Hombach (ed.): *Bildwissenschaft. Disziplinen, Themen, Methoden*, Frankfurt/M.: Suhrkamp, p. 37-51.

Löw, Martina (2008): "Der Reiz der Großstadt. Sexualisierung durch Bildproduktionen". In: Sigrid Brandt/Hans-Rudolf Meier/Gunther Wölfle (eds.): *StadtBild und Denkmalpflege. Konstruktion und Rezeption von Bildern der Stadt*, Dresden: Jovis, unpaginated.

Mittelstraß, Jürgen (2003): "Die deutsche Universität verliert ihre Seele. Über den modernen Wissenschaftsbetrieb, das Humboldtsche Bildungsideal und ein forschungsnahes Lernen". In: *Frankfurter Rundschau*, no. 145, 26.6.2003, p. 7.

Neumann-Braun, Klaus/Mikos, Lothar (2006): *Videoclips und Musikfernsehen. Eine problemorientierte Kommentierung der aktuellen Forschungsliteratur*, Berlin: Vistas.

Paech, Joachim (2005): "Medienwissenschaft". In: Klaus Sachs-Hombach (ed.): *Bildwissenschaft. Disziplinen, Themen, Methoden*, Frankfurt/M.: Suhrkamp, p. 79-96.

Peverini, Paolo (2004): *Il videoclip. Strategie e figure di una forma breve.* Roma: Meltemi.

Rösing, Helmut (2003): "Bilderwelt der Klänge – Klangwelt der Bilder. Beobachtungen zur Konvergenz der Sinne". In: Dietrich Helms/Thomas Phleps (eds.): *Clipped Differences. Geschlechterrepräsentationen im Musikvideo. Beiträge zur Popularmusikforschung* vol. 31, Bielefeld: transcript, p. 9-25.

Schierl, Thomas (2005): "Werbungsforschung". In: Klaus Sachs-Hombach (ed.): *Bildwissenschaft. Disziplinen, Themen, Methoden*, Frankfurt/M.: Suhrkamp, p. 309-319.

Schmidt, Siegfried J. (2000): *Kalte Faszination. Medien – Kultur – Wissenschaft in der Mediengesellschaft*, Weilerswist: Velbrück Wissenschaft.

Schmidt, Siegfried J. (2002): "Medienwissenschaft und Nachbardisziplinen". In: Gebhard Rusch (ed.): *Einführung in die Medienwissenschaft. Konzeptionen, Theorien, Methoden, Anwendungen*, Wiesbaden: Westdeutscher Verlag, p. 53-68.

Schmidt, Siegfried J. (2007): *Histories & Discourses. Rewriting Constructivism*, (translated from the German by Wolfram Karl Köck & Alison Rosemary Köck), Exeter (UK) and Charlottesville (VA): Imprint Academic.

Schmidt, Siegfried J./Zurstiege, Guido (2000): *Orientierung Kommunikationswissenschaft. Was sie kann, was sie will*, Reinbek bei Hamburg: Rowohlt.

Schmidt, Siegfried J./Zurstiege, Guido (2007): *Kommunikationswissenschaft. Systematik und Ziele*, Reinbek bei Hamburg: Rowohlt.

Schulze, Holger (ed.) (2008): *Sound Studies: Traditionen – Methoden – Desiderate. Eine Einführung*, Bielefeld: transcript.

Sumitra, Sheila (2007): "Interdisciplinary Teaching at the University Level". In: *Journal of Popular Music Studies*, vol. 19 no. 1, p. 110-112.

Weiß, Matthias (2007): *Madonna revidiert. Rekursivität im Videoclip*, Berlin: Reimer.

Wenzel, Ulrich (1999): "Pawlows Panther. Musikvideos zwischen bedingtem Reflex und zeichentheoretischer Reflexion". In: Klaus Neumann-Braun (ed.): *Viva MTV! Popmusik im Fernsehen*, Frankfurt/M.: Suhrkamp, p. 45-73.

Wulff, Hans J. (1999): "The Cult of Personality – Authentisch simulierte Rockvideos". In: Klaus Neumann-Braun (ed.): *VIVA MTV! Popmusik im Fernsehen*, Frankfurt/M.: Suhrkamp, p. 262-277.

**Lyrics**

Spears, Britney (2007): *Gimme More*, http://www.azlyrics.com/lyrics/britneyspears/gimmemore.html (04.03.2009).

*Fast Forward*:
The Future of the Music Video

# Get the Cut

On the Relationship between Visual Music and Music Video

CORNELIA LUND/HOLGER LUND

## INTRODUCTION

When considering the future of the music video, it seems a rewarding task to take a closer look at other audio-visual genres based on the same main characteristic as music video: the combination of music and moving images. One of these genres, one could say the older, yet much more vital cousin of the music video, is visual music.[1] While exploring some basic questions we have developed in the course of our research, this essay also investigates the actual relationship between music video and visual music and their possible future. How can we define the relationship between the music video and visual music? What characterizes their particular way of relating music and images? What are the limits of these particular ways, and where do they fail? What is the common formal standard for a combination of music and images in each genre? And where does this standard prove insufficient? Does the perception of this insufficiency lead to new combinations of music video and visual music which try to compensate for the shortcomings?

## MUSIC VIDEO AND VISUAL MUSIC – A SHORT DEFINITION

Simplifying things a little, one could say that most music videos conform to a basic formal standard: you see the people who made the music, you hear and you see them performing their music – at least they pretend to. Creating a sort of double link between visual and acoustic information, this standard is based on a double-sided principle of causality: what you hear is what you see and, at the same time, what you see is what you hear. One could speak of a mutual affirmation between the two media involved. This kind of medial ruse enables the standard music video to produce a real and causal synchronicity of visual and acoustic events or at least to simulate it.

In visual music, different kinds of images, taken from different sources, are combined with music, a combination which is very often characterized by two principles: what you hear has an effect on what you see, and what you see has an effect on what you hear. The synchronization of musical beats and filmic cuts, for example, suggests a certain synchronicity of what happens musically and visually. Sound and images may share the same rhythm, but the relationship between them remains nevertheless artificial and more or less arbitrary. In visual music, different ways of suggesting a close relationship between sound and image by proposing different forms of synchronicity can be observed. Apart from the rhythmical synchronicity of beats and cuts, the attempt to synchronize sounds and colors by associating colors with specific sounds, or to synchronize pitches with positions in space (such as high-low) or contrasts (such as warm-cold, bright-dark) can also be found.

Taking the short definitions above as a starting point for a comparative look at the relationship between music video and visual music, we can observe several differences between the two genres as well as similarities. The most important difference between music video and visual music is the illusion of a certain reality and causality on which the music video is based that contrasts with a relatively artificial and arbitrary relation between sound and image in visual music. The most basic similarity is that in both genres visual sequences are structured in time according to acoustic signals. In visual music, however, visual signals can also be used to structure the audio flow. Here, the visual part does not – as in the case of music video – necessarily follow the audio part.

## AESTHETIC INCONVENIENCES, OR HOW TO ESCAPE A DILEMMA

Already in the early days of music TV and music video's ancestors, with the "Soundies" and "Scopitones" of the 40's and 60's, an aesthetic dilemma became clear which was created by this basic rule according to which the musicians have to be seen while performing their song. An anonymous 1974 film, shot in Los Angeles during the recording of Elis Regina and Tom Jobim's *Àguas de Março*, provides a good example for the static situation in early TV music studios and the resulting despair of the cameraman.

*Figs. 1-3: Stills from the anonymous film for Elis Regina and Tom Jobim*, Àguas de Março, *1974*

The whole take is dominated by visual poverty, showing only the two singers singing in front of a microphone (fig. 1). When they start to whistle (fig. 2), the despair of the cameraman obviously reaches its climax, since he focuses on the microphone (fig. 3).

In some films produced for the "Scopitones", we can discern an early protest against the established standard even before music video proper came into being. Procol Harum's *A Whiter Shade of Pale* (16mm, Cameron Films International, C-104, about 1967), shot by Alain Brunet, is marked by an unmistakable attitude of denial: fixed camera positions, fixed positions and languid looks of the musicians who cross their arms instead of playing instruments, negating the principle of causality and even offending the expectations of the viewer by confronting him with the sole of the lead singer's shoe thrust into the foreground (figs. 4-6).

*Figs. 4-6: Stills from the Scopitone film by Alain Brunet:*
*Procol Harum,* A Whiter Shade of Pale, *ca. 1967*

The effect is the charming power of negation, an irony informed by the Fluxus movement, partly obedient to the standard of the music video, partly in denial: all the band members are present (as they should be), but almost nobody is performing music (as they should do).

About the same time, other musicians seemingly had a similarly bad feeling concerning the standard, as demonstrated by Peter Goldmann/ The Beatles' *Strawberry Fields* (1967) and the film for Pink Floyd's *See Emily Play* (Belgian TV, Brussels, 1968)[2]:

*Figs. 7-8: Stills from the film by Peter Goldmann: The Beatles,*
Strawberry Fields, *1967*

The Beatles are hopping around in a quasi-surrealistic landscape, playing on a rotten piano or being occupied by other mostly non-musical actions (figs. 7 & 8). In *See Emily Play*, the drummer is first playing on an invisible drum-set in a park (fig. 9), and at the end of the film the musicians are even playing cricket with their instruments (fig. 10 & fig. 11).[3]

Figs. 9-11: *Stills from the film by David Gilmour: Pink Floyd*, See Emily Play, *1968*

Throughout the history of the music video, this attitude of protest has lead to the point of an ostentatious refusal of performing music, as the following examples may show. In his video for the song *Survive*, directed by Walter Stern in 1999, David Bowie is present but keeps quiet throughout, even during long close-ups, when all the while you can hear him perform the song. A more recent example is the music video for *St. Helvetia*, directed by Anna Luif in 2007, where we can see Kutti MC moving to his own music on roller blades. His music video is fulfilling only half the standard: you can see the person responsible for the music; he is, however, not performing the song but listening and moving to his own music (fig. 12).

Fig. 12: *Still from the music video by Anna Luif: Kutti MC,* St. Helvetia, *2007*

The video for Fatboy Slim's *Everybody Needs a 303*, directed by Ron Kurtz in 1997, can be brought in as another example. In marked opposition to the standard, we are shown a person who is not singing, not moving, who is not even the musician. The man keeps still for more than half the time of the video until a woman's hand is seen slowly writing something on his forehead which can be deciphered at the end of the video as: "Why make videos?" (figs. 13-15)

Figs. 13-15: Stills from the music video by Ron Kurtz: Fatboy Slim, Everybody Needs a 303, 1997

So, where lies the problem? There seems to be a clear feeling of absurdity concerning the basic rules of music video, a feeling that seems to induce artists and directors to counter-react by revealing and ridiculing the artificiality of music videos in different ways.

But there is still another way of dealing with one's bad feelings about the artificiality of the standard. It is again a sort of protest against the rules, but, at the same time, it gives the directors of a music video the opportunity to do themselves a favor. Here also the musicians are not shown and nobody is performing music. Instead, a visual narrative is presented with such high intensity that the music becomes almost like the soundtrack to a film. The music seems secondary, as if it had been just added and adjusted to previously shot filmic images. An example is the video for The Chemical Brothers' *Elektrobank*, directed by Spike Jonze in 1997. This approach, however, remains problematic concerning the status of the music, exactly because it becomes secondary in relation to the images. One remembers the narrative much more than the accompanying sounds. This, however, can't be the aim of a traditional commercial music video which is meant to serve the music and not vice versa.

In most of the aforementioned examples, one of the key factors of traditional music video is strikingly present: they either show the musicians' performance or they are linked to the lyrics. Visual music, in contrast, is completely free in its choice of images and the manner of visualization. It is neither bound to narrative development nor to the lyrics. Unlike studio-produced music videos, visual music is very often performed live, as in Andy Warhol's *Exploding Plastic Inevitable* (1966), or in lightshows and expanded cinema domes, to name a few historical examples. But visual music is not limited to live performance and can also be produced under "studio conditions." Here one might think of the often-cited early examples by Oskar Fischinger or Len Lye, or examples such as *Beatles Electroniques* (1966–69) by Nam June Paik, Jud Yalkut, and Ken Werner, where found footage consisting of recordings of the Beatles (sound and images) is treated visually and acoustically.[4]

While the history of visual music seems less prone to protest against an inherent standard, it still is marked by a constant struggle with the basic problem of the genre: the lack of an inherent causality in the combination of sound and images. As an attempt to amend this, various technical tools and couplings have been employed throughout the history of visual music, such as, for example, the oscilloscope used by Mary Ellen Bute in the 1950's.[5] One might also think of the more recent Windows Media Player and the new digital means of visualizing sounds. Nevertheless, in most of these examples there still remains an unrewarding technical – automatic – character of the images, or better of the coupling of sound and images. And the fact that the relationship between images and sound is created by technical parameters does not really do away with the problem of the arbitrary character of the coupling.

Another attempt to bring images and sound together in a less artificial way is the improvisation in an audio-visual band. Here, the image becomes, so to speak, an instrument within the band, but since the whole context centres on the performative aspect, recording it is very difficult.[6]

As digital technologies offer more and more possibilities for audiovisual creation, more ideas to develop relationships between audio and video that do not suffer from the aforementioned lack of causality become possible.

A recent example for parameterization and interrelation of the control of audio and video has been developed by Jörg Koch, a German audio artist. For the audio-visual production *Road II* (2008), he wrote a computer program for sound generation and image treatment in MAX/MSP/Jitter. Taking single images as a starting point – photographs in the case of *Road II* – Koch's software first analyzes them and then generates and controls the audio according to predefined visual parameters. At the same time, some of the visual parameters controlling the music are fed back on other visual parameters. Brightness, colors, density, and other parameters provide the basis for the process of sound production *and* for the process of animation and alienation of the visual material. The program can be described as a mix-remix-machine, doing both the mixing and the remixing at the same time.

The sound production is mainly done by a synthesizer, which is controlled by the program. Additional software-based effects, field recordings, and samples are used for the work. The image treatment works mainly with traditional techniques such as solarization, keys, color management, and resolution reductions.

But even in this case, where a close parametrical interconnection is produced, the relation between the images and the music appears insufficient because it remains arbitrary and aleatoric, above all in the choice of the parameters. The result is a high degree of non-specificity concerning the images. The program is only a machine, as non-specific to the images as a turntable is non-specific to the music played on it.

## How could Music Video and Visual Music Come Together and Offer Solutions for all these Problems?

There is one form of joining music and images which has been explored lately by many artists and musicians. Making music and playing instruments is by no way forbidden in visual music, still we don't have the good old performance video in mind, but a form we might call "music on screen." Here, the making of the music is not a product of mere simulation (as in music video), but the music is instead produced by filmic means such as cutting and editing. The result is a music which is based on filmic procedures, inextricably linked to the images which have undergone the same processes.

As an early example one could refer to Jim Henson's *Time Piece* (1965); a more recent one is Thilo Kraft's *und* (2006), where sound and images are created together from the audio-visual material of a man saying "und" (which is German for "and").

Leading far away from the traditional realm of the commercial music video, these more experimental forms of audio-visual creation tend toward other contexts where the constraints of fitting into prescribed standards are less pressing. Consequently, these audio-visual forms are to be found mainly in artistic or cinematic contexts – where, by the way, visual music has always been at home. Such a development is not without consequences for either genre. One consequence might be the decommercialization of the music video, which – by becoming an artistic or cinematic product – can no longer function as a mere commercial.[7] Furthermore, the production of audio-visual entities in which image and sound are no longer published separately may rise in importance since this kind of production only becomes coherent as an audio-visual piece like Henson's and Kraft's films or the productions issued by Pfadfinderei & Modeselektor, such as their DVD *Labland* (2004) featuring music that has never been released separately on CD or vinyl.

These considerations permit us to close the loop and to take us back to the title of this essay: Get the Cut. To conceive of music as a product of filmic procedures by using filmic means such as cutting in order to create the score, while applying the same procedures to treat the images which have been recorded together with the music, and to thus create audio-visual entities: this can be regarded as a convincing strategy not only to bring music video and visual music together, but also to work on the inherent problems of how each genre can leave behind the aesthetic inconveniences discussed above.

# REFERENCES

**1** | Given the very heterogeneous field of contemporary audio-visual productions that can be seen as descendant from what is historically defined as visual music, we find it rather difficult to speak of visual music as a consistent genre (for the history of visual music see for example Brougher/Mattis/Strick/Wiseman 2005). We think, however, that visual music can be used as a sort of operative term encompassing all kinds of audio-visual productions that strive for a meaningful and equal relationship between image and sound (see also Lund/Lund 2009: p. 11–12). It is in this sense and with these reservations that we describe "visual music" as a genre and as counterpart of music video.

**2** | According to Povey 2009: p. 62 the song was released as a single on the 16th of June 1967; it was then re-released in 1968 and accompanied by this promo-film. Povey 2009: p. 91 reports that the film is part of a series of promo-clips, shot, in order to accompany a couple of songs, on the 18th and the 19th of February 1968 under the direction of David Gilmour for the Belgian TV in the Parc de Laeken in Brussels. Although never officially released by the band, the clip for *See Emily Play* significantly is the only one out of this series which was distributed via the video compilation *Rock & Roll - The Greatest Years - 1967* (VC 458) in 1989. See for this Povey 2009: p. 91.

**3** | The "non-performance" of the group in *See Emily Play* could have a wider background: Pink Floyd had already performed the song in the Pat Boone Show (CBS TV, USA, 1967), but Syd Barrett, while on stage, didn't mime his singing part during the playback of the music (see http://www.floydian.de/index.htm?/dokumente/konzerte/1967_festivals_tourneen_und_konzerte_radio_and_tv_auftritte.htm, last access: 29.12. 2009). Roger Waters, who then saved the performance during the Pat Boone Show by stepping to the microphone and, instead of Barrett, miming the singing part, had this situation perhaps in mind while doing the "non-performance" in *See Emily Play* for the Belgian TV. See for the Pat-Boone-performance also Povey 2009: p. 71.

**4** | For Andy Warhol's EPI see Joseph 2003; for Len Lye and Oskar Fischinger see Brougher 2005; for Nam June Paik/Jude Yalkut/Ken Werner see Herzogenrath 1999: p. 152.

**5** | For Mary Ellen Bute see Naumann 2009. For more information on sound-image-transformation see Thoben 2010.

**6** | According to the art theoretician Peggy Phelan, for example, a performance, once recorded, changes its status: "Performance cannot be saved, recorded, documented, or otherwise participate in the circulation of representations: once it does so, it becomes something other than performance." See Phelan 1993: p. 146.

**7** | The definition of music video as a commercial is, of course, very schematic and has been transgressed since the very beginnings of the genre. On the one hand, there are music videos, which switch to the art context such as Chris Cunningham's video for Björk's *All is Full of Love* presented at the Venice Biennale in 2002. On the other hand, many artists have been interested by the format of the music video. Damien Hirst made a video for Blur's song *Country House* in 1995,

Wolfgang Tillmans for the Pet Shop Boys' *Home and Dry* in 2002, to name just a few examples – for this topic of artists making music videos see the contribution by Antje Krause-Wahl in this volume.

## BIBLIOGRAPHY

Brougher, Kerry/Mattis, Olivia/Strick, Jeremy/Wiseman, Ari (eds.) (2005): *Visual Music: Synaesthesia in Art and Music since 1900.* Los Angeles: Museum of Contemporary Art; London: Thames & Hudson.

Brougher, Kerry (2005): "Visual-Music Culture", in: Kerry Brougher/Olivia Mattis/Jeremy Strick/Ari Wiseman (eds.) (2005): *Visual Music: Synaesthesia in Art and Music since 1900.* Los Angeles: Museum of Contemporary Art; London: Thames & Hudson, p. 88-177.

Herzogenrath, Wulf (ed.) (1999): *Nam June Paik. Fluxus/Video*, Bremen: Kunsthalle Bremen, Cologne: Buchhandlung Walther König.

Joseph, Brandon W.: "'My Mind Split Open'. Andy Warhol's Exploding Plastic Inevitable", in: Matthias Michalka (ed.) (2003): *X-Screen: filmische Installationen und Aktionen der Sechziger- und Siebzigerjahre.* Vienna: MUMOK; Cologne: Buchhandlung Walther König, p. 14-45.

Lund, Cornelia/Lund, Holger (eds.) (2009): *Audio.Visual – On Visual Music and Related Media*, Stuttgart: Arnoldsche Art Publishers.

Naumann, Sandra: "Seeing Sound: The Short Films of Mary Ellen Bute", in: Holger Lund/Cornelia Lund (eds.) (2009): *Audio.Visual – On Visual Music and Related Media*, Stuttgart: Arnoldsche Art Publishers, p. 40-54.

Phelan, Peggy (1993): *Unmarked. The Politics of Performance.* Routledge, London.

Povey, Glenn (2009): *Pink Floyd*, Paris: Éditions Place des Victoires.

Thoben, Jan: "Technical Sound-Image Transformations", in: Dieter Daniels/Sandra Naumann/Jan Thoben (eds.) (2010): *See this Sound. Audiovisuology Compendium. An Interdisciplinary Survey of Audiovisual Culture*, Cologne: Buchhandlung Walther König, p. 425-431 (also online under: http://beta.see-this-sound.at/kompendium/abstract/51).

# "Why Artists Make Clips"

## Contemporary Connections between Art and Pop

ANTJE KRAUSE-WAHL

"The Hours hope you'll agree that it's not just another 'pop video' as they are not just another 'pop' band."[1] This statement could be read on The Hours' website upon the release of the video *See the Light* (7:40 min.), advertising their new album *Sophomore* (2009). To underline their claim, they engaged the well-known artist Damien Hirst as their art director.

Several exhibitions have already drawn attention to the crossover phenomenon between fine art and music video. In 2004 the Queensland Art Gallery in Brisbane showed *Video Hits: Pictures came and broke your heart*, and in 2007 the Musée de la ville de Paris displayed seventy works under the title *Play Back*.[2] Both compilations indicate that the connections between music video and fine art are manifold. Aiming to differentiate these connections within the field, Kathryn Weir, one of the curators of the exhibition in Brisbane, made the following distinction: "Where visual artists have made clips for bands – plugging into the global distribution networks of music television – they speak to an exponentially expanded public. Other artists have 'digested' the form for an art audience. Their responses to music video draw on alternating currents of irony, nostalgia, critique, camp and celebration, and develop the genre further in an art context, whether citing music video style, commenting on its form, or challenging our perceptions of the relationship between music and images." (Weir 2004)

Following Weir's line of thinking, one can point out that such clips have been discussed in relation to the history of experimental film and video art (see, for example, Gehr 1993). The clips for an expanded public have come into focus for art history as well (Keazor/Wübbena 2007). But within these two histories the question as to "why artists make clips" has not yet been adequately answered. What has struck me during my research has been that the significance ascribed to clips made by artists themselves is not uniform: Robert Longo lists his clips for New Order and Megadeth on his website as part of his oeuvre.[3] For Isaac Julien and

n Evans, however, music videos are just trips on which they
ked at the beginning of their careers.[4] *J'aime les filles*, a video di-
ted by Philippe Parreno in 1998 for Dave Stewart, is mentioned on the
homepage of Parreno's gallery Air de Paris, but it has never been shown
on a music channel.[5] And, as Henry Keazor and Thorsten Wübbena note
in their essay on crossovers between art and music video, Jonas Åkerlund
took advantage of footage shot for Metallica in order to create several short
films at once, which were released in both the fields of music and of art
(Keazor/Wübbena 2007: p. 323–25).

Against this background, I will answer the following questions: How
can the interrelations between music video and an artist's oeuvre be described? What might be the reasons for artists to embrace this special format? And who benefits from these collaborations?

My essay will concentrate on the British art scene since the 90's –
where a continuous exchange between music and fine art can be traced[6] –,
focusing in particular on clips by Sam Taylor-Wood and Damien Hirst.

## Music and YBAs: Some General Remarks

At the beginning of the 90's, a group of young artists established themselves and were soon to become well-known and labeled as Young British
Artists (YBAs).[7] One common characteristic was their strong interest in
popular culture and in being part of this popular culture, with music as
an important source of inspiration. Gavin Turk, for example, created a
self-portrait entitled *Pop* (1993), a sculpture in which he slipped into the
role of Sid Vicious from the Sex Pistols, combining it with the Warholian
version of Elvis Presley. His sculpture was described as paradigmatic for
the attitude of this new generation of artists, who – with recourse to by-
gone subcultures – stylized themselves as, in this case, "punk rebels" or, in
other examples, as "working class heroes" (Legge 2000: p. 4).

Via their video works artists are also pointing out the role of pop music
in today's culture. Gilliam Wearing, for instance, can be seen in *Dancing
in Peckham* (1994, 25 min.) dancing in a shopping mall while appearing
to listen to music on her walkman, but in reality she is only imagining
the sounds of Nirvana, Queen, or Gloria Gaynor. Other artists appropriate
the formal characteristics of the music clip itself: Several of Tracey Emin's
videos can be called "clips" because her performance complies with the
length of the chosen song and her images are cut to suit the music rather
than the other way round. While *My Crystal Ship* from The Doors is playing, she is, with eyes closed, spinning around in her studio (*My Crystal
Ship* [1995]); during John Holt's reggae rendition of *Riding for a Fall* she is
riding on horseback along the beach (*Riding for a Fall* [1999]).

In both videos Emin tries to embody the song and its emotions expressed through the music and lyrics. Angela McRobbie has pointed out
that dance plays an important role in the construction of female identity

– it projects a dual relation, a fantasy of the self that is combined with a longing for the other. Thus, dance articulates adolescence, girlhood, femininity and sexuality at the same time. But because this process takes place within one's own body, it represents the fantasy of taking control, a resistance to the existing rules (McRobbie 1984). In *Why I never became a dancer*, a video that shows Emin dancing to Sylvester James's *You Make Me Feel*, the importance of music and dance for the construction of a female identity is particularly ostentatious. In the first part of the video Tracey Emin narrates with her voice the story of growing up in the small town Margate, accompanied by images from this location, including her sexual interrelationships with several men. The second part tells about her leaving. She is seen in a studio in a city dancing to lyrics like "You make me feel, mighty real", thus her "music video" becomes an expression of empowerment, an image of a female hero, controlling now her life and relationships – a story comparable to videos like Madonna's *True Blue* or Cindy Lauper's *Girls Just Want to Have Fun* (directed by Angel Gracia & Ciff Guest in 1986 resp. by Edd Griles in 1983).[8]

The significance of music in Emin's autobiography as well as the construction of her identity become apparent from a CD that she compiled in 2006 for the British furniture shop Habitat, which was given the title *Music to Cry to*. In the CD booklet she associates songs with personal experiences: "It's about being afraid of being happy" goes along with the above-mentioned song by John Hold, and "When my last boyfriend had an affair I played it really loud all the time" with Marianne Faithfull's *Broken English*. Tracey Emin's commitment to music and her adoption of the clip format shows how music, as part of the experience of growing up, plays an important role in constructing identity, but at the same time it is evident that for artists pop music opens up new options for becoming popular. This potential will be explored below.

## SAM TAYLOR-WOOD: THE CLIP AS A WORK OF ART

*Fig. 1: Stills from the music video by Sam Taylor-Wood: Elton John,* I Want Love, *2001*

In 2001 Sam Taylor-Wood shot a 35 mm film, later transferred to video, for Elton John's *I Want Love*, the single release from his album *From the West Coast* (fig. 1). The plot is minimal: The male actor, Robert Downey Jr., walks through empty halls of a historic and representative townhouse. He lip-synchs Elton John's song, lamenting a difficult search for love in the light of injuries already experienced. The video was made in one single shot, beginning with a zoom on Downey Jr., who with the second verse starts walking around, adapting to the rhythm. Due to the reduced and limited narrative, but also due to Downey Jr.'s minimal play, poses and mimics are emphasized: During the repeated phrase "I want love", he closes his eyes, leans theatrically against the window frame, sits down at the window, or looks longingly toward the imaginary sky. While he sings "I'm ready for the rougher stuff", he rumples his hair, and when "Other men feel liberated" sounds, he wraps his arms around himself.

Elton John songs are, as Simon Frith has written regarding *Candle in the Wind*, "infused with Elton John's personality and, for its emotional effect, infused too with a kind of collective sigh" (Frith 2007: p. 168). This claim of being a substitution for a broader public corresponds with the established performance of Elton John playing and singing at the piano. Taylor-Wood now has chosen an actor who obviously does not sing with his own voice but demonstrates emotional identification with the song through the movement of his body. One can argue that the actor replaces the emotional identification of the viewer/listener, but this explanation isn't sufficient, as a comparison with another work by the Taylor-Wood will show.[9]

Taylor-Wood commented in an interview that this video was an impulse for a new stage in her work, resulting in *Crying Men* (2002-2004), a photographic series made with the help of Elton John's connections in society (Taylor-Wood 2004).[10] In the sessions she asked male Hollywood actors to cry; since they visibly act out emotional states, the resulting pictures direct us to concentrate on these poses (fig. 2). Something comparable happens in *I Want Love* where the clichéd poses of a lovesick person are emphasized in a way that they become exposed as what they actually are: clichéd poses.

Sam Taylor-Wood also photographed Robert Downey Jr. for her *Crying Men* series. But in contrast to the other actors, whose eyes are filled with tears, Downey Jr. is lying in a rather erotic pose on a bed or, in the words of Linda Nochlin: "He doesn't let grief interfere with sensual self-display: he mourns lying down and lightly fraped, smooth-skinned and hairless, like a male odalisque or an epicene martyr, his arm raised provocatively over his head, his torso saucily twisted." (Nochlin 2008: p. 52-55) When in the video Downey Jr. lasciviously rests against the window frame, this devoted pose is likewise fitting. The sensitive male protagonist is attractive for both men and women, thus confirming in a subtle way the fact that the lyrics never address a distinctively gendered subject.

*Fig. 2: Sam Taylor-Wood:* Crying Men (Michael Madsen), *2002–2004*

It is the topic of the pose that connects Sam Taylor-Wood's artistic concerns with this commissioned work for Elton John. But although *I Want Love* was shown in 2002 as part of her solo exhibition at Matthew Marks Gallery in New York, some uncertainty about the significance of the video within her oeuvre existed. This became apparent when the video was banned to the corridor.

Since 1997 Sam Taylor-Wood has been working with the Pet Shop Boys when she designed their live show *Somewhere* at the Savoy Theatre in London,[11] and in 2003 they recorded together a remix of *Love to Love You Baby* under the pseudonym Kiki Kokova.

In 2008 Taylor-Wood produced *I'm in Love with a German Film Star,* an album containing four remixes of the hit by the post-punk band The Passions that entered the charts in 1981 – a trance-like song recounting a mystical encounter with a film star. In the video accompanying the "Radio Remix" – a piece whose sound is close to the original – we see the artist herself appropriating the famous pose of Marlene Dietrich sitting on a stool and wearing a tailcoat and a top hat (figs. 3, 4).

Fig. 3: Sam Taylor-Wood: Cover for the album I'm in Love with a German Film Star by the Pet Shop Boys, 2008

Fig. 4: Eugene Robert Richee: Marlene Dietrich in Morocco, directed in 1930 by Josef von Sternberg

This tableau vivant is animated only through the casual blinking of her eyes and the steady ascent of smoke from the burning cigarette that she is holding in her hand. But Sam Taylor-Wood is not only acting out her love for a star qua masquerade. The video contains both idleness und movement at the same time: while filmic time passes along with the smoke of the cigarette, the body is nearly frozen. Josef von Sternberg, the director responsible for shaping Dietrich's iconic image, has told how the actress was in agony while holding the airy poses he demanded – but that in precisely this holding of poses at length, in this tension between the passing of time and the pressure inflicted on the body to stand still, the glamorous aura of Dietrich emerged (Holert 2004: p. 63). In the picture time is condensed. Looking at cinema and the moving image, Gilles Deleuze has described those images that are capable of presenting direct images of time as "time-images". He argues, in short, that in classical cinema time is presented in movements referring to the external world, but that dealing with time-images means working with the *interstice*, the space between images (Deleuze 1989: p. 179-80). With her tableau vivant, Taylor-Wood is working with time in a twofold sense: she is exploring the importance of time for the auratic quality of one's pose. And she is creating a "time-image" in the Deleuzian sense as well. Mark Hansen has argued in an extensive article on time-images that, by interrupting our abstract thinking about time, they have an effect on the audience in providing it with an experience of the passing of time (Hansen 2004: p. 584-625). In this respect Sam Taylor-Wood's reflection on the interrelation between medium, glamour, and time further corresponds with the fact that a musical remake is at play here – something reenacted, like Dietrich's pose.

## DAMIEN HIRST: WHO IS ADVERTISING WHOM?

Like Taylor-Wood, Damien Hirst has collaborated with several musicians. In 1994 he designed the covers for Dave Stewart's single *Heart of Stone* and his album *Greetings from the Gutter* using his own artwork. The accompanying music video *Heart of Stone* was shot in an exhibition with several of the artist's works framing the stage for this piece. Dave Stewart himself devoted the song *Damien Save Me* to the artist.

In 1995 Hirst directed Blur's *Country House* from their album *The Great Escape* (1995). *Country House* tells a story of a prosperous townsman "caught in a rat race", who tries to escape by moving to a "country house". But this doesn't prove to be a viable alternative – he watches reruns on TV and collects receipts from his psychiatrist. The video's narrative plot is framed by the zooming in and out of a suburban high-rise window from an apartment where members of the band are gathering together around a table on which a parlor game titled "Escape from the rat race" is spread out. When the curtains of the windows are pulled closed at the beginning of the video, one member of the band, holding a book with an image of the castle Neuschwanstein on the cover, introduces the internal plot with "And so the story begins". This sentence is an allusion to the BBC children's series, *Jackanory*, which starts off with the following nursery rhyme: "I'll tell you a story, about Jack-a-nory; and now my story's begun" – the song text also refers to this show. The central setting is an oversized replica of the already mentioned game, on which various people are frolicking, including the members of Blur, the "city dweller" played by actor and musician Keith Allen, some lightly dressed women (among others Sara Stockbridge, a model for Vivienne Westwood, and Joanne Guest, actress and poster girl of *Loaded* magazine), a doctor (played by the famous British comedian Matt Lucas), and lastly a parade troupe with different farm animals.

From the game's board Damon Albarn comments on what is happening in parallel to the lyrics: When he sings "no limit", the protagonist is running against a street sign with the same inscription, and at "caught up" the girls running across the playing field are caught in a cage; during "in touch with his own mortality" the "city dweller" falls into a kind of torture chamber, and at "takes herbal baths" the band members can be seen together with girls in neatly arranged bathtubs. The noticeably repetitious structure of the music, both in the verses but also in the melody, are accompanied by actions in fast motion, thus visualising the "rat race".

The video is full of references to popular culture.[12] Next to *Jackanory*, the most noteworthy are those to the Benny Hill sketches: Their stage-like structure, the typical short skirts worn by the girls, sexual jokes, and even the usage of fast motion alienate the movements, transforming the action into an impression that is likewise intensified through the rhythm of the music. Damien Hirst carries the quoting of popular culture to the extreme, as John Harris has pointed out: "The result was a collision of *Carry On* and *Loaded* magazine: three minutes so in tune with the spirit of the age that it both dominated the airwaves and dated at speed." (Harris 2003: p. 234)

Compared to Sam Taylor-Wood, who uses the video clip as a medium for exploring the relation between moving and still images, Hirst employs images and scenes from popular culture, combining them with a story. Blur's lyrics and music meet Damien Hirst's pictorial narration in its ironic attitude regarding the quirks of British society. Success – Blur's song turned out to hit number one in the charts – came with consequences. In 1998 Keith Allen, Blur's bassist Alex James, and Damien Hirst launched the band Fat Les, whose song *Vin-Da-Loo* became the unofficial British hymn of the 1998 World Cup. The video (including, among others, also a cameo by the above mentioned comedian Matt Lucas) parodies the plot of Walter Stern's famous 1997 clip for *Bitter Sweet Symphony* by The Verve and is, at the same time, a mockery on British fan culture with similar visual jokes.[13]

In 1995 Damien Hirst was already established as a well-known media personality, not only for his sharks and cows preserved in formaldehyde, but also for his medicine cabinets filled with colorful pharmaceuticals as a metaphor of longing for a *Great Escape*. If in *Country House* Hirst's artistic inventions are only suggested through the animals or by showing a crazy doctor, he used them extensively when he started working with The Hours in 2007, a band linked to the Britpop context as well.[14] Damien Hirst, their "longtime friend and champion", designed the cover of their CD *Narcissus Road* by placing a skull with two clocks in its eyeholes in front of one of his "spin paintings", paintings that he had been producing regularly since 1995 by pouring paint onto a potter's wheel (fig. 7).

The collaboration was intensified in 2008 with the music video for the song *See the Light* (fig. 5). This video (directed by film director Tony Kaye and artistically designed by Hirst) directly enters the Hirstian pictorial world with blood being poured onto a revolving "spin painting". The term "spinning" is used not only in a literal sense, but also in the phrase "someone's head is spinning", which is central to the story told by the music video. It starts with actress Sienna Miller moving around in a deserted Prada shop, dressed in a hospital gown. She seems to be desperately trying to escape the fashion world. After leaving the shop, she roams the streets, only to find herself in a psychiatrist's parlour lamenting about how her life doesn't make sense. Another scene plays in an examination room where she is pushed into a magnetic resonance tomograph. This is linked to the following sequence where she is settled in a room with three slashed and still-bleeding cows hanging on the wall. Upon finding herself awake in the hospital, she starts destroying its furnishings, only to be seen again in a street at night, where she experiences a nervous breakdown. The video ends with a view into the white, glowing tomograph.

*Fig. 5: Stills from the music video by Tony Kaye (Art Director: Damien Hirst): The Hours,* See the Light, *2008*

Until 2008 Hirst extensively used – alongside the already mentioned medicine cabinets – medical utilities, like air tanks or anatomical models, transforming them with an intent to question the role of medicine as a kind of *ersatz religion.* Moreover, he has recently combined allusions to Christian iconography with the monetary value of art. In an exhibition at Gagosian Gallery in 2005 he gave one of his "spin paintings" the title *Beautiful Bleeding Wound Over the Materialism of Money Painting* (2005). His well-known diamond skull *For the Love of God* (2007), a life-sized cast of a human skull encrusted with 8,601 pave-set industrial diamonds with a total weight of 1,100 carats, has been described as a traditional vanity motif, reminiscent of the transience of all earthly values (Fuchs 2007) (fig. 6). Also, Hirst's pickled animals are increasingly embellished with Christian symbolism: *God Alone Knows,* a triptych of formaldehyde-filled glass units containing the eviscerated carcasses of sheep pinned in the extended T-positions of the cross, is described on the website of his London gallery White Cube as follows: "Hirst re-presents the visceral brutality of Christ's death, and yet there is an unexpectedly quiet beauty in the way the forlorn and tragic figures appear to float against their mirrored grounds, as if resurrected."[15]

In *See the Light,* on the one hand, distinctive scenes are reminiscent of individual works by Damien Hirst but, on the other hand, a story of a possible healing is told. As in the case of the skull, which combines earthly values with the vanity-symbol and as such tells a story about life and death, the video narrates a process – from a Prada shop (as the representation of 'false' redemption, ultimately driving only to despair) to a crucifixion up to a possible redemption.

In the 7:40 minutes of the music video, the only verses being constantly repeated are: "Can you see the light", "hold on", "there will be light", "please hold on, baby hold on", "there is light in us". The melody is also repetitive and together with the texts resembles an incantation, accompanying from the off the story of a desperate soul. When Damien Hirst in his catalogues – with telling titles such as *New Religion* or *The Elusive Truth* – raises the question about the role of religion and medicine in our society, connecting this with a possible spiritual dimension of fine art,[16] this seems to go hand in hand with The Hours' music, which is capable in both text and melody of bringing the spiritual dimension to the fore.

Fig. 6: Damien Hirst: For the Love of God,
Platinum, diamonds and human teeth,
17.1 x 12.7 x 19.1 cm, 2007

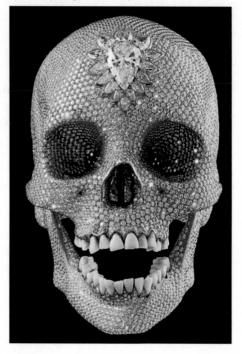

In light of this explicit treatment of Hirst's transformed iconography, the question of the objective of this collaboration can be put forth: the crossover between music and fine art in Britain since the 1960s has been analyzed by Simon Frith and Howard Horne in their comprehensive sociological study Art into Pop (Frith/Horne 1987). To explain this phenomenon, they point to the "art school connection", thus calling attention to the fact that since the 1960s the cultural producers in the field of music have been strongly aligned with art schools.[17] Frith and Horne make the assumption that this crossover arose out of a conflict: on the one hand, creativity and autonomy are considered high values in art education, yet on the other hand pressure to be economically successful can be noted in relation to the penetration of mass culture in art-educational contexts. Uniting both aspects seems to be possible in musical contexts since music makes it possible to be both creatively and commercially successful at the same time.

Pierre Bourdieu's theory of art production, however, makes clear another perspective on the connection between art and pop music. Bourdieu's interest lies, in view of the formation of avant-gardes, in describing the structure of the field of art, including its social constructions. He understands the field as a kind of "playground", a set of objective connections between individuals or institutions, both competing for the same thing: they're all longing for a position in the field of power. The specific individual position results from a complex interplay of the economic, cultural, and symbolic capital that already exists or has to be gained (Bourdieu 1996). It has already been argued that the YBAs have a strong connection to mass media and the advertising industry.[18] Michael Grenfell and Cheryl Hardy have systemized this by reverting to Bourdieu. They have made a distinction between the "field of cultural production", the "field of political power", and the "field of commercial enterprise" (Grenfell/Hardy 2003: p. 26) and have shown, how the YBAs occupy an outstanding position since they relate to all fields structuring the field of power. Grenfell and Hardy name the parameters that make it possible to attain power: "Wide circulation of products from the various fields as fashion objects or popular ideas" and "Connections with the fields of publishing and pop music." (ibid.: p. 27)

In this regard, music videos by artists do not only advertise pop albums – they are also part of and signify the accumulation of capital, necessary to occupy a dominant position in the field of art. Sam Taylor-Wood's *I Want Love* and Hirst's *Country House* and *See the Light* all connect to the different fields, for not only are artists and musicians collaborating, but well-known actors with high visibility in the media have also participated. Due to his drug addiction, Robert Downey Jr. was at the time of the video release just as famous as Sara Stockbridge, and as Sienna Miller is today.

But in terms of success *Country House* is an outstanding example. It was Blur's first number one hit, and the video not only adopted a range of popular issues, but was itself adopted by the media in turn: "Even in the two-dimensional media, the video did its work: *The Sun* ran a series of stills, in which Blur were dwarfed by a photo of Sara Stockbridge, headlined 'May Bust Men Win'" (Harris 2003: p. 234). In the same year, Damien Hirst was the winner of the Turner Prize. Thus, Blur and Hirst obviosuly had the benefit of gaining public attention from their joint collaboration.[19]

Compared to this accumulation of power, the collaboration between The Hours and Hirst can be viewed from a different perspective. While in the early 90's Hirst was still establishing himself, in the second half of the decade he professionalized his artistic output. As Donald N. Thompson has shown, Hirst is even today still working on different groups of works that all slightly alter a single motif – animals in formaldehyde, spin paintings, spot paintings –, all having become trademarks for the artist, carriers of the Hirst brand, so to speak, like Prada or Gucci (Thompson 2008: p. 73).

The motif of the skull is a carrier of the Hirst brand as well, and in 2007 it played a decisive role for the artist. At the June opening of the exhibition space White Cube 3 in London, he presented the already mentioned life-sized cast of a human skull entitled *For the Love of God* (2007). It caused a sensation because of its production costs, estimated at around 12–15 million pounds. White Cube was also offering limited edition silk-screen prints and produced a catalogue under the title *For the Love of God: The Making of the Diamond Skull* (Hirst 2007). But Hirst also went with this image in the fashion market and developed a *Warhol Factory x Levi's x Damien Hirst* collection sporting diamond skulls.

*Fig. 7: Damien Hirst & Jason Beard: Cover for the album* Narcissus Road *by the The Hours, 2007*

Even if the album cover for The Hours shows only a "naked skull" (fig. 7), since it was stocked in shops at the same time the exhibition was running, it makes just as much of a contribution to the valuation of the artwork as does Hirst's collection for Levi's Jeans, which are imprinted with skulls and "spin paintings" in the Damien Hirst x Levi's® collection.[20] Or is this fashion line an advertisement for The Hours? This example illustrates how comparable music, art, and fashion are in their need to work with brands. The Hours has benefited from Damien Hirst's brand and from his popularity,[21] for he has attained the status of a pop star among the artists, at least in Great Britain. And – as Mira Fliescher has argued – with this spreading of the motif, Damien Hirst is acknowledging the uniqueness and value of the single object: the encrusted diamond skull (Fliescher 2008).

## Leaving the UK

Researchers on YBAs point out that the above-described connections are a peculiarity of Great Britain but, considering the boom of the art market, the above phenomena do not apply to Great Britain alone. An example that might illustrate the accumulation of popularity on a global level is the collaboration of the rapper Kanye West, who in 2007 hired the Japanese artist Takashi Murakami and his company Kaikai Kiki to design the video for *Good Morning* accompanying his album *Graduation*.

Kanye West had already used the aesthetic of Japanese animés in *Stronger* (directed by Hype Williams in 2007). Whereas the music was a sample of Daft Punk's *Harder, Better, Faster, Stronger* (2001), West also seemed to be inspired by a Daft Punk music video drawn by Leiju Matsumoto.[22] But, first of all, West borrowed scenes from the animé classic *Akira* and loosely strung them together in combination with real-life adaptations of these borrowed scenes. The dark atmosphere of this animé and the story of Akira, whose awakening might bring the end of the world, are transformed into a love story embodying typical attitudes for a male rap star.

Compared to *Stronger*, *Good Morning* has a decidedly different aesthetic. While West is rapping about his ascent to fame and its related obstacles, the animé narrates the story of Teddy aka Kanye West, who can be identified through the white sunglasses he was wearing as his trademark in 2007. He gets up early in the morning to go to Hip Hop University and undergoes some serious mishaps: he misses the subway, his tuned car crashes, it starts raining, etcetera. In the end he obtains his university diploma and celebrates with his friends in the wide world opening before him. Even if the credits emphasize that Kanye West has written the story, Murakami uses images and signs in the clip that he has developed throughout his artistic career. Since 1994 he has worked with his signature character MR. DOB, a Mickey-Mouse-like figure with Manga eyes, whose name is written on the ears and along the oval of his face. MR. DOB was developed as a critical commentary on the role of trademarks in adding value not only to goods but also to artwork as well. But MR. DOB, who has undergone several mutations, has been simultaneously used as a merchandising article by Murakami himself, thus becoming a brand and making it difficult to distinquish clearly between art and advertising.[23] *Good Morning*, which is designed in colors and patterns typical for Murakami and also reveals many other figures that Murakami uses in his artworks, ends with an image showing the Teddy aka Kanye West on a huge MR. DOB flying into space.

*Fig. 8: Takashi Murakami: Cover for the album* Graduation *by Kanye West,* 2007

*Fig. 9: Takashi Murakami:* Homage to Francis Bacon (Study of Isabel Rawsthorne). *Acrylic on canvas, wood, 120 x 120 x 5 cm, 2002*

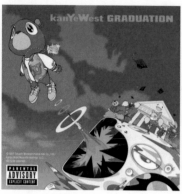

In *Good Morning* the story of Kayne West is told, but Murakami does not actually invent a new animé for the musician; rather, he is working with his own imagery – even if the cover for the album *Graduation* (fig. 8) is at least a variation of Murakami's *Hommage to Francis Bacon (Study of Isabel Rawthorne)* (2003; fig. 9). This is especially noticeable since Kanye West is well-known for his need to create his own strong means of self-expression. One might argue that Murakami and West are playing out a kind of competition as to who is more visible in the market, but this argument fails to take the music into consideration. West's music, his rapping, is not only famous for its distinctive style, but now works synergistically with a personality from the field of visual art in a way that both 'brands', via music and via image, are guaranteeing success for both the musician and the artist: *Good Morning* was not only prominent on MTV, but was also shown in the Murakami exhibition touring America and Europe, which in the United States was also accompanied by a performance by West at the opening (fig. 10).[24]

*Fig. 10: Still from the installation of the music video by Kaikai Kiki: Kanye West,* Good Morning, *2007*

I have shown that the crossovers between art and music video are manifold. But three aspects seem of particular importance to me. An obvious
point is that clips are part of popular culture; like magazine images or
ads, they are materials that artists work with. But, secondly, it is noticeable that artists producing music videos don't invent something solely for
the musician, but rather they explore their own artistic interest further
– especially if the artist is constantly working within the filmic medium.
In this respect, artists – and this is the third point – are now aiming at a
medium that is widely distributed and using it to disseminate their own
images as well.

Referring to the study by Frith and Horne, John Walker describes the
music video as an auditive and visual form that depicts the experimental
crossover (Walker 1987). Though as Diederich Diederichsen, in considering the role of music in fine arts today, critically remarks: "Music is able to
provide an update that could hook up the fine arts with a new public, but
also with other new, creative opportunities beyond those provided by galleries and other traditional venues." (Diederichsen 2008: p. 276)[25]

In this respect, music videos made by visual artists must be viewed
from a twofold perspective: they may be experimental, but music videos
are trailers as well, not only for a musician's album but also for the visual
artist.

## REFERENCES

**1** | See http://www.thehours.co.uk/seethelight/ (last access 20.12.2009).

**2** | See http://qag.qld.gov.au/exhibitions/archive/2004/video_hits (last ac-
cess 20.12.2009); also see Dressen 2007.

**3** | See http://www.robertlongo.com/work/gallery/1120 (last access 20.12.
2009); New Order, *Bizarre Love* (1986), Megadeth, *Peace Sells* (1986), or
R.E.M., *The One I Love* (1987).

**4** | Cerith Wyn Evans worked together with Derek Jarman for The Smith and for
Throbbing Gristle, Isaac Julien made the clip for Des'ree, *Feel So High* (1991).
But this information is only difficult to obtain, thus the videos never became
famous because of their later famous directors.

**5** | See http://www.airdeparis.com/pdave.htm (last access 20.12.2009).
For this video clip, Parreno combined the performance of the 1980's pop star
with an advertisement for candy. During a lecture at the Städelschule Academy
(31.1.2002), Parreno stated that this video had been commissioned by Dave
Stewart, but Stewart thought that the video represented mockery.

**6** | One representative example might be the CD from The @mbassadors *We
Love You* (2000) containing collaborations between artists and musicians:
Tracey Emin & Boy George, Marc Quinn & Brian Eno, Chris Ofili and Add N to X,
Gavin Turk mixes by Dub Pistols, etcetera.

**7** | On the formation of YBAs, the role of artists like Damien Hirst and of the
collector Charles Saatchi, and the context of New Labour, critically compare

the catalogue *Sensation: Young British Artists from the Saatchi Collection* (Rosenthal 1998); Ford 1998: p. 130-141 or Stallabrass 2001.

**8** | One could argue that Emin acts in this video like a fan, referencing popular dance videos of the 1980s. Jonathan Fiske wrote that in 1988 MTV asked Madonna fans to make their own videos for *True Blue* and the participants worked with the fantasy of empowerment in their pieces (Fiske 2000: p. 119).

**9** | Other music videos work with lip-synching as well. For example, David Fincher for George Michael's *Freedom! 90* – see for this for example Keazor/Wübbena 2007, p. 423-424.

**10** | See "Elton John: When I met Sam Taylor-Wood, I fell in love with her," *Telegraph*, http://www.telegraph.co.uk/culture/art/3563174/Elton-John-When-I-met-Sam-Taylor-Wood-I-fell-in-love-with-her.html (last access 20.12.2009).

**11** | For their show, Sam Taylor-Wood used three parallel screens that also resembled her own installations; see, for example, Frohne 1999.

**12** | Other quotes are from Charlie Chaplin and from Queen's *Bohemian Rhapsody*.

**13** | Fat Les produced other videos as well, such as *Naughty Christmas* (2000) and another soccer hymn *Jerusalem* (2000). In the latter there is a short sequence with Hirst himself, searching for the right display window for his camera.

**14** | Singer Antony Genn played the guitar in the band Pulp.

**15** | See www.whitecube.com/artists/hirst/ (last access 20.12.2009).

**16** | See, for example, the 2005 catalogue on Damien Hirst, *The Elusive Truth*.

**17** | Graham Coxton worked next to Damien Hirst at Goldsmith College.

**18** | See the chapter "The market and the state" in Stallabrass 1999: p. 170-196.

**19** | That artist and band are both the epitome of Brit Art/Britpop might be demonstrated by their *Mission to Mars*. In May 2003 a Damien Hirst's "spot painting" was used as an instrument calibration chart on the British Beagle lander, accompanied by a track by Blur, to be played from the probe as a signal that the Beagle had landed.

**20** | Respecting covers, further coincidences can be seen: For instance, on the exhibition catalogue cover of works from Damien Hirst's collection, published in 2008 under the title *In the Darkest Hour There May Be Light*, a Grim Reaper is depicted displaying notable similarities with the clocks on the *Narcissus Road* cover. See Hirst 2008.

**21** | Even if I couldn't trace the exact connections, Damien Hirst's artworks garnered a high profit during a Sotheby's auction in February 2008, and The Hours played during this event as well. See Sotheby statistics at http://chelseaartgalleries.com/auctions/with?sale=S25 (last access 20.12.2009).

**22** | The video accompanying the single became part of the musical section of the Daft Punk animé musical *Interstella 5555: The 5tory of the 5ecret 5tar 5ystem*. See Keazor/Wübbena 2007, p. 400-404 and http://en.wikipedia.org/wiki/Interstella_5555 (last access 20.12.2009).

**23** | For Murakami's ambivalent use of mass-market strategies, see Rothkopf 2007.

**24** | Just how effective this collaboration has proven is illustrated by the fact that Kanye West has designed sports shoes for Louis Vuitton, whose head designer Marc Jacobs works closely with Murakami.

**25** | My translation; originally in German: "Musik steht für ein Update zur Verfügung, das die bildende Kunst an ein neues Publikum, aber auch an andere, neue Verwertungsmöglichkeiten jenseits der Galerie und der Originale anschließen könnte."

## BIBLIOGRAPHY

Bourdieu, Pierre (1996): *The Rules of Art*, Cambridge: Polity Press.

Deleuze, Gilles (1989): *Cinema 2: The Time-Image*, Minneapolis: University of Minnesota Press.

Diederichsen, Diedrich (2008): "Echos von Spiegelsounds in goldenen Headphones". In: Diedrich Diederichsen, *Kritik des Auges: Texte zur Kunst*, Dresden: Fundus, p. 274-304.

Dressen, Anne (ed.) (2007): *Play Back*, Paris: Musées.

Fiske, Jonathan (2000): *Lesarten des Populären*. Vienna: Turia + Kant.

Fliescher, Mira (2008): "Skull Market: Kunst Markt Strategie", lecture held on October 15, 2008 at the Museum for Modern Art, Frankfurt am Main.

Ford, Simon (1998): "The Myth of the Young British Artist". In: Duncan McCorquodale et al. (eds.): *Occupational Hazard: Critical Writing On Recent British Art*, London: Black Dog.

Frith, Simon/Horne, Howard (1987): *Art into Pop*, London et al.: Methuen.

Frith, Simon (2007): *Taking Popular Music Seriously: Selected Essays*, Aldershot/Burlington: Ashgate.

Frohne, Ursula (ed.) (1999): *Video Cult/ures: Multimediale Installationen der 90er Jahre*, Cologne: DuMont.

Fuchs, Rudi (2007): *Rudi Fuchs in Damien Hirst: For the Love of God The Making of the Diamond Skull*, London: Other Criteria and Jay Jopling/White Cube.

Gehr, Herbert (ed.) (1993): *Sound and Vision: Musikvideo und Filmkunst*, Frankfurt am Main: Deutsches Filmmuseum.

Grenfell, Michael/Hardy, Cheryl (February 2003): "Field Manoeuvres: Bourdieu and the Young British Artists". In: *Space and Culture* 6, no. 1, p. 19-34.

Hansen, Mark (Spring 2004): "The Time of Affect, or Bearing Witness to Life". In: *Critial Inquiry* 30, no. 3.

Harris, John (2003): *Britpop! Cool Britannia and the Spectacular Demise of English Rock*, Cambridge, MA: Da Capo Press.

Hirst, Damien (2005): *The Elusive Truth*. Montreal: Transcontinental Litho ACME.

Hirst, Damien (2007): *For the Love of God: The Making of the Diamond Skull*, London: White Cube.

Hirst, Damien (2008): *In the Darkest Hour There May Be Light: Works From Damien Hirst's Murderme Collection*, London: Other Criteria.

Holert, Tom (2004): "Silver Cube: Transfusion". In: Tom Holert/Heike Munder (eds.): *The Future Has a Silver Lining*, Zurich: Migros Museum.

Keazor, Henry/Wübbena, Thorsten (2007²): *Video thrills the Radio Star*, Bielefeld: transcript.

Legge, Elisabeth (Summer 2000): "Reinventing Derivations: Roles, Stereotypes, and Young British Artist". In: *Representations* 71, p. 1-23.

McRobbie, Angela (1984): "Dance and Social Fantasy". In: Angela McRobbie/Mica Nava: *Gender and Generations*, London: Macmillan, p. 130-161.

Nochlin, Linda (2008): "When the Stars Weep". In: *Sam Taylor-Wood: 1995–2007*, Cleveland: Museum of Contemporary Art, p. 52-55.

Rosenthal, Norman (1998): *Sensation: Young British Artists from the Saatchi Collection*, Ostfildern-Ruit: Hatje Cantz.

Rothkopf, Scott (2007): "Takashi Murakami: Company Man". In: Paul Schimmel (ed.): © *Murakami*, Los Angeles: Museum of Contemporary Art, p. 128-159.

Stallabrass, Julian (1999): *High Art Lite*, London: Verso.

Taylor-Wood, Sam (2004): *Crying Men*, Göttingen: Steidl.

Tompson, Donald N. (2008): *The $12 Million Stuffed Shark: The Curious Economics of Contemporary Art and Auction Houses*, London: Aurum.

Walker, John A. (1987): *Cross-overs: Art into Pop, Pop into Art*, London et al.: Methuen.

Weir, Kathryn (2004): *Jump cut: music video aesthetics*, http://qag.clients.squiz.net/exhibitions/past/2004/video_hits/jump_cut_music_video_aesthetics2 (last access 20.12.2009).

## Photographic Sources

Fig. 1, 2: Taylor-Wood, Sam (2002): *Sam Taylor-Wood*, Göttingen: Steidl

Fig. 4: John Kobal Foundation/Getty Images

Fig. 6: Courtesy Jay Joplin/White Cube, London. Photo: Prudence Cuming Associates Ltd.

Fig. 8: © 2007 Takashi Murakami/Kaikai Kiki Co. Ltd./Kanye West/Mascotte Holdings, LLC

Fig. 9: ©2002 Takashi Murakami/Kaikai Kiki Co. Ltd. Courtesy Galerie Emmanuel Perrotin, Miami/Paris

Fig. 10: © 2007 Takashi Murakami/Kaikai Kiki Co. Ltd./Kanye West/Mascotte Holdings, LLC./Museum für Moderne Kunst, Frankfurt am Main. Photo: Axel Schneider

# "It's the End of Music Videos as we Know them (but we Feel Fine)"

Death and Resurrection of Music Videos

in the YouTube-Age

Gianni Sibilla

> "The music video is a dead medium. It is what it is, and I think anyone who refuses that is an idiot in 2008. We can all agree as a medium music videos really found their place in pop culture in the 1990's, and have been replaced by the Internet in the 21st century."[1]

This statement was made last June by Michael Stipe, frontman of R.E.M., not only one of the most prominent rock bands of the last 20 years, but also one that used music videos in a truly innovative way, beyond its mere promotional function.

Given the fact that we still see music videos everywhere, then if they had died, they must also have been resurrected. But what caused this process?

The answer is to be found in two main factors: the crisis of the music industry, and the advent of digital music and media (see also Sibilla 2008).

Music videos were one of the most interesting things that happened in the media landscape of the eighties and the nineties.[2] However, the "golden age" of the music video is long gone, and the Internet has caused the end of music videos as we knew them. But music videos are born again in a new form and in a new space: YouTube.

Music videos have their origins in the radio programming of popular music. The idea behind modern music videos was to produce a "clip" of images for repeated programming on TV in order to promote songs as done on radio.

A music video is conceived as a short film paid by the music industry to be shown by TV channels. On one side, the label, the PR and the management of the artist, in this way, are able to construct and control the "image" of the artist. On the other side, a lot of time (and money) is saved: the artist itself doesn't need to be taken around in different TV shows to present his song.

MTV was born in 1981 on the following premise: a TV channel made *of* music videos, and *like* a music video, made of material not paid for and not produced by the TV channel itself, but by someone else, the music industry. Even if the first TV shows, made of music videos had by then already existed, it was MTV that gave a real boost to the format, introducing an "audiovisual slang" that was later adopted by many other TV channels that wanted to appeal to a young audience.

The economic crisis of the music industry in the late 90's, due to the advent of digital formats and the rise of music piracy, has stalled music videos. But in the last few years it has found a new young audience in what many call the "Web 2.0": a term intended to represent a new model of the Internet that abandons the "old" idea of a digital space to expose goods in favor of a space of sharing things, ranging from communication to content like music, videos and so on. In this new space there are no more boundaries between the professional producer and the consumer. We all are "pro-sumers", and spaces like the video-sharing site YouTube represents an enormous community that uploads, creates, manipulates content and shares suggestions and stories. In particular, YouTube represents a community that has made the music video – a new type of music video: self- resp. hand-made but more inventive – one of the objects which contributes to make *user generated content* a wide-spread phenomenon.

## MUSIC VIDEOS AND THE MUSIC INDUSTRY

The drop in music sales left the music industry with much less money to spend in marketing and promotion than in the 80's and the 90's, the "golden age" of music videos. Moreover, MTV and other music TV channels have transformed into "mainstream" channels with less and less space for music. In this sense, music videos are dead: they no longer serve as a tool for launching an artist and/or expressing a form of visual creativity that accompanies music. Finally, the advent of digital music and media changed the distribution pipeline of music and musical media dramatically.

It all began as a simple idea: shoot a short film to illustrate and accompany a song with some images, with a conceptual style sometimes opposed to the narrative style of cinema (Hebdige 1988). However, music videos have a promotional function that stands above the artistic expression.

In the traditional industrial pipeline, music videos are commissioned and paid for by the artist's label or management. Once the song has been chosen – usually the "single" used to promote an album in the media – the label asks different directors for their ideas; sometimes the artists them-

selves request the visual development of some idea they have had for the
song.

At this point, the directors and the production companies take over:
they write the "treatment" of the song, find locations, actors and props
and produce and post-produce the video, usually in a short amount of time
before finally delivering the finished product to the label and to the artist.

The music industry then takes care of the last step of broadcasting by
delivering the video to music TV channels, asking for the programming of
the clip. The TV stations decide how and how often the video will be broadcasted, according to their editorial mission, the "sexyness" – in musical
terms and image – of the artist, and/or the quality of the video itself.

MTV is (or rather: was) the ideal destination for every music video. But
MTV has selective *criteria*: the music video must have a good production
quality (for example, they must be shot on film, not on digital media), and
its programming is mainly focused on mainstream artists; "cult" or indie
artists are often programmed only by night or on secondary channels.

The TV landscape has changed a lot in the last few years: "traditional"
TV is now accompanied by digital, satellite and cable TV. But in these spaces music TV channels remained a secondary target for the music industry,
due to the somehow "limited" audience of these channels.

In other words, the music industry tried to spread music videos across
different channels and spaces, but the ideal destination remained broadcast TV: with his "broad" audience it could justify the big money invest-
ment the production of a music video requires.


## From Industry-Made Music Videos to Hand-Made Music Videos: The Rise of User Generated Content

The production and distribution so far described is that of the typical "in-
dustry-made" music video. This format has a high budget: nowadays, the
average cost for a industrial music video in Italy is between 20.000 and
30.000 Euros. In the eighties, however, artists like Michael Jackson spent
millions of Dollars on a single music video.

Thanks to MTV, the rhythmic and 'schizophrenic' audiovisual language introduced by music videos during the 80's spread across every
segment of TV programming and influenced, for example, commercials
and "idents" (short clips made to promote not single programs but the
channel itself and its brand). Moreover, MTV became a model for many
others music TV channels.

MTV itself was cloned into "sister" channels, devoted to specified musical genres (adult rock, hip-hop, and so on) or to specified territories. In
1987 MTV opened in Europe, starting its globalization process in which its
world famous brand was adapted to different markets and cultures.

At the end of the 90's this system had already mutated: from a creative
point of view, music videos were stalled in a series of stereotypes on which

both the industry and the media relied upon. MTV has transformed from a Music Television to a television that now focuses mainly on fiction and reality shows and only occasionally presents music. The music industry, on the other side, has, as already stated, fewer funds to invest in the production of music videos.

At the beginning of the new millennium, the Internet became the new stage for music videos. Initially, Internet sites were used as a new distribution space for music videos which had received only a small amount of television rotation. Then came iTunes: an Apple service which sells music in a digital format for use on the iPod. From 2005 on, iTunes also began to sell music videos, charging 2 Euros or 2 Dollars per clip. Music videos became goods that one could buy and own, rather than something to be watched for free on TV.

iTunes still sells videos, but YouTube now offers an even easier way to watch music videos via the Internet. Thanks to this site, music videos are born again, in a new format, as a *user generated content*, which means: as "crafty" videos, made mainly by users with low budget or no budget at all, and basic tools such as a camera and an editing program.

Soon after, the Internet changed: cheap software that can help to easily make music and videos became common; the results are products that look almost professional, but are made in a bedroom, instead of needing professional and expensive facilities. This change is part of the transition towards the so-called "Web 2.0" where the user becomes the "star".

YouTube is one the most well-known sites of Web 2.0. YouTube was founded in 2005 as a video-sharing channel: every user can easily post a video online without any knowledge of web programming. In this way, videos are shared with the world or just within your friendship network. Additionally, every user can comment on other videos, share information or tell stories. On YouTube, as video-sharing channel, the emphasis is on sharing just as much as it is on video.

YouTube has many faces. As an enormous archive of clips from television and film, YouTube consists of pre-existent content that has disappeared from collective memory and been brought back to life and visibility from some user's private archive. Because this content is often under copyright, this form of sharing is controversial. Many broadcast and entertainment industries have initiated legal battles to protect the rights of their material uploaded on YouTube without their consent. Others have decided that if you can't beat the enemy, you have to become its friend and have opened "official" channels on YouTube where they post their own material.

The other side, perhaps the most interesting one, concerns the *user generated contents*. Thanks to the simple new digital instruments and software, many users have started to create home-made (or "hand-crafted") content. It might sometimes be entirely original or consist of "remixed" materials; one can here even think of "bricolage" as Claude Levi-Strauss used the term in order to describe the reworking of pre-existent material by using non-professional tools.[3]

This process has had an enormous impact on music video. Many artists are producing music videos now solely for YouTube, following different standards than in the case of clips intended for TV. It focuses less on photographic quality, and more attention is paid to the originality of the idea which is fundamental for attracting and keeping the attention of the viewer and in order to start a word-of-mouth process. Some videos of this type have had incredible results. The clip for the song of the Brazilian band CSS (an abbreviation for "Cansei De Ser Sexy")[4] *Music Is My Hot Hot Sex* (posted as an unofficial fan-made product by the Italian music blogger and photographer Clarus Bartel in 2008)[5] maintaining for a while the highest record of single views on YouTube. The high number, which exceeded one hundred million, raised in the end even many doubts, prompting YouTube itself to conduct an investigation into the possible manipulation and inflation of the numbers.[6] Similarly, the music video for the song *Here It Goes Again"* by the American band OK Go (choreographed by Trish Sie and directed by her and the band) with its simple idea of a single-shot choreography on eight *tapis roulants* has gained the band visibility first on the new and then also on traditional media.[7]

But there is a lot more: the entirely *user generated content* music videos. Sometimes they are made of a simple shot of someone singing his song or doing a cover of a famous song. In other cases they consist of shots made and edited by a user and cut to an artist's song. Take, for example, the song *Fake Empire* by The National. A user called "Verypalpablehit" has cut various images of contemporary society's decadence to the song, also the topic of the song's lyrics, thereby garnering almost 150.000 views and many positive comments. In other words, he has produced a hand made music video for a famous song.

The result is that the Internet is now undoubtedly the main promotional tool for music, and that music videos are now made primarily for this channel, which requires less focus on technical quality and budget, and greater focus on ideas.[8] But the goal is the same: spread the name and the music of an artist as widely as possible.

## MARKETING, PROMOTION AND DIFFUSED CREATIVITY OF MUSIC VIDEOS IN THE YOUTUBE AGE

The contemporary scene of music videos is marked by a new aesthetic. Music has transformed from a mono-medial object – originally intended primarily for listening, then also adding visual elements – to a cross-medial object; its language becomes more complex, intended for a multidimensional space like the web.

These pages were opened by a quote by R.E.M.'s lead singer Michael Stipe, regarding the music video as a "dead medium": it is interesting that such a provocative statement comes from the same band that helped directors such as Tarsem Singh and Spike Jonze to establish themselves.

But *it is* a provocation since the "traditional" music video is still alive and it is still being made, especially by and for "blockbuster" artists. For them, making expensive videos is almost a statement, a way to reassert their power in the music industry and in the media.

A rebirth of music videos from these ashes is beyond doubt: there is a trend to use the "low-fi"-aesthetics of user generated clips which means a recourse to an audiovisual language that genuinely comes from the web and not from TV.

An interesting example is that of Coldplay: the English band is currently one of the most loved and successful. In the space of eight years and four albums, Coldplay has become one of the most powerful b(r)ands in music, even from an industry point of view. During the promotion of the last album *Viva la Vida* (2008), Coldplay decided to also have a low-budget, "low-fi" YouTube-style music video for the title track. It was directed by the photographer and director Anton Corbijn who was asked by the band to recreate the idea and the scenes of his music video for the song *Enjoy the Silence* by Depeche Mode, which was shot more than a decade earlier in 1990.[9] Shortly after, Coldplay asked their fans to make a *user generated content* video themselves for the band's new single *Lost!* via a contest on the web.

Ultimately, R.E.M. presents the most interesting case in this media landscape. In March 2008, they released the single *Supernatural Superserious* in anticipation of *Accelerate*, the band's 14th studio album. A "traditional" music video was produced, shot by French director Vincent Moon. It is partly made of scenes that show the band playing in a studio and lip-synching to the song and presents a "low-fi" aesthetic by using handheld shots that follow the three musicians on a night in New York's SoHo. The "Director's cut" was sent to music channels, but at the same time the band opened a web site, www.supernaturalsuperserious.com, from which users could download 12 high definition visual tracks from which the "industry" version was edited. Users and fans were asked to re-edit the video and to post their own version on YouTube.

In other words, music video was re-mediated (Bolter 1999): techniques, technologies and social forms of the traditional medium have been transferred and re-adapted to a new digital space. By now, there are as many versions of a music video as there are users who have worked with and upon it. At the same time, the "traditional" music video tries to approach and embrace the "new" music video.

In this way, the musicians are achieving different goals:

1. Promotional: the music video is present both on traditional and on Internet spaces, respecting the individual 'language' of each medium.
2. In the digital space, the music video becomes a "viral marketing" tool, spreading like a virus that triggers a word-of-mouth-advertising.
3. The musicians get closer to their fans, giving them the opportunity to manipulate and remix their music starting from the master-footage, the original material.

4. In this way, the user generated music vide becomes a semi-professional *bricolage*, a semi professional remix of the original one.

Remixing and manipulating a music video is much more challenging and difficult than remixing just audio tracks. It doesn't necessarily require more skills or more money. Easy and cheap editing software is now easily found. But remixing and manipulating music videos requires *images*. Giving the web-community professional visual tracks is a way to stimulate diffused creativity, but also a way to control the final output which is something not possible in the case of entirely *user generated* music videos.

Also, the result is very interesting from another perspective: the "new" music video is a continuous work in progress that stimulates repeated exposure to the song. This, in the end, was the promotional goal of "traditional" music video and it is still the goal of "new" music video.

# REFERENCES

**1** | Billboard 2008.

**2** | The scholarly literature on music videos has grown a lot in the last few years, not only in English speaking countries. As starting points in the 80's and 90's see for example Behne 1987, Bódy/Weibel 1987, Kaplan 1987, Deville/Brissette, Goodwin 1992, Frith/Goodwin 1993 and Hausheer/Schönholzer 1994.

**3** | Lévi-Strauss 1966, p. 19.

**4** | "Cansei De Ser Sexy" means "I got tired of being sexy" which is apparently a comment made by singer Beyoncé Knowles in 2003 when the band formed. See Hutcheon 2008.

**5** | See Baio 2008. As Hutcheon 2008 states, CSS, in the context of a contest, launched by the Italian online video channel Quoob (which is produced by MTV Italia), had invited Italian fans to use footage of the band in order to create their own videos, using, however, another song, titled "Alcohol". In the interview, published by Baio 2008, Bartel tells that, although he did not participate in the contest, he did nevertheless download "the footage in order to edit it and (...) added a different track"; he then did "cut out some scenes where they were singing, added some effects to the background, and then (...) uploaded it to YouTube". Bartel says that he himself was astonished "that such an ugly video, made on a whim, would make it to the top of the charts".

**6** | See Hutcheon 2008.

**7** | The video debuted on YouTube on July 31, 2006 and had been viewed until November 2009 over 48 million times; it did win the 2007 Grammy Award for "Best Short Form Music Video" and the 2006 YouTube awards for "Most Creative Video". See Wikipedia "Here_It_Goes_Again" and "Trish_Sie".

**8** | See for this also the article by Kathrin Wetzel and Christian Jegl in this volume.

**9** | See for this also the article by Paolo Peverini in this volume.

# BIBLIOGRAPHY

Baio, Andy (2008), Interview with the creator of YouTube's new #1 video (5/6.3.2008), online under http://waxy.org/2008/03/interview_with/ (last access 15.1.2010).

Behne, Klaus-Ernst (ed.) (1987), *Film – Musik – Video. Oder die Konkurrenz von Auge und Ohr*, Regensburg: Bosse.

Billboard (2008): "R.E.M. Premieres New Video At New York Show", in: *Billboard* (20.6.2008), online under http://www.billboard.com/bb-com/news/article_display.jsp?vnu_content_id=1003819312 (last access 15.1.2010).

Bódy, Veruschka/Weibel, Peter (eds.) (1987): *Clip, Klapp, Bum – Von der visuellen Musik zum Musikvideo*, Cologne: DuMont.

Bolter, Grusin (1999): *Remediation. Understanding New Media*, Cambridge/London: MIT Press.

Deville, Nicolas/Brissette, Yvan (1988): *Rock'N Clip – La première encyclopédie mondiale du vidéo-clip*, Paris: Seghers.

Frith, Simon/Goodwin, Andrew/Grossberg, Lawrence (1993): *Sound and Vision. The Music Video Reader*, London/New York: Routledge.

Goodwin, Andrew (1992): *Dancing in the Distraction Factory. Music Television and Popular Culture*, Minneapolis: University of Minnesota Press.

Hausheer, Cecilia/Schönholzer, Annette (eds.) (1994): *Visueller Sound – Musikvideos zwischen Avantgarde und Populärkultur*, Lucerne: Zyklop.

Hebdige, Dick (1988): *Hiding in the Light*, London: Routledge.

Hutcheon, Stephen (2008): "Numbers don't add up for top-rating Hot Hot Sex YouTube clip", in: *Sydney Morning Herald* (6.3. 2008), online under http://www.smh.com.au/articles/2008/03/06/1204402619704.html?feed=html (last access 15.1.2010).

Kaplan, Ann E. (1987): *Rocking Around the Clock. Music Television, Postmodernism, and Consumer Culture*, New York/London: Methuen & Co.

Claude Lévi-Strauss (1966²): *The Savage Mind*, Chicago, IL: The University of Chicago Press.

Sibilla, Gianni (2008): *Musica e Media Digitali*, Milan: Bompiani.

Wikipedia:
http://en.wikipedia.org/wiki/Here_It_Goes_Again
http://en.wikipedia.org/wiki/Trish_Sie (both last accessed 15.1.2010)

# Music Video and YouTube: New Aesthetics and Generic Transformations

## Case Study – Beyoncé's and Lady Gaga's *Video Phone*

Carol Vernallis

Not much is left of the music video industry. Profits have fallen, budgets have been slashed and fewer videos are being made. Videos today can look like they're aping devices of the 80's, as if what we saw then wasn't reflective of musical styles or a zeitgeist but rather economics.[1] While it has always been difficult to make a living directing music video, now even the top directors tend to say, "I'm going on vacation – I'm going to direct a music video" because they don't get paid for what they do.[2]

I'm hopeful, however. Artists and technicians within other genres and media are laboring under similar constraints (*The NY Times* recently cut 10% of its staff and shut down foreign bureaus: yet within a year the company predicts an uptick).[3] Music video has always been mutable. I think it will survive this transition. Perhaps also, this moment presents an opportunity. If we listen carefully and attend patiently, we'll learn new things about the possibilities of the form.

I've claimed that music video is strange and getting stranger (Vernallis 2004: p. 6). Perusing the Internet produces unusual experiences: as we come across videos set adrift between election news clips, exhortations about how to keep your mate sexually engaged, and the newest fad diets; or click among streams of text, snapshots, and other YouTube links, music videos can now become the anchor rather than the source of discontinuity. Has the form of music video become the supertext? Music video's elongations and instances of condensation, its alternating thickets and wide-open spaces map onto the web's larger structures. Do the web's simultaneous windows and jumpy advertising also shape music video aesthetics? On a webpage, music videos compete with lurid pop-up ads and other scrolling devices. So why do the song and image project further than they ever did? The videos themselves still want to claim a liberatory otherness: "I kissed a girl and I liked it."[4]

Does music video's true home now reside elsewhere – in the film trailer, the mashup, the wedding video, the visual arts flash project, the DIY (do it yourself) aesthetic? Does this mean the genre has new means of realizing itself? We might first ask what music video is today. Older definitions don't seem to work. In the 80's and 90's people knew what a music video was – a song set to memorable imagery, paid for by the record company to promote the song or musicians, and screened on cable. Now, however, with YouTube's cornucopia of clips, DIY aesthetics, and new digital cinema's musical segments, the boundaries have been blurred. In *Auto-Tune the News*, newscasters with their voices processed through Auto-Tune "sing" their stories accompanied by tracks built in Fruity Loops, an inexpensive music-production program.[5] While some elements suggest prior understanding of the music video, others don't, as the experience leans close to watching news footage with a musical twist.  Music videos have always blended genres, incorporated other media, and adopted experimental techniques, but now indicators of production, reception, and intent go missing. While commonsense definitions of "music video" no longer hold, no other term has taken its place. I'll often describe short clips with lively audiovisual soundtracks and rich audiovisual relations as music videos or their siblings.

Given the number and variety of clips on YouTube, it's hard to draw a border between what is and isn't a music video. Clips I would once have considered as belonging primarily to another genre, perhaps because they appeal to different constituencies or foreground different techniques, now seem to belong firmly within the music video canon. Two examples: *The Badger Song* and *The Duck Song* most resemble children's cartoons.[6] Yet many music videos today use just as inexpensive and schematic animation, because it's easy to do and projects well on the web (the music video, directed by Hype Williams in 2008 for Kanye West's *Heartless* with its simple, block-like forms, achieved via the rotoscoping animation technique, seems to reference these). *The Duck Song*, a somewhat sophisticated tune with more than a wink at *Sesame Street*, is performed by an adult singer-songwriter on the guitar. Who am I to say this is a children's cartoon? My students listen to *The Duck Song* as much as anything else, and singer-songwriter Bryant Oden also sells his tune on the Internet.[7] The clip *Haha Baby* can be experienced as a music video – the father's and child's laugh becomes a singable melody.[8] Short-form clips with striking musical accompaniment, like *Kung Fu Baby*, and *Dramatic Chipmunk*, strike me as music videos, even more so than *The Duck Song*.[9] *Evolution of Dance* and *Charlie Bit My Finger*,[10] at first glance seem outside of the genre, but once they've been remixed through Fruity Loops, they begin to work like music videos.[11]

In this article, I won't be able to define all the generic features of today's music video, but I'll make a first foray in that direction, arguing that clips on YouTube now reflect an aesthetic different from those of earlier genres on television or cable. We can begin to understand music video as a part of a new mode and platform if we identify some of the aesthetic features that define YouTube: 1) reiteration and pulse; 2) irreality and weightlessness (tied to low-resolution and the digital); 3) scale and graphic values; 4) unusual causal relations; 5) parametric volubility and intertextuality; 6) sardonic humor and parody; 7) condensation; and 8) formal replication of the web. I'll apply these YouTube-oriented features to a music video most viewers would identify as traditionally belonging to the genre (here, a performance set against a pre-recorded song, released by a major record company, and designed to draw attention to the song and sell it). This process should help us identify the ways music video is changing and the ways YouTube reflects a new mode and platform. My case study will be the recent video by Hype William for Beyoncé's and Lady Gaga's song *Video Phone*, shot in October 2009.

But what is YouTube? How we might think about it?[12] Music video is making a strong global comeback because of YouTube. The number of clips on the site stretches to the sublime – YouTube streams 1.2 billion videos a day, enough for every person on the planet with Internet to watch a clip each day (Arrington 2009). As the site's number one streamed content, music video consumption is dramatically up. It's the perfect form to quickly set the pulse of our daily lives, as well as grab a moment's respite while websurfing or engaging in repetitive work. We may even look to music video clips on YouTube to match the pulse of today's world: perhaps in our heteroglot, diversified, but linked environment, we hope music video clips will help world citizens find a shared rhythm. YouTube and music video raises many questions, more than this article can address. These include new forms of attention; cross-cultural exchange; shifting ideological content; changed professions and forms of participation for industry personnel, media makers, musicians, and audiences; budget, bandwidth and screen size; and so on.[13]

Scholars have presented viewpoints on YouTube, but these still map but a glimmer of what YouTube is. Alex Juhasz describes it as a space for crass commercialism and further reification of mainstream media. For her, YouTube fails to build communities (Juhasz 2009). Michael Wetsch, on the other hand, writes on how much YouTube fosters community and acts as an agent for self-expression: the site makes possible new identities, sexualities, and modes of interaction (Wetsch/Heffernan 2008). Virginia Heffernan could be considered a connoisseur who classifies clips as high-art and elite, the indie, quirky, and the outsider (Wetsch/Heffernan 2008). These authors, I feel, have been the best at mapping YouTube's landscape. Since YouTube remains open territory, some of YouTube's aesthetic features (listed above) are a place to begin. Any clip – YouTube or music video – may embody some of these features, though not all. Sometimes a YouTube clip can seem to possess many of the elements commonly present in music video, though in a recent music video clip or a YouTube clip these can appear even more distorted and strange. As we'll see, this is strikingly so for Hype Williams's video for *Video Phone*, by Beyoncé and Lady Gaga.

## 1. REITERATION AND PULSE

The new prosumer YouTube aesthetic often emphasizes insistent reiteration[14] (forms like AAAAAAAAAAAAAAAAA, or variants, AAABAAAB-CAAAA are good examples.) Many YouTube genres have taken up an obsessive pulse. Crazy or overly anthropomorphized animals as in *Sneezing Baby Panda*, *Gizmo Flushes*, and others, show animals acting repetitively in videos sometimes punctuated by a sudden departure from the pattern.[15] The homemade documentaries with personal testimonials linked one after another often lead to something even more repetitive: people make compilation clips with the best smiling faces or the funniest falls out of chairs. Mashups are built up through videos spliced together, anywhere from two clips to hundreds. Clips start forming a regular progression. A march-like obsession and equal opportunity take hold. Reiteration in political viral web media occurs in clips like *APT Obama Obama*, where Obama's name is sung over and over again. *Barack Obollywood*, an homage to Bollywood, reiterates the word "acha" as the imagery disperses into kaleidoscopic replication.[16] Straight ahead music videos also have been taken over by an insistent pulse. *El Sonidito* is one of the most marked examples – others include *Chacarron Macarron* and *Sunday Afternoon*.[17] Why would reiteration be such a predominant feature of today's media? Let me give several reasons tied to production practices, contemporary labor conditions, and aesthetics.

The production practices of YouTube – including the DIY aesthetic – exert a strong influence. Fans with no training want to make something. With favorite materials – things to be deformed and reconfigured anew – they start projects but they may not know how to put materials together. Cultural forms like the pop song are products that have been studied and taught. In contrast, today's makers eschew these constructs, instead jumping in with their editing software and just get going. In the midst of alternating their materials, a realization dawns near the two-minute mark that they'd prefer to make something resembling a pop song and they peter out. Professional makers with more training may pick up on the style, even if it's primitive, because it seems like the next big thing. Such processes seep in, sometimes on a subterranean level, transforming culture on a global scale.

Reiteration also suits our time – YouTube clips project what we are and where we may be heading. The pace and demands of business and leisure time have been accelerating and the number of inputs continue to proliferate. Experiences are based on quick, overlapping hookups: the e-mail to which we must respond, the cell phone text message calling for an answer, the tweet that demands immediate attention, the voice of the person next to you, the song coming up on the iPod, the slot you occupy in the queue for the IVR phone bank. As a shot of repetition, YouTube works like a tonic. Jammed into that space for a minute, sped up and locked into a jackhammer mode, the web surfer, suddenly released back into the everyday media sphere, experiences wide open spaces.[18]

Competition among media also encourages obsessive repetition. YouTube's response to the hyperintensified-CGI laden-blockbuster seeking-new digital cinema and to video games may reveal a sharp competitiveness. The nagging quality may not only pull viewers away from other YouTube clips and more distant websites but also away from all external screens. One sort of reiterative form is a psychedelic, mind-twisting approach. These clips may provide a low-fi, low-cost blockbuster experience in miniature.[19]

Reiteration has an aesthetic function as well. The marks surrounding the YouTube clip and the frames strewn across the computer monitor can create a sense of baroque obsessiveness. YouTube links must respond to everything on the page: all the tiny graphs and signs repetitively laid out, and everything else on the monitor's screen. Together these establish a cluttered field from within which the clip must seize attention. Reiteration has also to do with consumption compulsion. When the mega popular YouTube *Shoes*'s lead singer, dressed in drag, sings "Shoes" in the most affectless style possible, over and over, s/he suggests that repetition is tied to the impulse to buy, buy, consume, consume, start over.[20] Yet as Gilles Deleuze would argue, with the Darwinian turn can come a slight difference (Deleuze 1995: p. 75). YouTube clips can mysteriously trip themselves into another place – frequently darker. In *Shoes* we start from a suburban family zoned out on couches as if they're on 'luudes, to finally a frenzied rave. Perhaps the reiterating word "shoes" has raised the family's level of delirium.

Repetition may reflect sociocultural changes. Howard Hawks's 30s screwball comedies were popular in an era when the popular press and other sociocultural forces encouraged couples to become help- and friend-mates. Today's repetition may help with the cultural disruptions many of us experience as we switch jobs from city to city, and become unmoored from friends and family. Similarly, childhood memories like those of coping with a steady stream of legal and biological parents may have a chance to be revealed and tamed. These forms of repetition are often accompanied with lost objects or surrealism. Clips like Dan Deacon's & Liam Lynch's *Drinking Out of Cups* seem to have the sense that a moment might be dislodged and held. If we control repetition we can insulate ourselves a little from outside forces. Drug culture may play a role too. The new drugs, like Adderall, Ritalin and Focalin, help us exceed at repetitive, slightly odious tasks. YouTube's reiterative 1's (their consistent, unremitting pulse) sync with our drug-influenced rhythms.

## The Case Study – Beyoncé's and Lady Gaga's *Video Phone*

Pop music has always employed techniques of reiteration. But something is different now. Many bloggers and journalists have noted that Beyoncé's most recent songs contain earworms – *Single Ladies (Put a Ring on It)* seems to get lodged in people's brains and won't let go.[21] *Video Phone* sounds like a one-off of *Single Ladies*. Perhaps simple phrases like "put a ring on it" and "video phone" repeated over and over, embedded in an overdubbed, chattering chorus of real and synthesized voices, help drive the sound into the brain (the sounds both ring and reverberate, suggesting obsessive demands for action). In these videos, Beyoncé's hips circling around and around alongside the musical hook reinforces the pattern. Other sources of repetition: Lady Gaga's songs, no matter how well crafted, are close siblings of one another (arrangement and presentation diverge little). Due to Gaga's predictable musical voice, simply her appearance in *Video Phone* reinforces a sense of repetition. The *Video Phone* song proper also contains much repetition. (In the upper registers, a synthesizer patch spends most of its time cycling among a few pitches, for example).

Many elements in *Video Phone*'s imagery feature reiteration. The opening, strobing overlays as a *Reservoir Dogs*-like bevy of men and Beyoncé strut past lonely warehouses (fig. 1), suggest instability. Once the video starts proper, the first series of Beyoncé's multiplying are formed through two types of visual imagery 1) echoed grayed-out heads filling out the left- and right-hand sides of the frame (as if they were scroll bars for videogames: fig. 2), with these gray heads beginning to multiply and 2) Beyoncé's dancing in the center of the frame with echoed, streaming images trailing after her. Together these suggest an infinite regress. Cameramen with their camera heads also begin to reproduce (fig. 3).

*Figs. 1-3: Stills from the music video by Hype Williams: Beyoncé ft. Lady Gaga,* Video Phone, *2009*

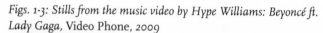

Beyoncé and Gaga, as women lined up in chairs, become exchangeable, rotatable. Visually this video suggests 80's music-video aesthetics, with its constant deployment of different dresses, set-ups, and color backgrounds (the videos for Whitney Houston's *I Wanna Dance with Somebody*, directed in 1985 by Brian Grant, and for Neneh Cherry's *Buffalo Stance*, directed in 1989 by John Maybury, are touchstones). But this video seems more adept and concerted in its effects. The set-ups feel reiterative. Though there is some cross-bleeding, the basic pattern is one after another in a series, with the series becoming more important than teleological drive.[22] But here the reiteration is able to carry us into new realms. More is at stake: sex for profit, pleasure, acceptance, power, or war.

On YouTube, repetition is often combined with boredom and tedium. Repetition, of course, can also be paired with a kind of jacked-up, unrelenting excitement, like the songs of Katie Perry, but *Video Phone* is a case of the former. The finger snaps are desultory, often lagging behind the beat. The synthesizer patch in the upper register conveys ennui, and the exotic melody in the mid-range sounds like an inexpensive 8-bit Casio sound from the mid 80's – thin and tinny. The drums in the rhythm section seem cheap – sometimes sounding like the banging on trash can lids, and sometimes like the tapping on heavy plastic. This arrangement does not suggest money or luxury – there are no live strings, for example. "Watch me on your video phone" sounds like a corporate slogan we're consigned to hear over and over.

## 2. DIGITAL SWERVE – IRREALITY AND WEIGHTLESSNESS

The digital itself produces an intensified audiovisual aesthetic – its both buzziness and weightlessness. Even though, as Lev Manovich argues, film possesses some digital features – the single frames (all 1's), the film projector's beam of light as it flashes on and off (0, 1's), and celluloid's succession (more 0's and 1's) – for many theorists, it remains distinct from digital media (Manovich 2001: p. XV, 20). André Bazin, for example, argued strongly for celluloid's analog component (Bazin 2004: p. 96-97). Film functions as a mask of the world, an analog, a replica; light falling on the randomly placed silver halides leave a mark or trace, something *directly* from the world remains on the film. Extending Bazin's argument, Laura Mulvey claims that film possesses contradictory pulls that shadow our own biological processes (Mulvey 2006: p. 17-33). One of cinema's aspects is teleologically driven, an Eros. The motoric film projector (and the camera as it records) drives forward, it purrs. The frame's constant passaging, filled with changing configurations that press forward and away, resembles our own life drives for power, sex, reproduction. Cinema's motoric nature is also why we see so often literalized, trains, cars, people running, people walking. Yet half of the film is comprised of stillness – a black, a darkness that occurs in the transition from frame to frame. Cinema itself, replicating so many of our beloved narrative forms, has a teleological drive – just as much toward Eros and power as toward a death-drive, a willingness to embrace cessation.

But the digital possesses different properties, as David Rodowick argues (Rodowick 2007: p. 93-99, 163). The digital is a transcriptive, rather than an analog process. Think first of a grid, a fine tic-tac-toe lattice, and within each block resides a pixel that flips on and off within its slot. The grid remains constant even as the pixels switch. Our experience is that of the grid's continuous burn, and the weightless fluctuations of pixels blinking on and off. The electronic light continually oscillates, appearing and vanishing, yet never completely rests. One way to give this digital weightlessness, life, is through phantasmagorically embodying it, making it musical. The digital music in tandem with the digital image creates a monstrously hybrid automaton. This phantasm is literalized in *Hellboy 2: The Golden Army* (2008, Guillermo del Toro): here the Green Monster that terrorizes the city, once shot down, becomes flowers' spores and green goo rolling and drifting away – nothing but dreams and nearly substanceless puff and stuff. Similarly, *Hellboy 2's* clunky robots crumble like wet meringues as soon as the switch is flipped off. In *The Day of the Earth Stood Still* (2008, Scott Derrickson) the globe and locusts seem comprised of gossamer. In *Transformers: Revenge of the Fallen* (2009, Michael Bay), metal machine monsters melt into ball bearings or turn into filament-dust. In *Speed Racer* (2008, Andy and Lana Wachowski) cars careening into each other sometimes go right through another as if they were ghosts. The digital images' swerve or momentum calls for a shadow schema, a filling in.

As Lawrence Sterne claims, the soundtrack is digital as well – we might say we have digital on digital – but perceptually the soundtrack provides a more continuous function, more closely aligned to our analog experiences (digital sound samples from both the top and the bottom of the wave form, creating a stronger illusion of continuity).[23]

## Beyoncé's and Lady Gaga's *Video Phone*

A lo-res aesthetic hovers over the video. The grayed-out images of Beyoncé's head against the more luridly colored ones remind us that we might be, or ought to be, watching on a video phone. Flickering images in the video's opening as well as its first verse (here the lyrics state: "cologne in the air") destabilize the video. The materials of *Video Phone* – plastic, lycra, and tiger prints – seem cheap, as do the more working-class, Wal-Mart, mass-marketed colors. These visual touches raise questions about whether we can receive pleasure from mainstream, commercial products. Props and costumes might look tossed together; the blue hooded mask and pink jacket suggest an irreality. Beyoncé's occasional harder chest thrusts, hip bumps, and knee bends seem like an attempt to lock the video down, to stop it from floating free.

## 3.  SCALE AND GRAPHIC VALUES

YouTube's aesthetic values include bold or strongly projected graphic design and well-judged scale. This may be related to the medium and its mode of delivery – a clip's limited length, its level of resolution, and the forms of attention it encourages. Small environments with low quality audiovisuals may tend toward a fuzziness or an ungroundedness that encourages makers, viewers, and consumers to seek stronger definition. YouTube clips must often garner attention in a competitive environment; many struggle to gain legibility.

What makes a successful YouTube clip? If we can imagine the forms traced as a cartoon – crudely outlined and colored in very simply – and it still speaks, my bet is it has a better shot at success. *Panda sneezes*, *Haha baby* and *Evolution of Dance* would all make popular cartoons. Of course these already have cartoon remakes yet they lack the same charm (and view counts), perhaps because their shape, color, movement, and proportion don't fall into exactly the right ratio. "Best of YouTube" clip homages with celebrity medleys like Weezer's music video *Pork and Beans*[24] or South Park's cartoon skit seemingly convey little of what's magical, charismatic or wonderful about the top-ranked YouTube clips.

YouTube clips tend to feature simplistic and evocative representations of the body and shape – either as face, body part or body whole. Clearly legible objects trigger rich affective responses, and help quickly give the performer a pseudo-context – (chairs, cups). Contrasting textures – the shiny and the dull; the smooth, brittle and rough – also help clips come forward. Color schemes differ from television. There might be an array of unified tones, the blues in *Laughing Baby*, the muted greens in *Numa Numa*;[25] these clips might also be luridly pastel or monochrome, but whatever color scheme, there is less room for the widely various, free or ad-hoc. Space contracts. While long-form media take us in and out of corridors, alleys, countrysides and intimate spaces, YouTube sticks to single frontal views (the differences in art and design between CD covers and album covers mirrors YouTube clips in relation to television – both YouTube clips and CD covers tend to project reduced, telescoped information).

### Beyoncé's and Lady Gaga's *Video Phone*

Since the early 90's, one strand in Hype Williams's oeuvre has been minimalist. He's often worked with simple set-ups such as a few performers before a blank cyclorama. Nevertheless, his earlier videos were different: the men and women came up to and backed away from the lens; figures in the background established a dense interplay with those in the foreground. The Beyoncé video is all frontal – all direct address. The video seems to be a primer on how to do frontality (you can pan up the body. Place two heads on the side. Shoot a composition with ¾ of the body. Use a close-up on the eyes. Create a tableau of three figures, and so on). Details are blunt: chairs, guns, a large bulls-eye. Costuming works emblematically to trigger fast associations – all details perform work (Beyoncé's red pumps have little bows on them – Gaga's yellow pumps don't). Yet subtlety is also important, at least on one register. The shapes of shadows shift from shot to shot – circular, ribbed and curved, boxy, or sweeping down from the top of the frame.

## 4. Causal Relations

Music video can raise questions of cause and effect, foregrounding relations so ambiguous that the music seems to be the engine mobilizing people, objects and environments (Vernallis 2004: p. 6). Yet YouTube clips raise questions of cause and effect even more sharply than do music videos – one sometimes wonders if this is the primary hook energizing the clip. A quick glance at the most popular YouTube clips bears this out. In *Panda's Sneeze*, did we know a panda could sneeze? And so hard that it would blow away both mother and baby? What animates that dancer in *Evolution of Dance*? Mexican jumping beans? Perhaps some wiry worms wiggling inside him, or mysterious powers rippling throughout his limbs? Why would the little boy in the car's backseat be so punch drunk, as if a parent had possibly malevolently slipped him a mickey?[26] One might argue that many media in their infancy focused on mysterious relations of cause and effect.[27] Since YouTube is just getting started, its development might trace its sibling's, the cinema's, first steps, which began with a "cinema of attractions"; here, a fascination with the basic mechanics of things like the Lumiere's earliest film strips with a train coming into town; Thomas Alva Edison's *Mr. Ott's Sneeze*; Georges Méliès's figures popping in and out alongside puffs of smoke (Gunning 1989). Music video first featured male musicians who terrorized women alongside awkward animation that made things appear and disappear (like the video for The Cars' *You Might Think*, directed in 1984 by Jeff Stein & Alex Weil).

David Rodowick provides a reason for the emphasis on causal relations (Rodowick 2007: p. 151). Our experiences of screens have changed with the computer's multiple windows we can activate, click through, resize, move and hide. In video games, too, we enact spatial transformations of the environment within the frame. The ways our gestures transform coordinates as we surf through the web, and participate in the game experience, might, through contagion, be transferred to YouTube. Though we cannot truly modify the inner workings of a clip, the top all time YouTube clips seem intensely bound up with powerful, obscure causal relations that are in play. We have the illusion that we might control these at a meta-level.

The scale of YouTube clips contributes to our sense of power. *Make McCain Interesting* and *Yes We Can* have small dimensions that create an illusion of our authority over annoying or overly dependent characters (we can snub them out in an instant).[28] Chris Crocker of *Leave Britney Alone*, Fred Figglehorn of *Fred Loses His Meds* and Gary Brolsma of *Numa Numa* may be tolerable in miniature, but they'd be unbearable on television.[29] The clips wouldn't have as much charm if they were closer to our size.

*Chocolate Rain* is a music video that emphasizes causal relations and fits the scale of YouTube. In this video, singer Tay Zonday leans back from the mic.[30] Zonday must have found this gesture so baffled viewers that he needed to add a clunky kyron-text generated disclaimer: "I step away because..." A mystery remains, especially since the recording equipment remains off-screen. How does this shape our experience of the music and understanding of its sources? (Imagine if we saw Zonday at the mixing board. How much allure would that have?) The adult voice in a young person's body adds to the enigma. And the screen's yellow tint? Does it speak with the lyrics? Does *Chocolate Rain* become golden? Occasional synth attacks in the upper register might suggest the beginning of falling rain. The lyrics have an apocalyptic bent – perhaps Zonday is an emissary from the future. *Chocolate Rain* is powerful because it elicits so many responses – awe, envy, affection.

## Beyoncé's and Lady Gaga's *Video Phone*

Beyoncé immediately raises questions about power and control: "Can you handle this?" or "Do you dare watch me?" Are we playing her, or is she playing us? Is she on our phone? Why would a miniature version of Beyoncé, as experienced on YouTube or a cell phone, be more threatening than if she were on cable TV? (Madonna's *Human Nature* and *Open Your Heart* both directed by Jean-Baptiste Mondino in 1995 respectively 1986 have nothing on this).[31] Inexplicably sometimes the guns go off and sometimes they don't. We hear sounds that suggest orgasm, but can't be sure. What are the triggers that push Beyoncé into a sexual state? Is her path always the same to orgasm? Does she need us at all? What if we could random access this music video? Would we have a better experience?

And is Beyoncé more of a top or bottom? She appears to have power here. Chewing gum, she's the bored, jaded sex-worker. But we can't quite gauge her actions – if she wants to, she might walk away. Gaga's relation to Beyoncé is unclear. Are they colleagues sharing a medley or competitors for fame, money, or sexual favors? (Gaga is performing too hard to chew gum.) Perhaps most uncanny are the soundtrack's voices. We hear women's moans throughout, but it's not always clear to whom they belong. Are two Beyoncés pleasuring themselves? Is it Lady Gaga, Beyoncé, or backing-track singers who moan increasingly as the song progresses? What is the status of the child-like robo-voice saying "You wanna video me?"

## 5. PARAMETRIC VOLUBILITY AND INTERTEXTUALITY

On all fronts YouTube is loquacious. Avid YouTube users are well familiar with the endless riffs on popular clips (these often overwhelm the original, making it near impossible to locate a sought-after clip). Intertextuality and hybridization occur across platforms, among users, and within clips. Let me show the ways YouTube's loquaciousness functions internally within a clip, fracturing its contents even more than music video ever did; while music video often showcased a moment-by-moment shifting aesthetic, YouTube cranks the volubility up a notch. One musical genre on YouTube simply multiplies: performance occurs within multiple frames within the clip, or a figure is multiply duplicated (*Enter Kazoo Man: Metallica Enter Sandman* and *Michael Jackson Medley* are good examples).[32] I predict we'll see these layering practices proliferating. We can look to film trailers first. For example, the film trailer for *The Spirit* (2008, Frank Miller) possesses key features of the new audiovisual aesthetics. Hyper-stylized, it follows a series of affective flashpoints, nimbly crossing media. (Alfred Hitchcock quipped that film was like life with all the boring bits cut out: he wanted to play audiences like an orchestra, propelling them along the paths of his moods. *The Spirit* approaches the segment Hitchcock dreamed of). An animated line comes into focus and the sound before the drawing helps us identify it as a heart monitor's flatline. The music and animated line swell and generate a tree turning into birds taking flight. Something streams with a whoosh across the frame. We follow it as it becomes a figure leaping off a building. The words "Silken Floss" impress themselves on the frame – the inky blacks, firehouse reds and strongly bolded text suggest S & M. We might feel as if we were like a stone skipping across the water.

The movement across medial surfaces makes it seem as if *we're* the hot potato. Intermediality can create an experience in which we shift our attention so rapidly among media that our experience is of only touching surfaces, never ground.

Trailers are a great form of parametric volubility, especially blockbuster film trailers. *The Transformers* trailer keeps us busy. We hear a sound, our attention turns toward it, something leaps across the frame, we follow it, and then another sound fills in what we heard. But our attention is already elsewhere. Trailers of this sort, including the one for *Miami Vice* (2006, Michael Mann), often become full-fledged music videos toward the end (they tend to open with enigmatic sounds of machine noises, heart beats, or suggestions of drumming, and two-thirds in work themselves into pop songs). Perhaps because YouTube is small and often made by prosumers without advanced skills, cross-mediality is not the most emphasized of techniques. But I'd argue it may be the wave of the future that will soon infiltrate all genres. *Barack Obollywood*, a 2008 presidential campaign clip, and the opening of LL Cool J (ft. Wyclef Jean)'s *Mr. President* music video showcase this style.[33]

Mashups form a subset of the new intermediality. In a mashup, the edited shots and sounds of a performer can hang as fragments. Other materials sweep past, but the musical hook or image lingers like a pungent smell. If you needed to pare down and carry forward an animal presence of your beloved performer, this would be it. Often one medium seems to retain its liveliness – a song lyric, the body moving, a musical hook, the other freezes in mechanical repetitions. The live bit pulls apart from a wash of other material pressing through. Any moment can teeter toward something revelatory or lost. A mashup can be unpredictable. On YouTube there are thousands of mashups including ones for the pop songs of the year as well as for the 2008 campaign.[34] Prosumer work is growing exponentially – in the future there will be more.

## Beyoncé's and Lady Gaga's *Video Phone*

Mashups too may have influenced *Video Phone*. One of YouTube's most popular mashups, *Tick Toxic*, features rapid cutting between Gwen Stefani and Britney Spears, each shot first establishing, and then giving ground to the second performer.[35] The clip's rapid change in mood or tone may have been picked up by *Video Phone*.

As mentioned, volubility and intertextuality occurs across all fronts. *Video Phone* takes place within many forms of conversation. This is the first video Hype Williams made with Beyoncé after the 2009 Grammy Awards, when Kanye West interrupted Taylor Swift's acceptance speech for "Best Female Video of the Year" by shouting that Beyoncé had one of the best videos of all time. Within a few days, President Obama, off-mic, called West a "jackass." The tapes were distributed widely through media outlets. Hype Williams may have felt a special pressure to stand by Beyoncé and make the "mother" of all videos, extending the range of people and places she might represent. At the same time as *Video Phone*, Lady Gaga's *Paparazzi* and *Bad Romance* were in play. The immensely popular Gaga/Beyoncé *Telephone* (directed by Jonas Åkerlund) soon followed, with a promise to serialize these events. In *Telephone*, we might imagine Gaga's serving prison time for all of her "bad" deeds like sex trading with Beyoncé in *Video Phone*; poisoning her lover in *Paparazzi* (directed in 2009 also by Åkerlund); selling herself and then killing her trick in *Bad Romance* (directed in 2009 by Francis Lawrence: as Beyoncé in *Telephone* notes, she's "been a bad, bad girl"). Similarly the man played by rapper Tyrese may be poisoned in *Telephone* for responding inappropriately to *Video Phone*'s women. *Video Phone* and *Telephone* share many aesthetics including a sonic low eight-bit rate, collaborative or competitive dancing (my students claim Beyoncé was not allowed to dance in *Telephone* so Gaga could shine), and a visual and aural stuttering and breaking up of sound and visual imagery. *Video Phone* is just as intertextual as *Telephone*.[36]

## 6. SARDONIC HUMOR AND PARODY

Parody permeates the web. Examples include the legions of versions of *Single Ladies* and the remakes of political ads like *john.he.is* and *Raisin' McCain*.[37] The aesthetic has so suffused web production, one could easily devote a chapter just to this topic.[38] Parody may be so prevalent today because so many untrained producers are participating in the art form – an event never occurring to such a great extent in history. I imagine many YouTube users are like college students enrolled in their first production class.[39] DIYers embrace compositional strategies that are easy to implement. You take the commercial or the television skit and you redo it: you can restage it or remix it – easy approaches include intercutting two or more clips and adding or deleting layers. In the anonymity of the web, YouTube makers are in search of a ground – your sarcastic take immediately places you in relation to a select group of viewers as well as the producers and fans of the original material. Your parody, now tied to original content, piggybacks on an already accrued attention (Sconce 2002). Sarcasm also pierces us. Anything that pushes against social norms tends to grab attention.

### Beyoncé's and Lady Gaga's *Video Phone*

Since any clip might be parodied, remixed, or just made to look generally stupid, many YouTube clips adopt a sarcastic, snide, knowing stance. *Video Phone* works this way. You might attempt a campy remake with young, plump, college-bound males, but the video has already anticipated that. It's already envisioned all the permutations. Already, there are spoofs and parodies of *Video Phone* on the web. It's something two or more boys or girls can do in their bedrooms. Props are easy to make. Do you have some sheets and several pairs of tights? Some wigs might help.[40] *Telephone's* funny gowns made of unhemmed swatches of cloth pay homage to this.

## 7. CONDENSATION

YouTube clips that have garnered over a million hits elicit unconscious desires and wishes in the deepest Freudian sense. YouTube is full of puns, jokes and returns to childhood. In *Numa Numa* a subtle allusion here to Humpty Dumpty is going on. Gary Brolsma's singing karaoke alongside a high, male but feminine-sounding falsetto pushes what's unfolding into a state of delirium. His facial gestures are so quick and malleable he becomes a Disney animation (watch: he's good with choreography for the camera, judiciously moving back from and toward the camera's lens in relation to the music. He's expert at navigating the small space he's been given). The fact that the clip conjures forth childhood fantasies, along with more adult anxieties concerning control and sexual desire, and that we sense we can click away from the clip and remove his audience, makes it overwhelmingly attractive.

### Beyoncé's and Lady Gaga's *Video Phone*

To give a sense of the ways condensation works in *Video Phone*, let me provide a more extended analysis of the clip, focusing on the social issues and psychic material called forth in this clip. Music video has always worked with condensation and a plurality of meaning, but *Video Phone* seems like a departure from the past, with its reduced materials and complex signifiers that fail to add up. If we take seriously the video's multitude of visual and aural signs, Hype Williams, Beyoncé and Lady Gaga seem remarkably expansive, willing to take over vast swatches of global and national discourse. One of two trajectories for *Video Phone* may not be progressive. In the clip, Beyoncé becomes our new Betty Page, our all-around, American pin-up girl for the troops in Afghanistan and Iraq (fig. 4). Her power and beauty can transsubstantiate our guilt over Abu Ghraib. Cameramen shoot her buttocks, and then she threatens men who are hooded and bound (fig. 5). We take the pictures on our cell phone. Yet her roles as B-girl and shy pin-up along with the semiotics of her costume – an oversized t-shirt embossed with an alien's head drawn in third world colors, sporting the word "peace," a jaunty beret and both male and female gender-symbol earrings – provide a more hopeful second trajectory (fig. 6). The video's color palette – moving through a trajectory from red and black to deep pink, blue and gray, pastel colors of baby pink, blue and yellow to third-world (possibly Jamaican) colors of orange, green, red and black, as well as the rising sun emblem of WWII Japan, point to a transnational, third world, perhaps more politically progressive and inclusive politics.

*Figs. 4-6: Stills from the music video by Hype Williams: Beyoncé ft. Lady Gaga,* Video Phone, 2009

A history of popular culture and performance, including African American culture, is also encapsulated. Beyoncé's first dance is a direct homage to Josephine Baker. Beyoncé's movements, long waving braid and flared miniskirt are a few references (one might be tempted to expand the exotic elements, adding drum beats, palm trees, and dinosaur bones). Howard Hawk's film *Gentlemen Prefer Blondes* (1953) is also referenced through Beyoncé's and Gaga's costumes of long satin gloves and dress, the performers' carefully choreographed work with chairs, and Beyoncé's readjusting of her breasts and bra. Many odd elements which might seem like loose ends appear too – early-80's album covers by Roxy Music and The Residents, 1980's big-shouldered military-style fashion, the work of Robert Mapplethorpe and Kenneth Anger, femme fatales like Yvonne De Carlo, films like Quentin Tarantino's *Reservoir Dogs* (1992), Roger Vadim's *Bar-*

*barella* (1968), and the 007-series, as well as an homage to women participating in more male working class pursuits such as welding, motorcycle
riding and driving big cars. Can all of these varied images of pop culture,
sexuality and global power be put into a meaningful relation?

*Video Phone* gains cohesion through its suggestion of an arc of desire
culminating in orgasm. Music video directors have become more skilled
at suggesting such an arc: Francis Lawrence's video for Lady Gaga, entitled
*Bad Romance* (2009), similarly, suggests a wide range of types of pleasures, all within 5 minutes. *Video Phone's* closing shots perhaps allude to
Luis Buñuel's opening for *Un Chien Andalou* (1929) with its slash through
the eye. Both a gun in *Video Phone*, and a knife in *Un Chien Andalou*, suggest penetration.

*Video Phone* could be seen as gay identified. Beyoncé and Lady Gaga
are divas loved by both the gay community and young women, rather than
by a large male contingent (many in the gay community consider her
transgendered; Lady Gaga has been compelled to deny this[41]). Beyoncé's
big t-shirt (fig. 6) might comment on Jamaica's homophobia: embossed
with an alien wearing both male and female gender-symboled earrings,
it might speak in code about present day international gay rights: for example, right now, in Uganda, a law is being passed to put homosexuals in
prison (Alsop 2009). Those convicted of "aggravated" gay activity or having AIDS can be executed. The American right is supporting this.[42]

For gay pornographer Paul Morris, *Video Phone* is all about Beyoncé's
chewing gum and Lady Gaga's genitals.[43] He notes Gaga is a very white
small male/tranny utterly outdone by Beyoncé. The camera guys are white,
the shirtless/headless men are black (except for at minute 1:46, where the
male might be black, Latino or white). The blue hoods (figs. 4 & 5) add
a softcore terrorism/torture reference, sexualized as blue/boyhood. The
bound boy at minute 1:46 (fig. 5) is wearing a blue/male hood, pink/fem
jacket, and no shirt. His legs are spread, suggesting strength, confidence
and male genitalia. The halo around him and the blue background suggest
blamelessness and anonymous identity. This moment (vulnerable anonymous masked white male, legs spread, torso bound) refers to the crux of
the video. Halfway into the clip, Lady Gaga spreads her/his legs to "prove"
to the camera the crucial absence of male genitalia. The lyric "You like
what you see?" really means "Do you like what you don't see?"

The video's lyrics contain puns and innuendos. "You wanna video me"
parallels "you wanna use me" or "you wanna fuck me" or "you wanna own
me." Since this clip concerns video phones, the "can you handle it" suggests, "can you masturbate to me," or can you handle the absence.[44] The
absence in Beyoncé is her vagina; for many gay-identified viewers, the
absence in Gaga is the effort to remove or deny male genitalia. An intima-
tion that the video considers sexual difference comes early. At the opening,
Beyoncé sings "uh-uh," or "no," while wearing a bandit mask and leading
her male posse (*Kill Bill* [2003/2004] and *Reservoir Dogs* references: fig.
1), her "no" takes on lethal force with the soundtrack's reference to Ennio

Morricone's scores for Spaghetti Westerns. After the slow dissolve to Beyoncé's eyes, we see a nervous camera-headed man straightening his tie (fig. 3) who might embody our subject position – we too might feel nervous when Beyoncé directly asks us: "Shorty, what's your name?"

I've claimed that music video is a heterogeneous medium, with many simultaneous, nearly equally engaging events (Vernallis 2004: p. 43, 129). With music video, we must chart our own paths through music and image to find meaning. Music videos also ask us to watch them repeatedly. Lacking in narrative devices, text, and with a shortened form, they rely on reduced materials to convey drama. On the web, resources for engaging attention may become even more attenuated. In *Video Phone*, Hype William foregrounds one of the most minimalist of materials – color – through several means, including raced bodies. Departing from standard industry practice, he does not balance Beyoncé's skin tone across the video, sometimes going for very deep, rich hues, sometimes a more lightly-complected, Lena Horne look. These changes often correspond to the song's rises and falls.[45] Beyoncé's irises sometimes shift to the deep brown or black, and in the pin-up section they are a grayish blue. Perhaps to foreshadow the turn to a more European American pin-up look, in the clip's *Reservoir Dogs* Spaghetti Western intro, one of the African American men in Beyoncé's posse is trailed by a strobing halo of curly blonde hair.[46] One might judge here that our imaginary for what constitutes American beauty remains white, Anglo-Saxon protestant.

Yet on a second register, Williams argues differently about color. After an opening in sexualized, hyper-aggressive reds and blacks, the video turns neutral white and black, and then shifts to deeper blues and pinks. Easter-egg, pastel colors sweep in (particularly with Lady Gaga), which suggest innocence and femininity. In the pin-up section, gemstone-like rich emeralds and darker gray turquoises appear. Beyoncé posing as a Betty Page-like pin-up strokes her machine gun up and down, and the shaft is a deep violet purple – a color of tumescence, of sexual excitement. If we keep our attention directed to the hues of her gun, we will eventually be carried along with a densely saturated blue and green that can lead us through surrounding fiery oranges, reds, yellows and magentas. This blue and green possesses special resonance for filmmakers. The two hues share little in common with skin tones so they can be used in matte backgrounds to key out unwanted parts of the frame (such as in the weatherman's blue-screen). For directors, chromakey blue and green have a special, race-neutral value. Following the video's changes of color, rather than its representations of people, may be the best way to experience it.

The song supports the image's dense web of signification. The music is unsettling and exotic.[47] Are there menacing elements at the periphery? The Morricone opening features a G-Phrygian ostinato (Bb, G, Ab, G), a mysterious, dark figure that hovers over the song like a cloud. The upper register ostinato's unsettling quality derives partly because it appears on the off-beats, with its highest pitch on the offbeat of beat two. When

Beyoncé states "Shorty, what's your name?" we suddenly shift to a happier Mixolydian mode in Eb (a scale with a major 3rd and a flat 7th), yet the Phrygian ostinato still remains. (Beyoncé will sing more of the Mixolydian scale's pitches at "cologne in the air"). Both Mixolydian and Phrygian are somewhat exotic. The Mixolydian occasionally turns to the flat side and, at one point (when Lady Gaga asks "Can you handle it?"), both the flat 3rd and the major 3rd occur simultaneously. In the rhythm track the more muffled drum hits sound like an irregular heartbeat (belonging to us or to the bound man?). However exotic, the song is redundant, so small changes seem big. The showbizy horns where Beyoncé and Lady Gaga dance, and the overdubbed women's voices completing a major triad ("take a cameo") register as key events.

## 8. MIRRORING THE INTERNET, ELICITING PARTICIPATION

Successful YouTube clips attempt to embody, depict, and participate in the network. The self-similarity of reiteration makes it possible for videos to sync up with others, creating a more frictionless path through the web's nodes and links. Each clip should excite, but also elicit an urge to continue on through YouTube. *Haha Baby*, *Charlie Bit My Finger*, *Evolution of Dance*, *Chocolate Rain*, and *Sneezing Panda*, put people in a rhythm as well as in an excitable state that carries them forward. Like a wind-up toy, a web user needs to keep moving through the web to diffuse energy and affect. A second point: viewers and uploaders tend to experience the web in isolation, as monads (each person with a computer peers into and attempts to draw information out of the network). Clips like will.i.am's *Yes We Can*[48], *Haha Baby*, *Charlie Bit My Finger* and *Panda Sneezing* are directed to solo viewers. Last, YouTube clips aim to connect with one another and the world. Viewers and content seem to project a dream of the construction of a total media library. YouTube's range of clips, with their trailing panoply of video blogs, all spanning the healthcare crisis, religion, and the latest pop concert, are concerned with getting linked up. Parodies on high-ranking clips and how-to's on the most banal topics – like modes of washing kitchen utensils, including more than one spoon (and then remakes of that), reveal a wish to fill in all the chinks.

### Beyoncé's and Lady Gaga's *Video Phone*

The frontal images and images of infinite regress in *Video Phone* both speak to the viewer and suggest diverging paths that all lead into the network. The dancing camera-headed men underscore the gathering images, which can be relayed out into the web. The clip's sexual excitement, against its intimations of boredom, may create enough anxiety and drive to keep viewers streaming through at a regular pace, continuing through to other web links. In response to YouTube's encyclopedic drive, this video's catalogue of women performers could be an attempt to retain and organize an array of visual imagery. *Video Phone* also reflects the hunger for people and clips that can be seen, heard, discussed and played out. Is *Video Phone* a comment on the last Presidential election and today's politics? It might reflect American culture's darker side that a campaign video like *Yes We Can* failed to address – what's been left out and put aside, in *Video Phone*, seems found and brought near. One might feel ambivalent about the Abu-Graib type of imagery – photographing torture shouldn't be sexualized or made desirable. Nevertheless, many contemporary films depict torture (*Star Trek* [2009], *The Bourne Ultimatum* [2007], *Slumdog Millionaire* [2008]). It's part of our history and our psyche. Can these images be put in relation with sexuality, gender, and nationalist movements?

## 9. POLITICS, MUSIC VIDEO AND YOUTUBE'S EVOLVING DISCOURSE

The politics of *Video Phone* will seem objectionable to many. It can make viewers anxious, as the YouTube commentary shows.[49] Consciously or unconsciously, viewers know African American women have fewer choices of image than do European American women. Once they've aligned themselves with what's understood as the raunchy or the tawdry, they may be less able to move to more traditionally valorized subject positions (as Madonna has been able to do somewhat successfully). Beyoncé's videos have tended to be sexy but also classy – Beyoncé's older videos share little with *Video Phone*'s clashing models of good and bad sexuality. A woman may be allowed to take pleasure from bondage, but she shouldn't then be the around-the-way B-girl or pin-up for our boys overseas. She might move up from peep show artist to lounge performer to an even more redeemed state in a field of nearly-pure-whiteness, but she shouldn't turn it around again by becoming a B-girl and a pin-up, and then vulnerably approach orgasm while at the same time performing the role of a bored sex-worker and military trainer. But in order for clips to register on YouTube, such clashes with our cultural categories may become increasingly more common. Violence and stupid humor, sexual vulgarity and prissiness, are often conflated on YouTube.[50] On the site, repetition with jarring discontinuity holds viewers.

We may want to accept what *Video Phone* does with representations of gender and sexuality. Both Hype Williams and Beyoncé have made a range of work, some of it very progressive.[51] As long as makers and viewers critically engage with a variety of media, including those with positive representations, why not grant these artists the space to make a clip like *Video Phone*? Hype Williams rarely works with white artists; giving him some latitude may be wise. His engagement with gay culture and aesthetics may suggest a different subject position than that of other directors. *Video Phone* might be an opportunity to assemble loved icons, gathered from a history of looking at media. Williams's response to the song is appropriate: alienation, jadedness, and ennui belong to the song proper. Williams can make clips with great tenderness, pathos, humility or uplift.[52]

I can't predict where music video and YouTube will go. Many genres exhibit a cycle of birth and death and relatively short runs. Who would have thought music video, after its recent low points, would come back with such ferocity? Neither am I claiming that this article's description encompasses all of YouTube. The site's corpus is unfathomable, stretching from documentaries, to university lectures and to clips on opera. Nor do all contemporary music videos share these aesthetics. If bandwidth, screen size and budgets increase, music video may return to a more classical mode.[53] Given music video's uncertain future, it's a good idea to keep an eye and an ear on Hype Williams and Beyoncé. Few artists have been able to straddle large media shifts. Think of film's transition from the silent to talkies, or changes due to television. Hype Williams, more than any other director, has flourished as music videos have moved from cable to YouTube. Beyoncé too has been able to maintain her artistic and star status in a newly digitized, connected age. These are artists to follow.

## REFERENCES

**1** | Some stylistic techniques common in 80's music videos recur today: simple cyclorama backgrounds, primary colors, clothes changes, limited props, and a stripped-down premise.

**2** | E-mail correspondence with Amy E., executive director, the music video production association, Fall 2008.

**3** | Conversation with Aaron Retica, staff at the *New York Times*, Fall 2008.

**4** | This, of course, the title of Kate Perry's smash-hit from 2008.

**5** | *Autotune the News* is a series of clips, available on YouTube, where the Brooklyn musician Michael Gregory has taken a number of evening news broadcast snippets which he comments upon by turning them into R&B pieces. His own voice as well as the voices of the people appearing in the news clips (such as news presenters, politicians etc.) are electronically altered with the help of the software program "Autotune" which normally is used in order to help singers' voices to achieve "perfect pitch." See as an example *Autotune the News #2: Pirates. Drugs. Gay Marriage*: http://www.youtube.com/watch?v=tBb4cjjj1gI (last access 10.3.2010).

**6** | *The Duck Song*, music by Bryant Oden, animation by Forrest Whaley (2009): http://www.youtube.com/watch?v=MtN1YnoL46Q (last access 10.3.2010).
*The Badger Song*, a musical cartoon by British animator Jonti Picking, released in September 2003: http://www.youtube.com/watch?v=vPvRVK9YbZM (last access 10.3.2010).

**7** | Oden has even released a CD which he sells on http://www.cdbaby.com/cd/bryantoden2 (last access 10.3.2010).

**8** | For *Haha Baby*, a clip of a laughing baby, responding to the noises made by a male adult, see: http://www.youtube.com/watch?v=NzQUtEIQXX0 (last access 10.3.2010).

**9** | For *Kung Fu Baby*, a clip of a baby making Kung-Fu-like moves being accompanied by music, see: http://www.youtube.com/watch?v=bxAirY-5QCQ, for *Dramatic Chipmunk*, the clip of a chipmunk accompanied by a dramatic and rousing score, see: http://www.youtube.com/watch?v=a1Y73sPHKxw (last access 10.3.2010).

**10** | For *Evolution of Dance*, showing the performance of comedian Judson Laipply, who dances his way through the history of popular dances, see: http://www.youtube.com/watch?v=dMH0bHeiRNg; for *Charlie Bit My Finger*, showing a baby biting an older boy's finger (one of the most viewed videos in YouTube), see: http://www.youtube.com/watch?v=he5fpsmH_2g (last access 10.3.2010).

**11** | Liminal videos existing near the genre's borders include *Automatic Mario: Queen's 'Don't Stop Me Now'*, *Alice*, and *South Park*'s remake of *Pork and Beans* (a response to Weezer's original *Pork and Beans*). For *Automatic Mario: Queen's 'Don't Stop Me Now'*, an online advertisement, matching four parallel levels from "Super Mario World" with the pitch and beat of the Queen-song, see: http://www.break.com/game-trailers/game/new-super-mario-bros/automatic-mario-queens-dont-stop-me-now.html; for *Alice*, a song by the Australian Electronica musician Pogo, based on snippets from the soundtrack of Walt Disney's *Alice in Wonderland* (1951) and originally released on YouTube in 2007, accompanied by spliced scenes from the film see: http://www.yooouuutuuube.com/v/?rows=36&cols=36&id=pAwR6w2TgxY&startZoom=1 or http://www.youtube.com/watch?v=zP7bI8JJIVA; for the South Park characters Kyle and Stan performing *Pork and Beans* see http://www.youtube.com/watch?v=kekmyVT9HRs (last access 10.3.2010).

**12** | Over the last few years, music video has hit several nadirs. (Post-2000, many music video fans could only view music videos through high-tiered cable. Regular cable programming like MTV had switched to reality shows.) During YouTube's first years, music video sites like Launch, AOL, and MTV streamed videos but bandwidth was narrow and budgets were low. As advertising moves to the web, music video budgets will most likely continue to grow. Currently directors gain higher budgets by including product placement. During MTV's reign, product placement was not permitted.

**13** | I've spoken twice with a staff person in PR at YouTube, but still have many questions about the site.

**14** | A prosumer is a person in postindustrial society who combines the economic roles of producer and consumer – the notion has been coined by futurologist Alvin Toffler in his 1980 book *The Third Wave*.

**15** | For *The Sneezing Baby Panda* see: http://www.youtube.com/watch?v=FzRH3iTQPrk; for the *Gizmo Flushes* (a clip, showing the obsession of the cat Gizmo with toilet flushes) see: http://www.youtube.com/watch?v=WofFb_eOxxA (last access 10.3.2010).

**16** | For the *APT Obama Obama* (a remake of the Lil' Wayne's *A Milli*) see: http://www.youtube.com/watch?v=t7RZTlzXHmo; for *Barack Obollywood* (a clip, editing images of Barack Obama in a way that he seemingly performs a Bollywood song) see: http://www.youtube.com/watch?v=sA-451XMsuY (last access 10.3.2010).

**17** | For the Hechizeros Band, *El Sonidito* see http://www.youtube.com/watch ?v=-XgNFLo5WOl; for El Mudo, *Chacarron Macarron* (Crazy Music Video) see: http://www.youtube.com/watch?v=l12Csc_IWOQ; for Jon Lajoie, *Sunday Afternoon* see: http://www.youtube.com/watch ?v=4gx3nn6LS6g (last access 10.3.2010).

**18** | When music videos first appeared, many theorists and critics complained that they were incoherent or schizophrenic. At the time it seemed difficult to decipher what music videos might be saying or what their effects were. As mentioned earlier, music video on television has become less and less important, though more and more people are watching videos on the web. Strangely, part of the aesthetics of web-based music video lies in its grounding function. Clicking among sites and multitasking so regularly, a three-to five-minute moment of music can actually provide both ground and respite – a moment of emotional connection. Shared with others, videos take on a social dimension.

**19** | Here are some examples of psychedelic reiterative clips on YouTube: *Dan Deacon & Liam Lynch - Drinking Out of Cups*, see: http://www.youtube.com/watch?v=skCV2LOc6KO; for *Shrooms: A Trip Experience* see: http://www.you tube.com/watch?v=B4pIxnuUG1k&feature=related; for *Pick of Destiny Shrooms* see: http://www.youtube.com/watch?v=guCPHG2ys9k&featu re=related; for Fischerspooner *Get Confused* see: http://www.youtube.com/watch?v=tljmpp1wot4 (last access 10.3.2010).

**20** | For *Shoes* (directed and interpreted by the comedian Liam Kyle Sullivan) see: http://www.youtube.com/watch?v=wCF3ywukQYA (last access 10.3.2010).

**21** | *Earworms!*:    http://www.freedomgen.com/index.php/community/groups/viewdiscussion?groupid=38&topicid=53; *Dig Those Earworms Out*: http://www.herald-mail.com/blogs/schelle/?p=59 (last access 10.3.2010).

**22** | Note the video's beginning when Beyoncé wears a third-world influenced t-shirt while she intimidates a bound man. We'll return to this later in the video.

**23** | Conversation, Lawrence Sterne (professor in the Department of Art History and Communication Studies McGill University), Spring 2009.

**24** | See for this video also the introduction to this volume: p.7.

**25** | For the clip, showing a webcam video from 2004 of Gary Brolsma, who filmed himself while miming to the song *Dragostea Din Tei* by the Moldovan pop band O-Zone and thus gained worldwide cult status as the "Numa Numa Guy", see: http://www.youtube.com/watch?v=60og9gwKh1o&feature=fvst (last access 10.3.2010).

**26** | For *David After Dentist* see: http://www.youtube.com/watch?v=txqiwrbYGrs (last access 10.3.2010).

**27** | Much early photography depicted spirits. The record's spirals were also said to carry direct imprints of voices from the dead.

**28** | For *Obama and McCain – Dance off!* (a clip from 2008 by David Morgasen, featuring a fictitious dance duel between Obama and McCain) see: http://www.youtube.com/watch?v=wzyT9-9IUyE (last access 10.3.2010).

**29** | For *Leave Britney Alone!* (by Chris Crocker) see: http://www.youtube.com/watch?v=kHmvkRoEowc; for *Fred Loses His Meds* see: http://www.youtube.com/watch?v=m9MAOeW8yyw. For Crocker see also the article by Jacke in this volume.

**30** | For *Chocolate Rain*, composed and performed by Tay Zonday, one of YouTube's most all-time popular clips, see http://www.youtube.com/watch?v=EwTZ2xpQwpA (last access 10.3.2010).

**31** | In an email message, colleague Alan Finke (VP of Development at MShift, Inc., San Francisco) sent me the following: "Did you watch it on a video phone? I did. They told me to. It takes on a different quality. The minimalism becomes very sharp and clear, the 8-bit casio sound becomes very appropriate in a GameBoy way and the most interesting thing is the lighting. It turns an iPhone into a little box of light that you hold in your hand. There's a sort of 3d quality with a depth that extends behind the phone into your hand, and there's a cool moment near the end where a burst of fire from a gun breaks the frame (another penetration reference?) And there's a whole other quality to being able to hold the performers in your hand. You can possess them, but you can't touch them. They're in a flat frame, but they're in a 3d world and you can tap on the glass."

**32** | *Enter Kazoo Man: Metallica Enter Sandman performed on KAZOO by Mister Tim (multitrack)* is a clip in which the teacher, composer, conductor and performer "Mr. Tim" reinterprets the song *Enter Sandman* by Metallica on a kazoo; since his version was recorded on multitrack, the video is echoes this by presenting four musicians (all played by "Mr. Tim") in a split screen – see: http://www.youtube.com/watch?v=iC65ufGUvKM (last access 10.3.2010); a similar solution is presented in the *Michael Jackson Medley* – http://www.youtube.com/watch?v=R12QVtuBO_Q (last access 10.3.2010) – where the multitrack recording of Kurt Schneider's voice is visually represented by having Schneider appear parally six times on stage.

**33** | For the video for the song by LL Cool J (ft. Wyclef Jean), *Mr. President*, directed in 2008 by LL Cool J and Ron Lakis see http://www.youtube.com/watch?v=IE32yCxy87I (last access 10.3.2010).

**34** | See for example *HOT K-POP 2009 ~ special mashup pt. I ~ (23 songs in one)*: http://www.youtube.com/watch?v=wyZPpwLZeag, which features 23 of Korean hit songs from 2009. For *Obama Mashup Tribute: He Really Deed It* see: http://www.youtube.com/watch?v=LBh9c8cuthQ. See also *MASHUP - Obama/McCain Campaign Ads*: http://www.youtube.com/watch?v=IEehKNNMq_4, *Getting Nasty - John Bennett's entry in Campaign Mash Up*: http://www.youtube.com/watch?v=DB56hlJoHN4 and *Barack Obama: Unstoppable Momentum (Led Zeppelin Mashup)*: http://www.youtube.com/watch?v=g_NrAmqaShY (last access 10.3.2010).

**35** | For *Tick-Toxic: Mashup of Britney Spears and Gwen Stefani* which combines the music and the visuals from the videos for their songs *Toxic* (video directed in 2004 by Joseph Kahn) and *What You Waiting For?* (clip directed in 2004 by Francis Lawrence) see http://www.youtube.com/watch?v=gRHfd9YtoOA (last access 10.3.2010).

**36** | See the section on condensation for more discussion of *Video Phone*'s intertextuality. *Telephone* references *Kill Bill* (Quentin Tarantino, 2003/2004), *Thelma and Louise* (Ridley Scott, 1991), Noir, B-movies and YouTube fan culture.

**37** | See *John Rich – Raisin' McCain Music Video*: http://www.youtube.com/watch?v=qmKgITJejfg and *john.he.is*: http://www.youtube.com/watch?v=3gwq EneBKUs which parodies will.i.am's *Yes We Can*-video (see below note 48) in order to let McCain appear in a critical light.

**38** | Richard Dyer's book *Pastiche* is helpful here: Dyer 2007.

**39** | Many students in my production courses have never taken a college general education "Intro to Art" course: elementary through high school hasn't afforded them artistic training either. They're very excited but their skills are not very high.

**40** | See for example the *Video Phone Remix Beyoncé and Lady Gaga (Cordless Phone Spoof)*: http://www.youtube.com/watch?v=DfHh8jHsFOw (last access 10.3.2010).

**41** | "I look at photos of myself, and I look like such a tranny! It's amazing! I look like Grace Jones, androgynous, robo, future fashion queen. It's not what is sexy. It's graphic, and it's art." See http://popwatch.ew.com/2009/02/09/lady-gaga-inter (last access 10.3.2010). There are also ample references from gay sources citing Gaga as a gay icon. For example, her profile in OUT magazine says: "A life of glamour is an ethos to which every gay -- from the 17-year-old Dominican tranny voguing in his bedroom to the tanorexic middle-aged Miami circuit queen -- can relate. It's one reason we love Gaga. Another, of course, is that Gaga loves us back. Gayness is in Gaga's DNA." And: "Her devotion to gay culture is unparalleled by any other artist operating at her level of visibility or success." See for this: http://www.out.com/detail.asp?page=2&id=25720 (last access 10.3.2010). See also a youtube video alleging her transsexuality (1,231,978 views): "Breaking news: Lady GaGa is actually a MAN!": http://www.youtube.com/watch?v=P36i5BaAP6w (last access 10.3.2010).

**42** | It doesn't seem unreasonable to me that Williams, Beyoncé, and Lady Gaga or the clip's costume designers and other technicians might have added a subtle detail like this to the video. Many of my friends and colleagues in the gay community follow international gay rights closely. Choreographer Michael Peter's finger snaps in John Landis' music video for Michael Jackson's *Thriller* (1983) is one example of a touch added to speak to the gay community.

**43** | Interview, December 3, 2009.

**44** | The line "Can you handle it" is at the same time a clear reference to the song *Bootylicious*, interpreted in 2001 by Beyoncé's former group Destiny's Child.

**45** | Watch the video from minute 3:10.

**46** | Note the fourth shot into *Videophone*'s opening. The blonde-haloed man enters left of frame at minute 0:29 and exits at 0:37.

**47** | Conversation about the song and musical analysis offered by Charles Kronengold and Jesse Rodin (professors in Musicology at Stanford), December 10th 2009.

**48** | For this video see the introduction to this volume: p. 7.

**49** | 1alexandra12: "horrible... Beyoncé you dissapointed me.. and lady gaga you are an ugly slut...."

shakirap483: "Beyoncé owns the stage not lady gaga she's wired in head in so many ways" taytaygurl09 "this is a unique video, but what's with all the toy guns?"

1111GENESIS: "@taytaygurl09 the video is symbolic for the gay revolution."

MrSweetJuice: "lady ga ga is the worst fucking singer or w.e she is on the planet.....i mean the bitch is fucking terrible and all her songs sound the same and im pretty sure shes a fucking guy....fucking tranny cunt nigger, FUCK HER!! and honestly fuck her gay faggot homosexual fanbase, all you HIV carrying monkeys need to be put to death right along with niggers and Lady ga ga the fuckign tranny cunt!! oh and all u faggot fudge packers better not message my profile with homo messages OR ELSE!!!"

LiteSkin87: "Beyoncé is bad, thick, and delicious looking, but man, she is straight sleazy. She's married, for shit's sake. Stop talking about how niggas is hitting you up and you're assuming the position. Sit your ass down and have a kid somewhere."

norhophobia: "yep she's an official whore now. i wouldn't want my man or my daughters watchn her vids now..and would feel uncomfortable watchn w/ my momma around or anybody for that matter @liteskin87 i agree she's married wth this is disgusting....it's sad cuz she's so talented u can see she is pretty and "sexy" w/o her acting and lookn like a street walker in all her vids smh"

nautigirl2774: "apparently sex sells, but this a totally crap video. I used to think that Beyoncé had class, but now see that she'll do anything to make a buck. So much for being a role model to young girls, she looks like a tramp."

cobra902001: "Please Wake up people, this video is about Beyoncé and Lady Gaga promoting bi-sexuality, don't let the elite brain wash you any longer"

rainbowskies400: "Umm..not sure how to feel about this video. haha"

All of which are from just one copy of Video Phone: http://www.youtube.com/watch?v=btuRgzIaZso

**50** | See for this for example *Thomas the Taxi Driver*, a snippet from the children program *Thomas the Tank Engine*, combined with the vocal track from the scene in Martin Scorsese's film *Taxi Driver* where Harvey Keitel's character describes all the things his prostitute is capable of doing: http://www.youtube.com/watch?v=usfkjbsjNtk (last access 10.3.2010).

**51** | Examples include the videos for Beyoncé's *If I Were A Boy* (directed in 2008 by Jake Nava) *Irreplaceable* (directed in 2006 by Anthony Mandler) and Hype William's *Diamonds from Sierra Leone* for Kanye West (2005) and *The Rain (Supa Dupa Fly)* for Missy Elliott (1997).

**52** | See for example those for Ne-Yo, *Go On Girl* (2007), Wu-Tang Clan, *Can it Be All So Simple* (1994) and Taral Hicks, *Silly* (1997).

**53** | The video by Francis Lawrence for Lady Gaga's *Bad Romance* (2009), suggests this might be so.

# BIBLIOGRAPHY

Alsop, Zoe: "Uganda's Anti-Gay Bill: Inspired by the U.S." In: *Time*, December 2009 http://www.time.com/time/world/article/0,8599, 1946645,00.html?xid=rss-topstories (last access 10.3.2010).

Arrington, Michael (2009): "YouTube Video Streams Top 1.2 Billion/Day": http://techcrunch.com/2009/06/09/youtube-video-streams-top-1-billionday (last access 10.3.2010).

Bazin, André (2004): *What is Cinema?*, Berkeley: University of California Press.

Deleuze, Gilles (1995): *Difference and Repetition*, New York: Columbia University Press.

Dyer, Richard (2007): *Pastiche*, London: Routledge.

Gunning, Tom: "The Cinema of Attractions: Early Film, Its Spectator and the Avant-Garde". In: Thomas Elsaesser/Adam Barker (Eds.): *Early Film*, British Film Institute, 1989, p. 56-62

Juhasz, Alexandra (2009): "Learning the Five Lessons of YouTube: After Trying to Teach There, I Don't Believe the Hype". In: *Cinema Journal*, 48, Number 2, Winter 2009, p. 145-150.

Manovich, Lev (2001): *The Language of New Media*, Cambridge (Mass.)/London: The MIT Press.

Mulvey, Laura (2006): *Death 24x a Second: Stillness and the Moving Image*, London: Reaktion Books

Rodowick, David (2007): *The Virtual Life of Film*, Harvard University Press.

Sconce, Jeffrey (2002): "Irony, nihilism, and the new American "smart" film". In: *Screen*, Volume 43, Number 4, p. 349-369.

Vernallis, Carol (2004): *Experiencing Music Video: Aesthetics and Cultural Context*, New York: Columbia University Press.

Wetsch, Michael (Introduction)/Heffernan, Virginia (2008): "The Many Tribes of YouTube" and "Pixels at Exhibition": "An Anthropological Introduction to YouTube" (Lecture at the Library of Congress, 23. June 2008): http://www.youtube.com/watch?v=TPAO-lZ4_hU (last access 10.3.2010)

# Future Thrills the Video Star –
# The Future of the Music Video

Kathrin Wetzel/Christian Jegl

Fig. 1: *Future thrills the Video Star – Die Zukunft des Musikvideos*

## A View Back into the Future

Kathrin Wetzel and Christian Jegl started their Bachelor Thesis *Future thrills the Video Star – Die Zukunft des Musikvideos* (fig. 1) in October 2006. Within four months a dissertation evolved which deals with the current situation in the music video business as well as with the future tendencies of this medium. To gain a better insight into the genre, experts[1] in film, research, and music were interviewed about the evolution of the music video as a medium, the role of music channels, progressive and visionary ways of visualization and broadcasting. The thesis was developed at the HTWG, Constance, Germany, within the communications design course in the winter semester 2006/2007.

> "The art of prophecy is very difficult,
> especially with respect to the future."
>
> *Mark Twain*[2]

## FROM 'KILL' TO 'THRILL'

You saw ringtone commercials, reality, dating, and pick-up artist's shows besides comedy series on every music channel. Who didn't find himself in that situation? If you were lucky enough to actually see a music video on MTV or VIVA, it was reduced to three quarters of the whole screen and surrounded by a lot of colored, flashing elements, making it hard to even detect the actual music clip.

Fortunately there was YouTube and MyVideo which provided almost every music video at a mouse click – but to what effect? The compression led to immense loss in image and sound quality. The DVD-series *The Work of Director*[3] provided another opportunity to watch remarkable music videos. But there was hardly any up-to-date publication on the topic.

The well-known phrase "Video killed the Radio Star" almost could have turned into "Future killed the Video Star". During our research it more and more transpired that the music video is not threatened by extinction, but is in fact going through a change. Therefore "Future thrills the Video Star" will serve as a more appropriate expression.

## THE MUSIC VIDEO IS DEAD?!

The music video business struggles with this point of view already for a few years now. Not only the fact that music clips seem to vanish more and more from the music channels program, but also that there is an increasing number of telecasts unfurling the history of the music clip seems to indicate that the question could be affirmed.

However, the experts we asked agreed that the statement is wrong. For example, according to Christoph Mangler, "music and music video are inseparably linked with pop and youth culture. You cannot erase that!" (Mangler 2006: p. 185) As long as there are young people there always will be a youth culture – hence the music video will endure as well. Thus it is more the question: Will the music video continue to exist in the way we used to know it?

In what follows, we will discuss some of the factors influencing the future of the music industry and opening new paths.

## THE INTERNET

The transition has been going on for quite a while already: music channels started paying more and more attention to dating and Reality TV programs. At the same time, the Internet presented an acceptable alternative form of distribution for the music video, particularly in the form of the newly emerging YouTube and MyVideo platforms. A continuously growing data stream naturally allows a steadily improving quality in distribution. The advantage is, for example, that on the net the clip doesn't have to pass the slow and expensive procedures of traditional broadcasting. The Internet reaches people more directly: an international audience is at hands with the push of a button. "Especially newcomer bands dealing with small budgets benefit from that advantage at the moment", said Henry Keazor (Keazor 2006: p. 165). And this advantage still persists. One can state that by now the Internet has even become an essential marketing tool for musicians – and here for stars as well as for newcomers.

These new forms of online distribution also influenced a new form of music video: the self-made video. One of the most well-known example of this type might be the video for the song *Here It Goes Again* by the band OK Go. Comprised of one shot, eight treadmills, and the four band members dancing, this simple video won the YouTube award "Most Creative Video" in 2006 and a Grammy Award for "Best Short Form Music Video" in 2007.[4]

Commenting on this trend, Uwe Flade suggests that self-made music videos are easily distributed over the Internet. On the contrary, Flade claims, more artistic and emotionally involving music videos need instead a high-quality-platform to bring out their whole value (Flade 2006, p. 152-158). Hand-held camera, and limited image quality matched with a witty idea – that's what this type of music video looked like in the beginning. Nowadays one could counter that in some places using IP TV, Internet is equivalent to television and limitations of resolution and data-rate have disappeared. Mark Feuerstake sees this process in terms of an unstoppable trend in which "everyone can see that the quality improves from year to year. We are living in a very fast time. You just don't realize this, when you are smack in the middle of what's going on" (Feuerstake 2006: p. 146).

At the same time, it is possible that small-sized video screens, as found on YouTube and similar online platforms, already belong to the past. When we spoke to Zoran Bihac, he told us of the rather challenging nature of small-sized video screens, particularly the challenge of creation and design. "The look and the things happening in the video have to adapt completely. Everything has to be closer which means using more close-ups" (Bihac 2006: p. 133). To handle the divergency of screen sizes is getting more and more important. On the one hand there is a huge trend to buy and use wide flat screens, on the other hand watching videos on small sized displays of portable gadgets like cell phones or mp3 players is increasingly gaining popularity.

The success of the first generation of the Video iPod has demonstrated a major interest in 'pocket' music videos. Within the first 20 days following the release of the Video iPod, the iTunes Store already counted one million clip downloads.[5] Ilka Risse has a critical view on this way of watching music videos: "I don't respond to that. The quality is just too low. Why should I watch music videos on my cell phone?" (Risse 2006: p. 201). But Jamba, a company that sells such videos, confirmed that requests for Video Ringtones have indeed increased.[6] Christoph Mangler comments on Jamba's statement: "that's the trend. As a record label you must not miss that at all!" (Mangler 2006: p. 183).

Although Internet and television content designed for cell phones was sneered at in the past, they are now an essential part of the product offered by the majority of cell phone providers: Internet and television for cell phones and alike. Despite this development, size adaptation, as mentioned and claimed by Zoran Bihac, has been largely disregarded.

## INTERACTIVITY

Whether you are at home or on the move, the Internet gives another opportunity – to be an active user. Contrary to the passive and receptive behaviours dictated by television, the Internet enables active consumption. The keyboard and mouse are always seductively within reach. Bands like Radiohead seized this as an opportunity: in summer 2008 they released the outstanding clip for their song *House of Cards*. Inventive new technologies were applied: instead of using the usual cameras and lights, 3D plotting technologies collected information about the shapes and relative distances of the rendered objects and the video was then created entirely through a visualization of that data. Moreover, data fragments were then put at the disposal of fans in order to give them the possibility to generate their own visualizations of the video and to publish them on the web (Knoke 2008). By taking advantage of the possible interactivity and by involving the audience, Radiohead has raised the music video to a new level.

Some of our interviewees see a lot of potential for the clip in this sector as well. Zoran Bihac clarified this point by stating that "technology seduces people to play and have fun. The whole thing is about to become a kind of egocentric mania and everyone feels appointed to have more ability for taking decisions than others. Everybody wants to be a pop star, so there is cell phone software to easily create your own video" (Bihac 2006: p. 135) Thorsten Wübbena agreed and added: "I imagine several modules consisting of different elements with a certain already existing base and the rest to be variable" (Wübbena 2006: p. 171).

Henry Keazor's idea of an interactive music video is a mixture of a so-called "Tanzautomat" (a dancing machine) and the cyberspace. "A 3-dimensional projection of yourself into the music video would enable you to do a virtual dance with Jennifer Lopez" (Keazor 2006: p. 171). You would not only be close to your idol, but you could also participate in designing the clip yourself. That this is not a spaced out future thing can be seen by the proximity of such visions to our actual every-day-life. Game stations such as Nintendo Wii, for example, demonstrates this proximity by allowing users to interact with virtual teammates and fellow players.[7]

## OLEDs

A newer form of technology is called OLEDs, short for organic LEDs.[8] They might have the potential to thoroughly change our exposure to media in the coming years. By using OLEDs you have the opportunity to transform almost every surface into a display – ranging from textiles to paper or paint. OLEDs will make many new things possible and some of our experts did find the idea very inspiring. What would it be like if musicians would start sprawling on t-shirts, dancing towards us from walls and accessories or just appear via promotion video in a magazine? Markus Hauf's extremely critical of such developments and pointed out the unavoidable stimulus-overload. But at he same time he said: "Well, you also have to consider all the young people growing up with it. For them it would be just natural. Maybe they would not even question the whole thing" (Hauf 2006: p. 189f.). We have also talked to Thorsten Wübbena about this colorful and eventful world. He said: "I think you have to separate what is possible and will be offered, and what will be allowed just in certain contexts" (Wübbena 2006: p. 173). The musician Thees Uhlmann looked at the positive side: "Everything new and moving will make people go crazy for it first. People love pictures in motion. In that area possibilities will be pushed to the limits. But I consider it a great idea to have a shirt with a moving Tomte-lettering on it. I would definitely invest into that research" (Uhlmann 2006: p. 209f.).

## CONCERTS, MERCHANDISING, AND CINEMA

But there are more alternative forms, combinations and overlapping contents of music clips and other media, like concerts, different merchandising forms and the cinema, for example.

Zoran Bihac, for example, imagines that in ten years from now, the majority of people might prefer to watch shows, rather than music clips. Or perhaps the trend would undergo a reversion. "Five years ago nobody thought the vinyl record to come back" (Bihac 2006: p. 130). In that case high quality music videos would be published on special editions of tour DVDs only. Or perhaps music, film, and clip would merge not just on a live-DVD, but into a ninety minute music clip documentary. This would mean that a band would not have just a four minutes advert, but instead an entire advertising show which brings the band, its music and style closer to the fan.

A contemporary example of the interdependent relationship between commercials and music videos is the clip for the song *Grip* by Roel Wouters aka Xelor for the Dutch band ZzZ (Björn Ottenheim and Daan Schinkel). The entire scene is shot from above. While the two band members (lying on pedestals so that they face the viewer) seem to simply perform the song, acrobats are jumping on a trampoline, holding up chalkboards with words such as "Pulse", "Rotate and Pulse", "Flip and Pulse" etc. which at the same time dictate the movements of the gymnasts and the way the present their boards. All these elements were then later adapted by the advert company Krow Communications in their commercial for the "Fiat Grande Punto" car where also a portion from the song *Grip* is used on the soundtrack (Bürki 2008).

Another context to which music videos and their esthetics are applied to is the cinema since more and more (former) video clip directors tend to work for the film. David Fincher, Mark Romanek, Michel Gondry and Spike Jonze are now all well-known directors in both the video and the film industry. And also Anton Corbijn, the photographer and director, who shot many music videos, including videos for Depeche Mode and Joy Division. In 2007, Corbijn released his feature film *Control*[9], a movie about Ian Curtis and the band Joy Division. It clearly demonstrates the aesthetic influence of Corbijn's music videos and photography. And to get his work shown at cinemas is a dream of every German music clip director, too. In 2008, for instance, the movie *Nordwand*[10] by Philipp Stölzl was released as his second feature film in the cinemas.

In our interview with Henry Keazor, Keazor expanded on such developments, stating that: "These directors transfer some aesthetic parameters from the music video to the cinematic context where they appear as innovative, and this helps to further develop the aesthetics of the music video" (Keazor 2006: p. 159). A current example is the movie *Wanted*[11] by Timur Bekmambetov (formerly a director of commercials). *Wanted* feels like a very long music video. Bekmambetov already showed how to convey typical elements of a music video (such as fast-edited sequences and the hereby typical cinematography and aesthetics) to the cinema in his movie *Night Watch: Nochnoi Dozor*.[12]

The question is if there still will be directors like Gondry, Romanek or Chris Cunningham in the future, who brought the music video to such a high level. Thorsten Wübbena asked himself if aspiring directors with great potential would be prevented to come up in the future (Wübbena 2006, p. 159). And Henry Keazor added: "We are at a crucial point now where you can already see certain tendencies. On one hand the music video is said to die out, on the other hand there are more and more universities and production companies that provide video clip courses. It's paradoxical. More people are taught how to do video clips while the medium itself is considered dead." He also said that this trend could be a bit too late. You have to wonder what kind of perspectives those people will have (Keazor 2006: p. 159).

## IT'S THE END OF THE WORLD AS WE KNOW IT – AND I FEEL FINE[13]

These possible developments and tendencies show that music videos will persist. It will be more likely the common structures and formats like music channels that have to change.

> "I'm stunned how people aren't seeing that with TV, in five years form now, people will laugh at what we've had."
>
> *Bill Gates*[14]

The music video itself will make its way, going through different trends, and above all it will create new trends. This medium has been seen critically for a long time. Sometimes it hasn't been noticed at all. But via MTV the music video has left its mark on a whole generation. It has the power to reveal something – like a movie, a song or a book. Nobody can really tell how music videos will adapt to new ways of displaying. At the moment the music clip is in a transitional period, but it will survive. New directors will arise and create new visualizations.

> "Of course, I cannot say whether things will get better if they change.
> But this much I can say: things must change if they are to get better."
>
> *Georg Christoph Lichtenberg*[15]

The Bachelor Thesis *Future thrills the Video Star – The Future of Music Video* contains an interactive DVD, a booklet and a website (fig. 2). You can find further information about the project and download all of the interviews by visiting: www.time-to-thrill.de

*Fig. 2: DVD-Case, Booklet*

## REFERENCES

**1** | Interviews with experts: Asta Baumöller (Managing Director VIVA Schweiz/S Media Vision AG), Zoran Bihac (director), Mark Feuerstake (producer and director), Uwe Flade (director), Markus Hauf (visual fx artist), Henry Keazor (art historian), Christoph Mangler (director), Ilka Risse (cutter), Thees Uhlmann (singer and songwriter), Thorsten Wübbena (art historian).

**2** | Attributed to Mark Twain, see e.g. Samuelson (2001).

**3** | http://www.directorslabel.com (last access 10.12.2009).

**4** | http://en.wikipedia.org/wiki/OK_Go (last access 10.12.2009). See for this also the article by Gianni Sibilla in this volume.

**5** | http://www.apple.com/de/itunes, http://www.apple.com/de/ipod/ipod.html (last access 10.12.2009).

**6** | Ulrike Trommer (2006 - 2007: Manager Global Communications and CSR-Responsible at the Jamba! GmbH) in 2006 in an e-mail to the authors.

**7** | http://de.wikipedia.org/wiki/Wii (last access 10.12.2009).

**8** | http://en.wikipedia.org/wiki/OLEDs (last access 10.12.2009).

**9** | http://www.control-film.de (last access 10.12.2009).

**10** | http://www.imdb.de/title/tt0844457 (last access 10.12.2009).

**11** | http://www.imdb.com/title/tt0493464 (last access 10.12.2009).

**12** | http://www.imdb.com/title/tt0403358 (last access 03.03.2010)

**13** | The title refers – of course – to the song by R.E.M., published in 1987, and included on their album *Document*.

**14** | Quoted after: http://www.businessanthropology.info/gwp+and+internet+tv.aspx (last access 10.12.2009).

**15** | Originally in German: "Ich kann freilich nicht sagen, ob es besser werden wird, wenn es anders wird; aber soviel kann ich sagen: es muß anders werden, wenn es gut werden soll." From the so called *Sudelbuch K* , quoted after Wolfgang Promies, *G.C. Lichtenberg: Schriften und Briefe*, Vol. 2, Munich: Hanser 1971, No. K 293.

## BIBLIOGRAPHY

Bihac, Zoran (2006): Interview. In: Kathrin Wetzel/Christian Jegl, *Future thrills the Video Star – Die Zukunft des Musikvideos*, Konstanz: Bachelorthesis at HTWG Konstanz.

Bürki, Julia (2008): Fiat kauft Idee von VUCX-Regisseur Roel Wouters, http://www.online-artikel.de/article/fiat-kauft-idee-von-vucx-regisseur-roel-wouters-11648-1.html (last access 10.12.2009).

Feuerstake, Mark (2006): Interview. In: Kathrin Wetzel/Christian Jegl, *Future thrills the Video Star – Die Zukunft des Musikvideos*, Konstanz: Bachelorthesis at HTWG Konstanz.

Flade, Uwe (2006): Interview. In: Kathrin Wetzel/Christian Jegl, *Future thrills the Video Star – Die Zukunft des Musikvideos*, Konstanz: Bachelorthesis at HTWG Konstanz.

Hauf, Markus (2006): Interview. In: Kathrin Wetzel/Christian Jegl, *Future thrills the Video Star – Die Zukunft des Musikvideos*, Konstanz: Bachelorthesis at HTWG Konstanz.

Keazor, Henry (2006): Interview. In: Kathrin Wetzel/Christian Jegl, *Future thrills the Video Star. Die Zukunft des Musikvideos*, Konstanz: Bachelorthesis an der HTWG Konstanz.

Knoke, Felix (2008): Radiohead lässt Fans Videoclip remixen, http://www.spiegel.de/netzwelt/web/0,1518,565947,00.html (last access 10.12.2009).

Mangler, Christoph (2006): Interview. In: Kathrin Wetzel/Christian Jegl, *Future thrills the Video Star – Die Zukunft des Musikvideos*, Konstanz: Bachelorthesis at HTWG Konstanz.

Risse, Ilka (2006): Interview. In: Kathrin Wetzel/Christian Jegl, *Future thrills the Video Star – Die Zukunft des Musikvideos*, Konstanz: Bachelorthesis at HTWG Konstanz.

Samuelson, Robert J. (2001): "The Specter of Global Aging". In: *Washington Post*, February 28, p. A25.

Uhlmann, Thees (2006): Interview. In: Kathrin Wetzel/Christian Jegl, *Future thrills the Video Star – Die Zukunft des Musikvideos*, Konstanz: Bachelorthesis at HTWG Konstanz.

Wübbena, Thorsten (2006): Interview. In: Kathrin Wetzel/Christian Jegl, *Future thrills the Video Star – Die Zukunft des Musikvideos*, Konstanz: Bachelorthesis at HTWG Konstanz.

## About the Editors

**Henry Keazor**, after having studied Art History, German Literature, Musical Science and Philosophy, worked as assistant professor of the Kunsthistorisches Institut in Florence, then at the Art Historical Institute of the University of Frankfurt/Main where he did his habilitation in 2005. After working as Visiting Professor at the Institute for Art History of the University of Mainz and as Heisenberg-Fellow of the DFG, he got, in Fall 2008, the Chair in Art History at the Saarland University. His research fields cover Early Modern Art (especially French and Italian Baroque), Media, "The Simpsons", contemporary architecture (Jean Nouvel) and the music video.

**Thorsten Wübbena**, after having studied Cultural Sciences, Art History and History, did work at the Zentrum für Kunst und Medientechnologie in Karlsruhe (ZKM), before joining the Kunstgeschichtliches Institut of the University of Frankfurt/Main in 2000 as a collaborator. His main interests are new media and I.T. in the humanities (image databanks DILPS, ConedaKOR and the online edition "Sandrart.net").

Together they have published *"Video thrills the Radio Star": Musikvideos: Geschichte, Themen, Analysen*, Bielefeld: transcript 2005 (2nd edition: 2007), "'Kulturelle Kannibalen'? Videoclips in Kunst und Alltag", in: *Forschung Frankfurt*, 1, 2006, p. 44-47 and the chapters and entries about "Music Video", in: Dieter Daniels/Sandra Naumann/Jan Thoben (eds.): *See this Sound. An Interdisciplinary Survey of Audovisual Culture*, Cologne: Walther König 2010, p. 223-233 (also online under http://beta.see-this-sound.at/kompendium/abstract/44).

## About the Authors

**Saul Austerlitz** is a writer and critic in New York City. His work has been published in the New York Times, Los Angeles Times, Boston Globe (where he is a regular contributor), and other publications. He is the author of *Money for Nothing: A History of the Music Video from the Beatles to the White Stripes*, New York/London: Continuum 2007. His forthcoming book, *Another Fine Mess:*

*A History of American Film Comedy* has been published in September 2010 by Chicago Review Press.
www.saulausterlitz.com

**Bruno Di Marino** (born in Salerno in 1966) is an essay-writer and doing research on cinema and video (with a particular interest in experimental film and video); he works also as a teacher, organiser of exhibitions as well as retrospectives and director of festivals. Since 1986 he is also writing for several magazines and dailies. In 1993 he founded and managed until 2001 the audiovisual archives of the Museum of Contemporary Art at the University La Sapienza in Rome. Since 2001 he is the consultant of the Rarovideo home video's label. His publications include: *Sguardo, inconscio, azione. Il cinema underground e d'artista a Roma (1965-1975)*, Rome: Lithos 1999, *L'ultimo fotogramma. I finali del cinema*, Rome: Editori Riuniti 2001, *Clip! 20 anni di musica in video*, Rome: Castelvecchi 2001, *Interferenze dello sguardo. La sperimentazione audiovisiva tra analogico e digitale*, Rome: Bulzoni 2002, *Pose in movimento. Fotografia e cinema*, Turino: Bollati Boringhieri 2009 e *Film oggetto design. La messa in scena delle cose*, Milan: PostmediaBooks 2010.

**Laura Frahm** is a researcher and lecturer at the International Research Institute for Cultural Technologies and Media Philosophy at the Bauhaus-University Weimar. From 2005 to 2007 she was a doctorate fellow at the Transatlantic Graduate Research Program Berlin/New York "History and Culture of the Metropolis in the 20th Century." She holds a M.A. in Theater, Film and Television Studies, History of Art, and Spanish/Romanic Studies from the University of Cologne. Her areas of specialization are history and theory of media, spatial theory and topology, new media (music videos, media art). Recent publications: *Bewegte Räume. Zur Konstruktion von Raum in Videoclips von Jonathan Glazer, Chris Cunningham, Mark Romanek und Michel Gondry*, Frankfurt/M.: Peter Lang 2007, and *Jenseits des Raums. Zur filmischen Topologie des Urbanen* (Bielefeld: transcript 2010).

**Giulia Gabrielli** has made her Ph.D. at the University of Triest in Communication Science. She teaches the history of the cinema and of music video and works at the Italian online journal *Fucine Mute* (www.fucine.com), where she has published various articles on the directors and the aesthetics of music video.

**Christoph Jacke** is Professor of Theory, Aesthetics and History of Popular Music at the University of Paderborn, Germany. He before worked as lecturer at the department of "Culture, Communication & Management/Applied Cultural Studies" at the University of Münster, Germany, and was also guest-teaching at the University of Bremen (Cultural Studies), at the Free University of Berlin (Communication Studies), at the University of Paderborn (Popular Music and Media Studies), University of Vienna/Austria (Music Studies), and at the Hochschule fuer Musik, Cologne (Popular Music Studies). He writes as a freelancing contributor for the *Frankfurter Rundschau, De:Bug, Testcard and Telepolis.* Recent publications: *Populäre Kultur und soziales Gedächtnis: theoretische und exemplarische Überlegungen zur dauervergesslichen Erinnerungsmaschine Pop/Popular Culture and Social Memory: Theoretical and Empirical Analyses on The Oblivious 'Memory-Machine' Pop.* Special Edition SPIEL. Issue 2/2005, Frankfurt/M.: Peter Lang Verlag 2008 (eds. Christoph Jacke, Martin Zierold), *Einführung in Populäre Musik und Medien,* Münster et al.: LIT 2009. www.christophjacke.de.

**Christian Jegl** made an apprenticeship as an advertising technician in 1998, followed by a second apprenticeship in graphic design in 2002. In 2003 he began to study communications design at the University of Applied Science in Konstanz where he graduated as a "Communication Designer B. A.". Since 2007 he works as an Art Director in an advertising agency in Munich; he is also the founder of the design studio "dasneueschwarz". www.dasneueschwarz.net

**Antje Krause-Wahl** holds a Ph. D. in art history (*Konstruktionen von Identität: Renée Green, Tracey Emin, Rirkrit Tiravanija,* Munich: Schreiber 2006) and is currently teaching at the Academy of Fine Arts, Mainz. She has lectured at Heidelberg University, Frankfurt University and the Academy of Fine Arts Leipzig, curated several exhibitions and works regularly for the visiting program at the Museum of Modern Art in Frankfurt am Main. Her research topics are artist's identity, art education, art and fashion and artist's magazines. Recent publications include: "Between studio and catwalk – artists in fashion magazines", in: *Fashion Theory,* 13 (1), March 2009, p. 7-28 and "Touching from a distance – Andy Warhol, Alex Katz, Barkley L. Hendricks", in: Annette Geiger/Gerald Schröder/Änne Soell (eds): *Coolness – Zur Ästhetik einer kulturellen Verhaltensstrategie und Attitüde,* Bielefeld: transcript 2010, p. 219-236.

**Barbara London** founded The Museum of Modern Art's media exhibition and collection programs. Her recent MoMA exhibitions include "Looking at Music: Side 2"; "Automatic Update"; "River of Crime", an on-line project with the Residents; "Stillness: Michael Snow and Sam Taylor-Wood"; "Anime!! Masters of Animation: Hayao Miyazaki and Isao Takahat"; "Video Spaces: Eight Installations", and web projects undertaken in China ("Stirfry"); Russia ("InterNyet"), and Japan ("dot.jp."). Her latest projects (2009) were "Out on the Edge. Net Pioneers" (Linz: Ludwig Boltzmann Institute) and "Minimal Music Gave Us Maximal Video" (ArtForum, New York).

**Cornelia Lund** is an art historian and curator. From 2001 to 2004 she was a research associate at the International Center for Cultural and Technological Studies at the University of Stuttgart. Since 2004, together with Holger Lund, she has been running fluctuating images (Stuttgart/Berlin), a platform for contemporary media art. She is currently working on a DFG research project on documentary film at the Potsdam Film & Television Academy (HFF Konrad Wolf). Her topics are mediality and intermediality, as well as audiovisual art forms. She has published on the relationship of image and text, moving images and sound as well as dance and film, and she is co-editor, together with Holger Lund (see below), of *Audio.Visual – On Visual Music and Related Media*, Stuttgart: Arnoldsche 2009.

**Holger Lund** has studied History of Art, Compared Literature and German Literature at the University of Stuttgart. He has finished his Ph. D. on Max Ernst's collage novels in 2000. He has been fellow for artistic coordination at the Akademie Schloss Solitude, Stuttgart, in 2001/2002. Since 2002 he has been a lecturer at several institutions like the University of Applied Sciences DHBW Ravensburg, Stuttgart University and Heidelberg University and worked as an author and curator as well. Since 2008 he has a tenure professorship in theories of design at Pforzheim University, School of Design. In 2010 he will publish a vinyl record compilation on Turkish funk music from the 1970's.

**Klaus Neumann-Braun** has the Chair for Media Science at the University of Basel; before that, between 1992 and 2005, he had professorships at the universities of Trier, Frankfurt/Main and Koblenz-Landau. His main topics in his teaching and research are media- and communication sociology, analyses of popular culture, research concerning the audience, the impact and the reception of media phenomena and methods of interpretation. Together with Axel Schmidt (see below) he has edited the volume *VIVA MTV! Popmusik im Fernsehen*, Frankfurt am Main: Suhrkamp 1999; together with Lothar Mikos he has published in 2006 *Videoclips und Musikfernsehen*, Berlin: Vistas, and in 2008 he published (together with Axel Schmidt and Ulla Autenrieth) *Viva MTV! Reloaded*, Baden-Baden: Nomos 2009.

**Paolo Peverini** is Assistant professor in Communication at LUISS University in Rome, where he teaches Semiotics and Visual Semiotics. He is a Steering Committee member of the Centre for Media and Communication Studies "Massimo Baldini" (http://blogs.luiss.edu/communication/category/luiss/); the Centre is an institutional member of the ECREA (European Communication Research and Education Association) and affiliate member of the MeCCSA (Media Communication and Cultural Studies Association). He has, among other publications, written the book *Il videoclip. Strategie e figure di una forma breve*, Rome: Meltemi 2004.

**Axel Schmidt** is Assistant Professor at the Institute for Media Science of the University of Basel. In his publications he deals with popular culture,

TV, youth culture and -communication as well as with the qualitative methods of social research. His publications include *Popvisionen. Links in die Zukunft*, Frankfurt/Main: Suhrkamp 2003 (together with Klaus Neumann-Braun and Manfred Mai), *Die Welt der Gothics - Spielräume düster konnotierter Transzendenz*, Wiesbaden: Verlag für Sozialwissenschaften 2004 (together with Klaus Neumann-Braun) and *Viva MTV! Reloaded.* Baden-Baden: Nomos 2009 (together with Klaus Neumann-Braun und Ulla Autenrieth).

**Thomas Schmitt** has studied cinema technique at the École "Louis Lumiere" in Paris and works as a journalist and film critic; he has participated at various festivals on advertisements and promo clips in France and currently writes his Ph.D. about the "History of audio-visual short formats in France". He has been secretary of the SPPAM (Syndicat des Producteurs de Programmes Audiovisuels & Musicaux) the French union of video music producers in 2008 and teaches theory, history, economy and aesthetics of the music video at the International Film School in Paris (EICAR). He is also known as Tom Tom/Hephaïstos, member of the Paris based situationist steet art movement.

**Gianni Sibilla** teaches at the Catholic University of Milan, where he is the director of the post-degree course on Music Industry and Communication ("Master in comunicazione musicale per la discografia e i media"). He has published various books on the relation between music and media (among those: *I linguaggi della musica pop*, Milan: Bompiani 2003. *Musica e media digitali*, Milan: Bompiani 2008). He also works in the music industry as a journalist and writer: he is the deputy editor of on-line music magazine *Rockol.it*, and has been a writer on several TV and radio music programs.

**Carol Vernallis** is Associate Professor at the Film and Media Studies Program of the Arizona State University. She is the author of the book *Experiencing Music Video: Aesthetics and Cultural Context* (New York: Columbia University Press 2004); while preparing her forthcoming book *Accelerating Aesthetics: YouTube, Music Video and the New Digital Cinema* (Oxford University Press), she is currently also writing a book with the title *The Art and Industry of Music Video* which will contain interviews with music video directors as well as a description of the production and distribution of music videos.

**Matthias Weiß** has studied Art History and Theatre Studies. Since 2005 he works as a collaborator at the interdisciplinary research project "Kulturen des Performativen" at the Freie Universität Berlin. In the context of the topic of the present volume he has published, among other: *Madonna revidiert. Rekursivität im Videoclip*, Berlin: Reimer 2007, *Tanzende Bilder. Interaktionen von Musik und Film*, Munich: Fink 2008 (ed. together with

Klaus Krüger), "Images of Performance – Images as Performance. On the (in-)differentiability of music video and visual music", in: Cornelia Lund/ Holger Lund (eds.): *Audio.Visual – On Visual Music and Related Media*, Stuttgart: Arnoldsche 2009, p. 88-101.

**Kathrin Wetzel** began to study communications design in 2003 at the University of Applied Science in Constance where she graduated as a "Communication Designer B. A.". In 2007 she worked as a free-lance designer and began then, in 2008, a Master study course in "Creative Direction" at the HS Pforzheim. Since 2010 she works in the creative department of an advertising agency in Munich.
www.designwalz.de

# Index

BIBL.
LONDIN.
UNIV.